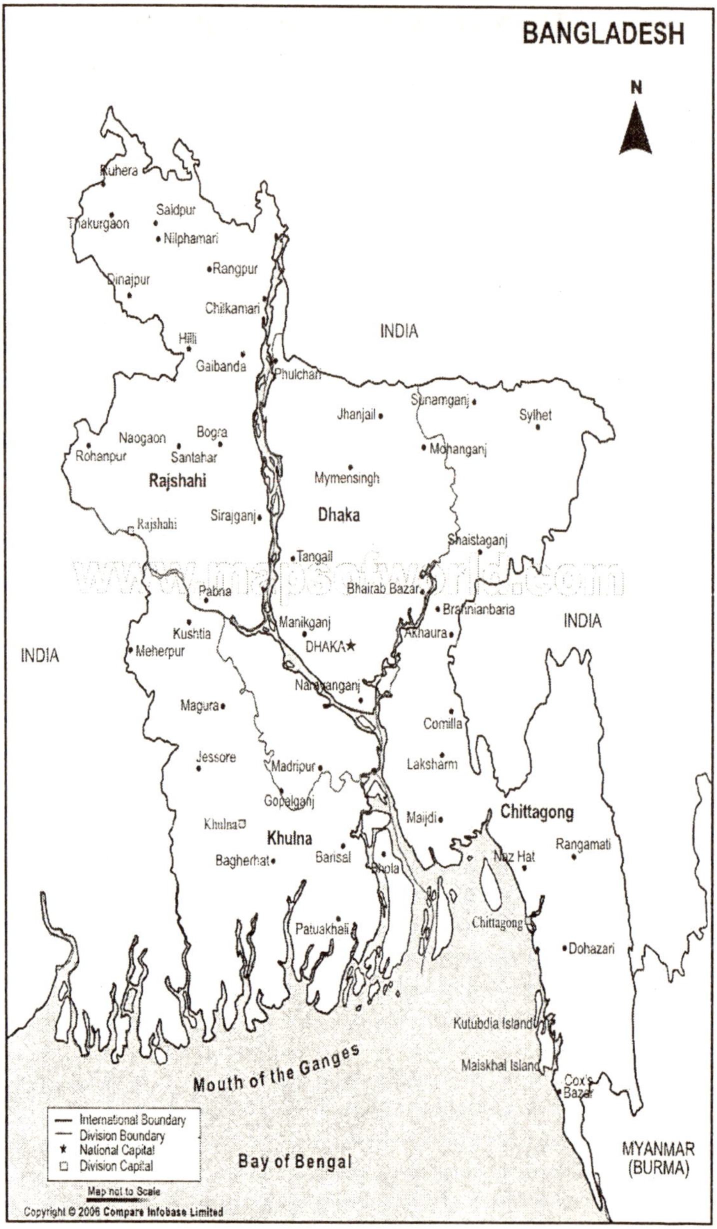
BANGLADESH
N
INDIA
INDIA
INDIA
MYANMAR (BURMA)
Kuhera
Thakurgaon
Saidpur
Nilphamari
Rangpur
Dinajpur
Chilkamari
Hilli
Gaibanda
Phulchari
Naogaon
Bogra
Rohanpur
Santahar
Rajshahi
Rajshahi
Sirajganj
Jhanjail
Sunamganj
Sylhet
Mohanganj
Mymensingh
Dhaka
Shaistaganj
Tangail
Bhairab Bazar
Brahmanbaria
Pabna
Kushtia
Meherpur
Manikganj
DHAKA
Akhaura
Narayanganj
Magura
Comilla
Jessore
Madripur
Laksharm
Gopalganj
Maijdi
Chittagong
Khulna
Khulna
Bagherhat
Barisal
Bhola
Naz Hat
Rangamati
Patuakhali
Chittagong
Dohazari
Kutubdia Island
Maiskhal Island
Cox's Bazar
Mouth of the Ganges
Bay of Bengal
International Boundary
Division Boundary
National Capital
Division Capital
Map not to Scale
Copyright © 2006 Compare Infobase Limited

FUNDAMENTALISM IN BANGLADESH:
Its Impact on India

ABU NASAR SAIED AHMED

OMEO KUMAR DAS INSTITUTE OF SOCIAL CHANGE AND DEVELOPMENT, GUWAHATI

&

AKANSHA PUBLISHING HOUSE

NEW DELHI-110002 (INDIA)

CONTENTS

PREFACE

The rise of Ayatullah Rohullah Khomeini at the centre stage of political Islam in the Middle East after dethroning Reza Shah Pehlavi in February 1979 is a watershed not only in the history of Islam but also in the post-World War II history of international politics. The impact of the rise of political Islam has been felt all over the world, more particularly, in the Islamic world from Algeria to Indonesian-Malaysian archipelago. The ascendancy of political Islam in Iran reverberated in the Islamic world which has a population of 900 million spread over 44 Muslim majority countries and in almost all countries of the world where they have a substantial population. A section of the Muslims suddenly found an outlet to express themselves with an assertive agenda of consolidating their religious identity by capturing political power in the Muslim majority countries. A still more aggressive group took recourse to a violent and militant path to enforce Islamic laws and practices, in both social and political domains, in their respective countries.

The West and the Islamic countries, as other countries with a substantial Muslim population, could not ignore the resurgence of political Islam. The recent changes in the social, economic and political landscape of the Islamic world, defined and delimited within the framework of fundamentalism, have captured the attention of academics, political activists and policy-makers. They are confronted with a nagging volley of questions as to why many of the educated and westernized

Muslims look back to century old medieval practices and traditions, why have their habit, education, political outlook and world perspective turned out to be Islamic, why have they become terribly anti-West, and why have they chosen terrorism to register their presence and to pursue political objectives?

In pursuit of academic explanation to each of such tangled questions the post-1979 world has seen countless publications, more so after the 9/11 deadly attack in the heart of the United States of America. The discourse on Islam has become a global agenda. Many of the issues, quite naturally, have not found an unassailable answer. Definitional problems on issues like 'Islamic fundamentalism', 'Islamic terrorism', 'militant Islam', 'political Islam' or 'Islamism" preclude a consensus. One positive dimension of such intellectual exercise is that the debates and discourses on Islam have generated enormous stockpile of data, information and analyses, which might eventually illuminate the way to the proper perspective on various aspects of this most misunderstood religion in the world.

India is surrounded by two Muslim majority countries – Bangladesh, where 89.6 per cent people are Muslims and Pakistan, which has a Muslim population of 98 per cent. Pakistan was created out of the Indian subcontinent on the basis of the 'two-nation theory'. Islam became the core foundation of statecraft of the new country carved out of British India. But it took less than a quarter of a century to be disillusioned with the efficacy of the theory; East Pakistan became Bangladesh in 1971 to prove to the rest of the world that religion is not the cementing force in a nation-building process. India fought three major wars (in 1947, 1965 and 1971), and also a major border skirmish (in 1999) with Pakistan. Besides, India has been facing the huge problem of proxy war waged by Pakistan. There are about 32 jihadi groups operating there. Most of these outfits have an anti-

India agenda. Naturally, everything that happens in that country is a matter for concern and of interest in India.

Bangladesh is still a low priority item in the national policy making process. That India liberated Bangladesh has now been a matter of the bygone past. Anti-Indian forces have ruled Bangladesh most of its post-colonial period. There has been a steady growth of Islamic fundamentalist parties and groups since the assassination of Bangabandhu Sheikh Mujibur Rehman on August 15, 1975. The rise is paradoxical in a country which emerged as a Bengali nation-state after discarding the religious identity. The Islamists, who collaborated with the Pakistani army and other terror groups and who faced public trials for atrocities committed against their own people, have occupied seats of power. The phenomenal rise of political and militant Islam is undoubtedly a major concern for India because of the geopolitical ramifications involved.

It is surprising that the issues related to the rise of Islamic fundamentalism in Bangladesh and its impact on India are not yet addressed academically. How could the Islamist capture imagination of a substantial section of the people of Bangladesh where the ethnic Bengali nationalism had superseded religious identity? The present study approaches the issue of Islam from a historical and political perspective. It includes aspects on the advent of Islam in present Bangladesh and its spread, primarily because of the Sufi saints who developed an accommodative model of Islam shaping the unique character of the Bengali Muslims, markedly different from the variety of those in northern and western parts of India. This distinctiveness enabled them to stage a massive revolt against the rulers in Islamabad and eventually rise as a distinct international personality. That is why it is intriguing to find that political and militant Islam has surfaced in a country where Bengali nationalism, to all intents and purposes, appears to be the paramount hallmark of national solidarity.

The study, therefore, concentrates on the rise of Islamic fundamentalism in Bangladesh in recent years and its inevitable ramifications not only in that country as also on the obvious impact on India, destined as we are to share the same geopolitical space in our sub-continent.

It becomes a pleasant duty to acknowledge with a sense of thanks and gratitude the role played by a number of persons who facilitated the present study from the day one to the last word written. To name some of them whose contributions permeated at every stage of this study is a fascinating task. They are André Béteille, Chairman, Indian Council of Social Science Research, Arjun Asrani, India's former Ambassador to Thailand and Japan, Ashok Jain, Chairman of Omeo Kumar Das Institute of Social Change and Development (OKDISCD), K.P. Ernest, Ambassador to New Zealand; the four Joint Secretaries in the Ministry of External Affairs, Mohan Kumar, Joymoni Bhagwati, Sunil Jain and Amrit Lugun, who spared their valuable time to discuss many of the issues covered in the study; the Librarians at Dhaka University, Asiatic Society of Bangladesh, Jawaharlal Nehru University and Ministry of External Affairs; Directors of Centre for Policy Dialogue, Dhaka, Bangladesh Institute of Development Studies, Dhaka, Bangladesh Academy for Rural Development, Comilla, Bangladesh Rural Advancement Committee (BRAC), Dhaka; Harun-or-Rashid, Sonia Nishat Amin, Nazmunisha Mahtab, Asha Islam Nayeem, Shaheen Ahmed, AKM Khademul Haq, Dil Roushan Zinnat Ara Nazneen of Dhaka University; Hasanuzzaman Chowdhury of Chittagong University and Meghan Guha Thakurta, a former professor of Dhaka University and now the Director of Research Initiative Bangladesh. All of them deserve my profound gratitude. A number of persons contributed to the outcome of the present study. They are Anuradha Dutta, my former teacher and currently my distinguished colleague, with whom I used to discuss regularly most of the issues dealt with in this work during the preparation of the first draft, Partha S. Ghosh, SIS, Jawaharlal Nehru University, whose academic inputs helped formulation of the framework of the study, and Indranee Dutta, Director of the Institute, who extended infrastructural facilities. Sirajul Islam and Sahjahan Miyan of Asiatic Society of Bangladesh deserve my profound gratitude. They made my research easy by offering me affiliation to the Society. Besides, I talked to a large number of people in Bangladesh, such as, rickshaw pullers, auto-rickshaw drivers, vendors, women selling tea and rice cake on footpaths of Dhaka, students, businessmen, Imams, religious leaders and women activists, political leaders who will remain anonymous. My proficiency in Bengali helped me a lot in interacting with them with ease. Their cooperation and open mind helped me understand their perception about religion, fundamentalism and militant Islam. I take this opportunity to thank my research associates, M.R. Kazi and Elizabeth Devi at OKDISCD, and Mridusmita Bora, a PhD student of Jawaharlal Nehru University, who worked hard to collect relevant data. My special thanks to Sahidul who was with me all along during my 21 day sojourn in Dhaka in November 2006. I had a long discussion with Manabendra Deb, President of Dhaka University Students Union, and some of his friends. Besides, I had interacted with some of the functionaries of Jamaat-e-Islami, a few faculty members of Dhaka University, businessmen, community leaders, priests in Dhakeswari temple and Kali Mandir, media persons, religious leaders who wanted to remain anonymous. I understand and appreciate their difficulties. Media person Aminur Rashid, a highly argumentative and articulate young man with a wide and positive perspective of the future of Bangladesh, presented me his publications on election politics; I acknowledge his gesture with thanks.

Faruq-sad-uddin Ahmed, professor at Gauhati University, went through the first draft of the study minutely and offered valuable inputs. I am grateful to him. Special thanks go to Ratna, my former Associate and now a faculty member of Indian Institute of Entrepreneurship, Guwahati, for her inputs to the formulation of Chapter II and Rustam Ali for his technical assistance. My wife Ruby and children Rosa and Sazhiv encouraged me to complete my study within the stipulated time frame.

Above all, I am indebted to the Ministry of External Affairs, Government of India, for the financial support without which this work would not have been possible.

I have dedicated the book to my teacher, mentor, philosopher and guide, an eminent social scientist, Professor Anuradha Dutta, who stands by me at critical moments in my life and who acts as a source of boundless inspiration. Currently as a Professor of Peace Studies at the Institute, she happens to be my colleague. This gives me a unique advantage of working with her, which, for me, is a rewarding and almost transcendental experience. The dedication is a humble tribute to an outstanding personality by her humble student.

I thank M.P. Misra, who agreed to publish the book in the shortest possible time. A timely publication of a study is necessary to keep alive the relevance of its content.

It goes without saying that the content, analyses and data are my responsibility. No one else is accountable for any misinterpretation, mistake, faulty analysis that might have crept into the body of the book inadvertently.

Abu Nasar Saied Ahmed

ABBREVIATIONS

AD	:	Anno Domini
BC	:	Before Christ
BCI	:	Business Competitiveness Index
BIMSTEC	:	Bay of Bengal Initiative for Multi-Sectoral Technical and Economic Cooperation, a conglomeration of seven countries (Bangladesh, Bhutan, India, Nepal, Myanmar, Sri Lanka and Thailand)
BNP	:	Bangladesh Nationalist Party
BOP	:	Balance of Payment
BRAC	:	Bangladesh Rural Academic Committee
CENESEAS	:	Centre for Northeast India, South and South East Asia Studies
DFI	:	Direct Foreign Investment
DGFI	:	Directorate General of Forces Intelligence
GCI	:	Growth Competitiveness Index
GDP	:	Gross Domestic Product
HuJI	:	Harkat-ul-Jihad-al-Islami
ICS	:	Islamic Chatra Sibir
IIG	:	Indian Insurgent Groups

IKNMB	:	International Khatme Nabuwat Movement Bangladesh
IOJ	:	Islamic Oikya Jote
ISI	:	Inter Service Intelligence
JMB	:	Jamaat-ul-Mujahideen Bangladesh
JMJB	:	Jagrata Muslim Janata Bangladesh
LDC	:	Less Developed Countries
NDI	:	National Democratic Institute of International Affairs
NGO	:	Non-Governmental Organization
OKDISCD	:	Omeo Kumar Das Institute of Social Change and Development
RAW	:	Research and Analysis Wing
SAARC	:	South Asian Association for Regional Cooperation
SAPTA	:	SAARC Preferential Trading Agreement
UNDP	:	United Nations Development Programme
VAT	:	Value Added Tax
WTO	:	World Trade Organization

LIST OF TABLES

1
INTRODUCTION

At the culmination of a terrible liberation war, a sovereign nation-state called People's Republic of Bangladesh, the youngest nation in South Asia, joined the community of nations as a new member on December 16, 1971. Politically this astounding development demolished the validity of the 'two-nation theory' that divided the Indian sub-continent in 1947 and paved the way for the creation of an unviable wing of Pakistan called East Pakistan, now Bangladesh. Religion, as the edifice of political unity with utter disregard to historical, cultural, linguistic, traditional and geographical dissimilarities and dissonances, does not act as a strong cementing force. It is neither paradoxical nor ironical but a universally acknowledged fact of political life of all nations that mere religious sentiment does not work as a decisive drive for nation-building. Had it been so, in the Middle East there would have been only one state and history would not have witnessed bloodshed for such a long time among the Muslim brethren.

The new state of Bangladesh inherited endemic problems of grave magnitude. Some are natural such as flood, cyclone and draught; and some are man made, such as the huge population, which probably could not be suitably accommodated within its limited geographical territory of 148,393 sq km out of which the land coverage is 133,910 sq km. only half of it (55.39%) is arable. Host of others include political instability as testified to by despicable political killings, military rule, political unrest of the recent variety, abject rural poverty, rampant corruption (Bangladesh, of course, is not the only corrupt country in South Asia) and rising Islamic militancy since 2001. Besides, problems of underdevelopment are visible in almost all walks of life in Bangladesh.

This land mass, known previously as East Bengal during the colonial era and East Pakistan from 1947 to 1971, located between 20.34^0 and 26.38^0 North latitudes and 88.01^0 and 92.41^0 East longitude, is surrounded by India (out of its 4246 km international boundary it shares 4053 with India and the rest 193 with Myanmar). In other words 95.45% of its land border is shared with India and the rest with Myanmar. It has an easy access to high seas with a long coastline of 580 km. This deltaic country is "Flat like a map" crisscrossed by countless rivers which run down from the Himalayas to meet the Bay of Bengal.[1] Except for the hilly tract in the north-east and south-east, the country is a low, flat and fertile land which has forest coverage of about 13%. It produces bamboo, timber and cane.

The country is divided into six divisions – Barisal, Chittagong, Dhaka, Khulna, Rajshahi and Sylhet and further sub-divided into 64 districts. Bangladesh has 507 Upazilas and thanas, 4,484 unions, 59,990 mouzas, 87,319 villages, 223 municipalities and 6 city corporations (Dhaka, Chittagong, Khulna, Rajshahi, Sylhet and Barisal).

Bangladesh is known as a land of rivers with 54 major rivers originating in India and about 230 other smaller rivers and rivulets under three mighty river systems: Ganges-Padma, Brahmaputra-Jamuna and Surma-Meghna. These river systems facilitate as water reservoirs and also as other sources of livelihood. Bangladesh is essentially a rural country with a rural population of 76.9% and hence agricultural as well. Agriculture contributes 9.5% to the GDP. It is one of the poorest countries in the world (GDP per capita $1770) and ranks 139th among the 177th countries listed in the UNDP, 2005. Nonetheless, christened a "landscape of disaster" in the early 1990s because of recurrent natural disasters, Bangladesh has gradually made an impressive improvement in matters of primary school enrolment, infant mortality, nutrition management of mothers, reduction of fertility rate and gender parity, due mainly to the interventions of the civil society, women organizations and certain government agencies and NGOs like Bangladesh Rural Advancement Committee (BRAC).[2]

The People

A country with an estimated population (July 2006) of 147,365,352[3] Bangladesh is the 8th most populous one in the world, with the highest density of population (over 1000 per sq. km). Taking several factors together, such as the current growth rate of population at 1.48%, the projected population for the next few decades, a hypothetical assumption of low fertility and hence gradual reduction in population, Bangladesh will, nonetheless, have a massive population of 192 million in 2051.[4] It would be a stupendous task to manage this huge population within its geographical limits and with its natural resources. Table 1.1 shows the decadal variations of population since liberation in 1971.

Bangladesh is essentially a Muslim dominated country (89.6%) most of whom adhere to the Sunni tradition. Islam is the state religion. It has the third largest Muslim population after Indonesia and India. The Hindu community constitutes 9.2 per cent of the total, with the Christian and the Buddhist and others being a mere 1 per cent of the total population (Census 2001). Ethnically Bangladesh is pre-eminently a

Table 1.1
Population statistics of Bangladesh: 1901-2001

Year	*Population*	*% of variation*	*Growth rate*
1901	28,927,786		
1911	31,555,056	9.08	0.94
1921	33,254,096	5.38	0.60
1931	35,604,170	7.07	0.74
1941	41,997,297	17.96	1.70
1951	44,165,740	5.16	0.50
1961	55,222,633	25.4	2.26
1974	76,398,000	38.35	2.48
1981	89,912,000	17.69	2.35
1991	111,455,185	23.96	2.17
2001	129,247,233	15.96	1.48

Source: *2004 Statistical Yearbook of Bangladesh,* p. 33.

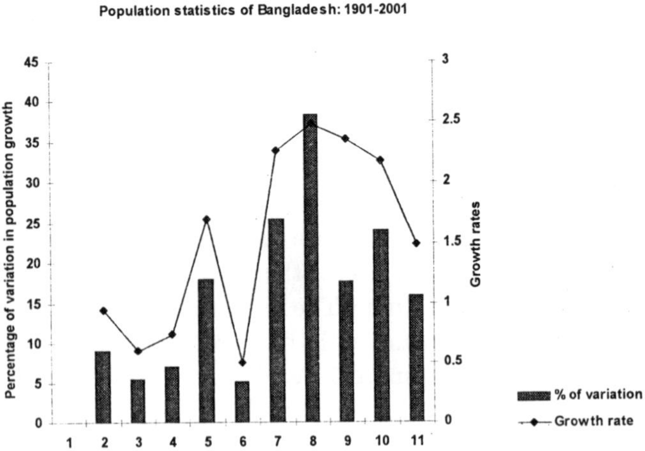

Bengali nation-state. Its Bengali population constitutes 98% of the total population, the rest are Urdu speaking Biharis and others. Bangladesh has a tribal population of over 1.2 million, who are distributed in Khagrachhari, Bandarban, Rangamati, Chittagong, Cox's Bazaar, Habiganj, Sylhet, Sunamganj, Maulavi Bazaar, Dinajpur, Joypurhat, Rajshahi, Naogaon, Ranpur, Bogra, Mymensingh, Barguna and Bhola districts. There are about 45 tribal groups and the most notable among them are Chakma, Garo, Hajong, Khasi, Santals, Maitei and Murgong. The tribal population constitute less than 1 per cent of the total. The Buddhists constitute the majority of the tribal population, followed by Hindus and Christians (Table 1.2).

Table 1.2
Distribution of tribal population by religion

Religion	*Per cent*
Hindus	24
Buddhists	44
Christians	13
Others	19

Source: http:www.discoverybangladesh.com

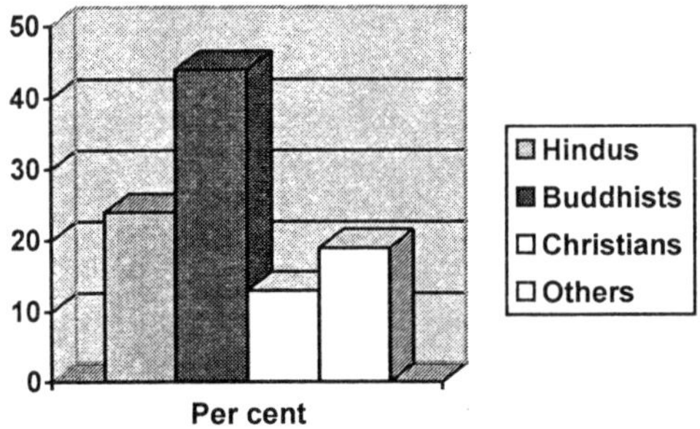

The geographical territory now known as Bangladesh once used to be called Bangalah and later Bengal, a term used by archaeologists, cartographers, geographers, historians and social anthropologists. It is difficult to reconstruct the history of Bengal owing to paucity of historical data. The first reference to the word Bengal was made in the early Vedic literature in the form of 'Vanga', an area covering the whole of lower Ganges.[5] It is believed that the advance of the Aryans during the period of 1500-800 BC did not touch Vanga which was under forest cover and was inhabited by indigenous people of proto-Australoid origin, later came to be known as Veddoid.

It is understandable that the terms Bengal and Bengali have origins from Vanga. As the name of the country suggests, Bangladesh is a land of the Bengali. The people are a mixture of Dravido-Mundo Longheads, Alpine Shortheads, Aryan Longheads and Monogolian Shortheads.[6] Stone tools found in various parts of present Bangladesh provide the earliest evidence of pre-Aryan human settlement. It is now believed that today's Bengalis are an admixture of Dravido-Mongolid races akin to the predominantly in the vast region of South East Asia.[7] Despite the fact that the people living in this country had resisted the Aryan attacks from time to time since the 5th century BC, the Sanskritization influence penetrated deep into the culture and religion of its pre-Islamic population. As such, the process of Aryanization or Sanskritization of the so-called non-Aryan impure 'barbarians' (*mleccha*) was quite late, considering the fact that the North India had already experienced the process in the middle of the second millennium BC.[8] It is because of Aryanization that, for the people, the historic tie with northern and western India is more pronounced than that with South East Asia.

Several geo-political dispensations covering a millennium shaped the history of modern greater Bengal, which got split into two – East and West Bengal during the colonial period and later on became parts of two independent countries. A brief narration might be useful in appreciating the contextual panorama presented in the subsequent Chapters.

Present Bangladesh was a part of an ancient political entity known as Prachya (East) which included Anga, Pundra, Vangal, Samatara, Khadi, Radha, Gauda, and of course, Pragjyotishpura.[9] At the same time, the major rivers and their tributaries created natural arteries of communication and transport and at the same time formed cultural sub-regions namely Vanga (which included present districts of Dhaka, Faridpur, Jessore, Bakarganj, Khulna and Nadia), Varendra (present districts of Malda, Pabna, Rajshahi, Dinajpur, Bogra and Rangpur), Bhagirathi-Hooghly Samatata (present districts of Midnapur, Howrah, Hoolgy, Burdwan Mirshidabad and Birbhum of West Bengal) and Haricale (present Comilla, Noakhali and Chittagong.[10] The vast region was inhabited by non-Aryan ethnic groups named after the places where they used to live. The Chittagong area was known as Haricale. Magadha conquered a major part of Vanga in 545 BC. Two centuries later Vanga not only attained some degree of political independence due to its inaccessibility caused by forests and rivers but also gained prominence for its flourishing trade and commerce. Its people drew the attention of the rest of the region as a sea-faring race famous for boat building.

Buddhism was probably introduced to Vanga during the period of 321-181 BC, although the first material evidence for the advance of Buddhism was found at a stupa of second century BC in Madhya Pradesh in which it was inscribed that the people living in that region have become devotees of Buddhism.[11] With the expansion of Buddhism, the region saw construction of roads, buildings, watch towers, towns, monasteries and universities in a planned manner. It is interesting to note that although the Kushans (300-100 BC) did not exercise full control over Vanga, the Buddhists culture conquered it.

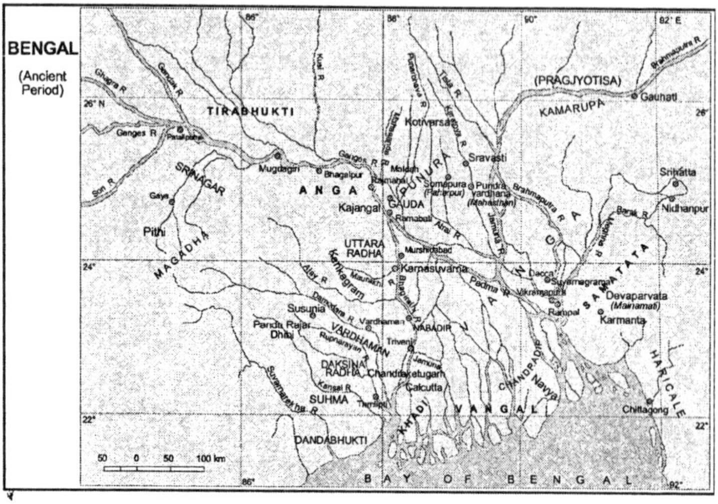

Source: Banglapedia, CD, 2006

Thus, historians claim to have unearthed a recorded history of Bengal which dates back to the fourth century BC on the basis of historical records and inferences that could be found from the time of the Mauryas who swayed over Bengal during 317-232 BC.[12] Later on they ruled a part of Bengal during the first and the second century AD, followed by the rule of the Guptas over a large part of Bengal for over two centuries (320-524 AD). During that period Bengal emerged as an important province. The Gupta period is known as the Golden Age of Indian history. Known for their efficient administration and benevolence, the Gupta kings brought prosperity and political stability to Bengal. The discovery of Gupta coins in different parts of present Bangladesh bears testimony to the fact that the Gupta rule was considerably extensive. It also proves the economic prosperity of Bengal in those days. The Gupta period was followed by the rule of the Buddhist Pala dynasty which covered a fairly long period (750-1155 AD). Legends say that local chieftains elected Gopala as the king of Vanga in 750 AD. With his coronation, the reign of the Palas commenced. The Pala kings - Dharampala (781-821), Devapala (821-861) and Mahipal (995-1043) were known for their military might and good governance. During this time the region came to be known as Bangala.[13] The decline of the Pala dynasty commenced with the end of the rule of Rampala (1082-1124).

During the long rule of the Buddhist Pala dynasty covering a period of four centuries, Bengal enjoyed the fruits of peace, development of art and sculpture, and religious tolerance. The two major religious communities – the Buddhists and the Hindus – lived in an atmosphere of amity and co-existence, culminating in the evolution of Tantric cult and practices among the Buddhists of Bengal. Vijoy Sena defeated the last of the Pala kings in 1195 and established the Hindu Sena rule.

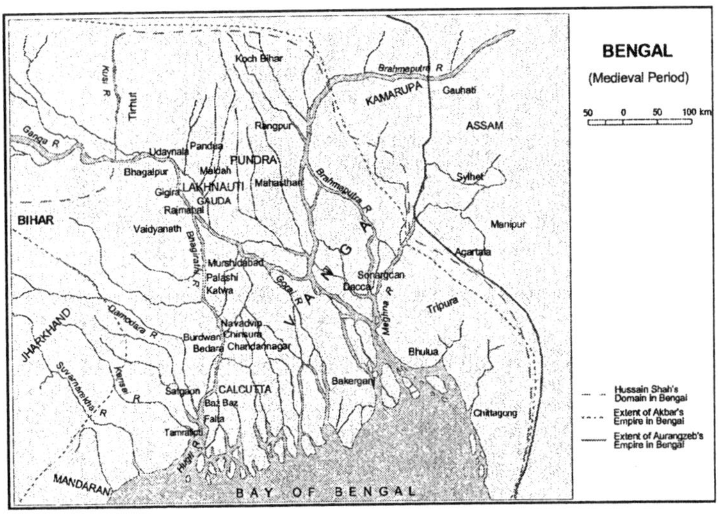

Source: Banglapedia CD, 2006

This was the time, as recorded by an Arab geographer Mas'udi (d. 956), the Arab traders landed in Bengal through sea routes and settled in the south eastern part of the delta ruled by another Bengali Buddhist named Chandras (825-1035)[14]. The advent of the Arab Muslims to this part of the delta and the creation of two trading Diasporas – one of Arab origin and the other, the Buddhist, brought about a composite and tolerant culture in the region. Along with the trading Arabs came the Muslim preachers to propagate Islam. Later on as the entire delta came under the Sena kings, many of the oppressed Buddhists and low caste Hindus embraced Islam to escape social discrimination and oppression at the hands of the ruling class.

Ikhtiaruddin Muhammad Bakhtiar Khilji, a representative of the Delhi Sultanate of Kutubuddin Aibak, conquered Lakhnauti in 1203-04. He entered the capital city Nadia[15] and defeated King Lakhmansena and inaugurated Muslim rule in Bengal. This conquest could be regarded as the precursor to the advent of the Muslims in Bengal. The Slave dynasty defeated the Hindu rulers and occupied Bengal in the 13th century. Then followed the successive Muslim rules by the Khiljis, the Tuglaks and finally the Mughals. The British took over Bengal after defeating Sirajuddaula on June 23, 1757 in the battle of Plassey.

The original Dravido-Mongoloid race of Bengal was exposed to a process of admixture due to the advent of the various religious and racial groups belonging to Buddhism, Hinduism and Islam. There was an inflow of substantial migrant population from Afghanistan, Persia and Turkey in the wake of the conquest by the Monghuls. At any rate, there are three distinct phases in the history of Bengal. The early Buddhist period started from the time of the Mauryas through the Palas. The Hindu period started from the date of the conquest of Bengal by the Senas who terminated the Pala rule. The Muslim period commenced from the 13th century and ended in 1757 AD with the defeat of Sirajuddaula at the hands of the British. By the time the Sepoy Mutiny broke out in 1857 the territorial limit of Bengal came to be known as Bengal Presidency, which included a vast territory covering parts of Bihar, north eastern part of Orissa and the whole of Assam as well. The East India Company engaged a British surveyor, James Rennell in 1784 to prepare a map of India. In this map he labelled Bangala as Bengal. The map showed a large territory covered by the British conquered territory of Bengal which extended up to Banaras in the west, Sylhet and some parts of lower Assam in the east, from the border of Bhutan and Nepal to Midnapore in the north and Bay of Bengal in the South.

India's first War of Independence, 1857-58, terminated the rule of East India Company and marked the beginning of direct British rule in India. The British Government made changes in the boundary of Bengal more than once, for political and administrative reasons that served their colonial interests. The most important change was the partition of Bengal in 1905. The new eastern province of Bengal with an area of 276,00 sq. km and a population of 31 million, majority of whom were Muslims (59.3%), laid the foundation for the partition of the country on religious lines in 1947 and eventually the creation of a separate sovereign state of Bangladesh in 1971.[16]

Prelude to dismemberment of Pakistan

Pakistan was created in 1947 with the division of the country on the basis of the 'two-nation theory'. The new state stood an absurd entity with fractured geography, wide social and cultural disharmony and incongruous historical tradition. Except religion, there was hardly anything called shared and common identity between the two parts of Pakistan separated as it was by the Indian territory over 1700 kilometres wide.

The differences and dissonances were so profound to provoke Rupert Emerson to comment that "by the accepted criteria of nationhood there was in fact no such thing as a Pakistani nation".[17] It, therefore, did not take much time for the edifice of a false nationhood primarily based on religion to get dismantled. To be precise, the contrasts overshadowed the apparent religious affinity. The political expediency based on emotions was consigned to flames of an uprising of Bengali Nationalism.

It is not merely geography that hindered the nation-building process in Pakistan. Although it is true that the geographical separation of the wings stood as a major source of difficulty and incipient alienation, later mistrust and misunderstanding played havoc. The location of the national capital in the western wing offering enormous advantage to the people living there, while causing hardship to the people of the other side had a negative impact on the national identity of Pakistan. The geographic separation initiated host of problems beginning with communication constraints in the movement of goods and population to problems of defence and security, adversely affecting the emotional integration of Pakistan as a nation.

The cultural, linguistic, and political contours of the two wings of Pakistan had been so diverse that a meeting point of all diversities could not be located. While West Pakistan had a larger territorial space of 496,644 sq km accommodating 45% of the total population, East Pakistan, with lesser geographic space, accommodated more people but with fewer resources were available. Added to this visible discrepancy, the most glaring sources of discontentment were linguistic conflict and unequal share of political power. Apparently, the Bengalis from East Pakistan enjoyed equal share of power in respect of induction of ministers and election of the members of the Constituent Assembly and National Assembly during the early period of united Pakistan.[18] That façade of co-sharing continued till 1970. But when the question of exercising real political power associated with the key positions such as those of the prime minister or the president arose, a Bengali would not be allowed to rise to the level. The tendency to deprive a Bengalis from occupying the real seat of power was visible, if not pronounced, even in the formative phase soon after the birth of Pakistan. It was a ceremonial position only that was given to a deserving Bengali. Soon after the death of Mohammad Ali Jinnah, Nazimuddin, a Bengali Nawab from East Pakistan became the Governor General leaving the powerful position of prime minister to be occupied by Urdu speaking Liaquat Ali Khan. The trend continued; in 1970 Sheikh Mujibur Rehman, despite his stunning electoral victory, not allowed to become the Prime Minister of Pakistan. This deprivation propelled Bengali nationalism to stage a massive revolt ultimately leading to dismemberment of Pakistan.[19] As Sufia M. Uddin writes "Bengali roots became a source of pride and national fervor that would lead to the creation of Bangladesh".[20]

Bengali nationalism emerged out of the linguistic differences between the two wings of Pakistan. East Pakistan is pre-eminently a Bengali speaking region where more than 80% people spoke Bengali. On the other hand, West Pakistan had no singular dominant language. At least four major languages *viz*, Urdu, Punjabi, Sindhi and Pushtu made West Pakistan a multi-lingual region. Yet Jinnah made a statement on March 21, 1948 while delivering his convocation address at the Dhaka University to the effect that to consider the demand for Bengali as one of the national languages was inimical to the interest of Pakistan. It could be marked as the turning point in the history of united Pakistan that eventually ignited the linguistic nationalism leading to the break up of Pakistan. He said:

> Let me restate my view on the question of a state language for Pakistan. For official use in [East

> Pakistan] the people of the province can choose any language they wish. The question will be decided solely in accordance with the wishes of the people of this province alone, as freely expressed through their accredited representatives at the appropriate time and after full and dispassionate consideration. There can, however be only one lingua franca – that is the language for intercommunication between various provinces of the state – and that language should be Urdu and cannot be any other.

Justifying his contention of placing Urdu at the national status, Jinnah said that Urdu

> has been nurtured by a hundred million of this subcontinent, [it is] a language understood throughout the length and breadth of Pakistan and above all a language which more than any other provincial language, embodies the best that is in Islamic culture and Muslim tradition and is nearest to the language used in other Islamic countries. [21]

Jinnah's attempt to make Urdu the only state language did not succeed. The efforts to impose Islamic nomenclature continued even after the death of Jinnah. There was an attempt to Urduize the Bengali script, when the Central Advisory Committee for Education recommended Urdu script for Bengali "in the interest of national unity and solidarity and the rapid advancement of general education in Pakistan".[22] Pakistan's Education Minister's comment on was highly provocative. He said:

> Not only Bengali literature, even the Bengali alphabet is full of idolatry. East Bengali letter is associated with this or that god or goddesses of Hindu pantheon...Pakistan and Devanagiri script cannot co-exist. It looks like defending the frontier of Pakistan with Bharati soldiers! To ensure a bright and great future for Bengali language it must be linked with the Holy Quran. Hence the necessity and importance of Arabic script.[23]

Such expressions foretold the unbridgeable divide of Pakistan even at the dawn of its creation and impracticability of efforts to Urduize the language which was shaped by a process of several centuries. At any rate, these developments gave the early premonition of eventual disintegration of Pakistan and emergence of a nation-state, People's Republic of Bangladesh.

Soon after the declaration of the Muslim League on January 26, 1952 that Urdu would be the only official language of Pakistan, the people of East Pakistan declared February 21 as the State Language Day even in the teeth of brutal military strength of the ruling regime of Pakistan. The demonstration in support of the linguistic solidarity on that day led to the killing of seven persons. Several hundreds were injured. The Swahid Minar near the Dhaka University and the commemoration of 'Ekushey' (twenty-first)[24] continues to remind what the Bengalis suffered during the language movement and the price paid for rejection of Urdu as alien to the Bengali Muslims, whose identity had been constructed through a long process of socio-political and cultural evolution. By definition the Bengali Muslims stood different from the West Pakistani Muslims because of their pronounced social, cultural and linguistic differences. The three components – culture, social process and language – created a syncretism that encompassed all other domains including religion.[25] These distinctive components led to the marginalization of religion and concomitant upgradation of Bengali identity that eventually laid the foundation of the nation-state. It did not take long to usher in the process of construction of Bengali nationalism based essentially on language.[26] The formation of Awami Muslim League in 1949 by Maulana Abdul Hamid Khan Bhasani, Hussain Shaheed Suhrawardy, Samsul Haq, Ataur Rahman and Sheikh Mujibur Rehman was a clear indication that Bengali nationalism was going to play the key role in deciding the fate of the then East Pakistan.

The only binding element of religion, Islam, was too fragile to hold Pakistani nationalism together. The West Pakistanis suffered from a sense of superiority complex and used to look down upon the Bengali Muslims as half Muslims.[27] Such a contemptuous attitude towards the Bengali community is reflected in the autobiography of Ayub Khan. He wrote that the Bengali Muslims "have been and still are under considerable Hindu and cultural and linguistic influence. As such they have all the inhibitions of down trodden races and have not yet found it possible to adjust psychologically to the requirements of the new born freedom."[28] To be more precise, the rulers in West Pakistan viewed the customs and traditions of the Bengali Muslims such as singing Rabindra Sangeet, wearing sarees and putting bindis on forehead by Muslim women, and speaking Bengali common to Bengali Hindus with disdain, and therefore, regarded the Bengali Muslims as somewhat less Muslim than their counterparts in West Pakistan.

With little in common to share, the two artificial wings of Pakistan were destined to fall apart under the weight of vast disparity in terms of development and discrimination in employment in bureaucracy and military.[29] The discrimination was profound not only in the higher ranks and files but also in the lower echelons of these two vitally important segments administration and national security. In 1956 there were only 2900 Bengali officers out of 42,000 officers in the central government of Pakistan. Since Islamabad was the capital of the country, far away from the eastern wing, the lion's share of government positions went to the people of West Pakistan. The disparity between the east and the west in administration widened day by day. In 1962 in the foreign services, Bengali officers constituted only 20.8% while in defence services only 10 per cent jobs went to Bengali officers. In the field of education the financial allocation for West Pakistan was Rupees 1530 crore during the period of 1948-1955. But East Pakistan got only Rs.240 crore which accounts for only 13.5% during the said period. The total expenditure during that period for the development of East Pakistan was only 10%. The Government of Pakistan spent Rs.5700 crore during the period of 1948 to 1955 towards the development of Karachi city and Rs.3000 crore for Islamabad during 1956-1967. A miserly amount of Rs.25 crore only was spent for the development of Dhaka city during the same period.[30] To state precisely, as Rehman Sobhan argues, the political and economic balance heavily favoured West Pakistan.[31] The Bengali psyche had always been haunted by a sense of relative and appalling deprivation. The disparity between East and West Pakistan in administration widened. The disparity was profound and palpable to say the least. It led to the formulation of a six-point charter of demands for autonomy of East Pakistan which was placed by Sheikh Mujibur Rehman at a convention of the opposition parties in Lahore on February 5 and 6, 1966. The rejection of the charter by the government of Pakistan intensified a massive movement in East Pakistan which was followed by a countrywide crack down.[32]

The language issue generated an emotional appeal for collective action towards realization of the ethnic pride of a nation. It paved the way for the articulation of a greater demand for autonomy. Simultaneously, it gave a distinct shape and personality to Bengali nationalism[33]. The refusal of the Pakistani military government headed by General Yahya Khan to respect the verdict of the people in the 1970 elections which gave absolute majority to the Awami League in the National Assembly of Pakistan became a point of no return. Bangladesh became a sovereign independent country in the real sense of the term on December 16, 1971 when the Pakistani brigades surrendered to the Indian forces and the Mukti Bahini after a brief war.[34]

A new nation emerged out of the ruins, devastation, general massacre of countless people and eventually military intervention. Those who collaborated with Pakistani army – the Jamaat-e-Islami (henceforth Jamaat), the al-Badar, the Razakars and a host of small Islamists groups – either disappeared or maintained a low profile. Many of them were summarily executed in mass frenzy. Some others were put behind the bars. Bangladesh emerged as a secular democratic country. Its constitutional arrangements had lived up to the spirit and philosophy on which the new republic decided to stand at that historic point of time. It cultivated a strong bond of fraternal relation with India, which had extended a helping hand at the most crucial time of its struggle for independence as also to secure its status as an independent international personality. The relationship between the two South Asian countries grew in a spirit of friendship and mutual respect during the Mujib era. But the process of internal democratization and secularization, and the cultivation of good neighbourly external relations with India received a massive setback with his assassination at the hands of a handful ambitious military officers on August 15, 1975. The successive regimes, with the exception of Sheikh Hasina Wajed's as the Prime Minister (1996-2001), demonstrated anti-Indian stance, as a matter of course. The relationship, thus, drifted from friendship to hostility with the pitch being queered by certain tangled issues, such as, sharing of river water, migration of Bangladeshi citizens to India, border skirmishes, displacement and rehabilitation of the Chakmas, and Bangladesh's role in providing the North East militant and jihadi groups with logistic infrastructure.

Is Bangladesh moving towards Islamic fundamentalism? If so, what impact will it have on India? The present study attempts to answer these two core questions.

There has been some controversy regarding the term 'Islamic fundamentalism' which is used mostly by the West to refer to a movement in the Islamic world demanding strict adherence to and observance of the teachings of the Qur'an and the Hadith and the Shariah laws. It is distinctively a modern phenomenon which believes revivalism and rejects copying western models and values, and advocates a return to the pristine fundamentals of Islam.[35] Many of the Muslim scholars would prefer terms such as 'Islamism' or 'Islamicism' to the over-used term 'Islamic fundamentalism' which, in these days, has gained currency in a spectacular manner ever since the Iranian revolution of 1979.[36] The spread of the idea of revivalism in social context and charging movement towards political Islam understood in terms of capturing state power by electoral practices or by violence, within a short span time covering the Islamic world which has a 900 million population living in 44 Muslim majority countries and some more countries where there is a substantial Muslim population, from Algeria to Indonesia, is a stunning development in the modern world. The revivalism involves increasing number of groups, associations, political parties and movements which denounce not only the West but also the secular rulers and governments in Muslim majority countries for not adhering to the fundamental principles of Islam, not promoting and safeguarding the interests and welfare of the *ummah* (community), and for indulging in corruption and for projecting themselves as secular. Therefore, the fundamentalists argue in favour of spearheading a massive movement, which could be an armed and a violent one, to spread ideas of Islamic theology and tradition in order to revitalize Islam and Islamic society and to overthrow the existing corrupt, inefficient, secular and liberal Islam. Islamic fundamentalism believes in strengthening the foundation of the religion. In doing so it wants to go deep into the roots of the religion in order to purify, expunge and renew it by propagating the principles as laid down in the earliest phase of Islam.

The Islamists in Bangladesh, both the political and the militant, aim at transforming their society and the polity so as to follow and practice the Islamic way of life in the rigid sense of the term. While the Jamaat has come forward to take recourse to parliamentary methods of transforming Bangladesh into an Islamic country, the militants want to change everything by violent means. There has been a steady rise of Islamists in Bangladesh since 2001 when the Jamaat became a partner in the coalition ministry headed by Begum Khaleda Zia. The rise has been checked to a considerable extent by the present care taker government. The decision to execute the six militants on the midnight of March 30, 2007 and crackdown on the militants show that the government meant business in putting a strong brake on the rise of the fundamentalists. Be that as it may, one cannot be sure that there would be no reversal of the process initiated by the temporary caretaker government; a future elected government might once again return to the political expediency of the pre and post-poll arrangement of 2001.

At any rate, Bangladesh has been facing a serious challenge to its democratic polity with the emergence of political and militant Islam in the recent years, more particularly after the 2001 general elections. It is paradoxical to find that the Jamaat, which collaborated with the Pakistani army, al-Badar and Razakars during the war of liberation, and had to stand on public trial after the liberation, slowly emerged in the national political scene owing to the patronage of General Ziaur Rahman. The Jamaat leader Golam Azam, who took refuge in Pakistan after the liberation, came back during the time of General Ziaur Rahman and secured a political space in Bangladesh. The party eventually became a coalition partner of the government headed by the Bangladesh National Party (BNP) in 2001. Its student wing, Islamic Chatra Sibir (ICS) has been spreading its wings to control a number of colleges and universities. The Jamaat is the most influential among the various Islamic political parties and groups like Islamic Oikya Jote (IOJ), rendering others almost redundant. Simultaneously, there is also a rise in militant Islam. Three hardcore groups - the Jagrata Muslim Janata Bangladesh (JMJB) once led by the dreaded Siddiqul Islam alias Bangla Bhai (who along with the supreme leader Abdur Rahman was arrested on March 1, 2006, tried and executed on March 30, 2007, on the charges of killing 64 persons including Muhammad Yunus, a professor at Rajshahi University and two judges), the Jamaat-ul-Mujahideen Bangladesh (JMB), which claimed to have triggered off August 17, 2005 serial bombing all over Bangladesh, in 63 out of 64 districts and asked the Government and the people to adhere to Islamic law and practices (its leader Abdul Awal was also executed on March 30, 2007), and the Harkat-ul-Jihad-al-Islami (HuJI), are reportedly making steady penetration countrywide as extreme rightist and militant Islamic forces. The tendency of the BNP to institutionalize religious fundamentalism in a covert form by accepting Jamaat as a partner in the coalition government and conniving at the subversive activities of militant Islam is bound to have far-reaching effects which India cannot afford to ignore.

The rise of Islamists, both political and militant, in Bangladesh has far reaching consequences for India since its shares with Bangladesh a long stretch of 4053 km border. The admittedly porous border adjacent to Assam, Meghalaya and Tripura provides easy entry-exit route to the jihadi groups as well as the militants belonging to North East making the entire the North East India vulnerable thus jeopardising India's national security. There has been a steady growth of Madrassas in Bangladesh – 7373 registered and state sponsored Madrassas and an equal number of private and unregistered Madrassas, with unregulated curriculum, scoring a phenomenal rise of 22.22% in five years from 2001 to 2006 in comparison to a mere 9.74 % growth in general educational institutions. This has been a major concern of the socially conscious citizens of the country. The abovementioned spurt is spectacularly evident in most of the backward north-western districts of Bangladesh. This is bound to have adverse impact in some of the districts of Assam such as Karimganj, Goalpara and Dhubri, which are close to the international border. The recent mushroom growth of private Madrassas in Assam, most of which are unregistered and with out-dated curriculum should invariably cause concern. There has been an unholy nexus amongst the jihadi groups, North East militants and the intelligence forces of Bangladesh and Pakistan. They all have a single-point agenda to create social and political instability in North East India. A dispassionate approach to the problems posed by the rise of Islamic fundamentalism might lead to the formulation of a concrete set of policy to deal with it and save the region from both foreseen and unforeseen turbulence.

REFERENCES

1. F.B. Bradley-Birt, *Dacca: The Romance of an Eastern Capital*, First published in 1914, (Guwahati: Spectrum Publication, 1992), p. 3.
2. *Human Development Report 2005*, p. 46 and 221.
3. https://ww.cia.gov/cia/publications/factbook/geog/bg.html. Bangladesh Bureau of Statistics, *2004 Statistical Yearbook of Bangladesh*, puts it to be 123.8 million (Census 2001) while the adjusted population stood 130 million, p. xx.
4. Centre for Policy Dialogue, *Demographic Dynamics in Bangladesh: Looking at the Larger Picture* (Dhaka: Pathak Shamabesh, 2003), pp. 6-7.
5. *Banglapedia*, CD Edition (Dhaka, Asiatic Society of Bangladesh, 2006).
6. R.C. Majumdar, *History of Bengal* (Dacca: University of Dacca, 1943), p. 374.

7. Kamruddin Ahmed, *Social History East Pakistan* (Dacca: Orient Longman, 1969), p. 8.

8. Romila Thapar, *From Lineage to State: Social Formations in the Mid-First Millennium BC in the Ganga Valley* (New Delhi: Oxford University Press, 1984) also her "Image of Early Barbarian in Early India", *Comparative Studies in Society and History*, Vol. 13, No. 4. (October 1971) and Puspa Niyogi, *Brahmamic Settlements in Different Subdivisions of Ancient Bengal* (Calcutta: R.K. Mitra, 1967).

9. For details of the political and physical sub-regions of Bengal see O.H.K. Spate and A.T.A. Learmonth, *India and Pakistan: A General and Regional Geography* (London: Methuen, 1967), pp. 571-573.

10. For a detailed discussion on the cultural sub-region in ancient Bengal see Barrie M. Morrison, *Political and Cultural Regions of Early Bengal* (Tucson: University of Arizona Press, 1970), Chapter 4.

11. For a detailed account of the growth of Buddhism in Bengal see Gayatri Sen Majumdar, *Buddhism in Ancient Bengal* (Calcutta: Navana, 1983).

12. Clarence Maloney, "Bangladesh and Its People in Prehistory", *Journal of the Institute of Bangladesh Studies*, Vo. 2 (1977), pp. 17-20.

13. R.C. Majumdar, *History of Ancient Bengal* (Calcutta: G. Bharadwaj & Co. 1971), pp. 99-100 and 159. It may be noted that the word 'Bengali' came from the word 'Bangala'. Today's Bengali language is an Indo-Aryan language which passed through a long process of evolution for several thousand years experiencing a chemistry of languages and dialects of many Austoasiatic, Dravidian and Sino-Tibetan groups living in the deltaic region. For a thorough discussion on the subject see M.H. Klaiman, "Bengali" in Bernard Comrie (ed), *The World Major Languages* (New York: Oxford University Press, 1990), pp. 499-511 and also S.K. Chatterji, *Origin and Development of Bengali Language*, Vol. 1 (Calcutta: University of Calcutta Press, 1926), pp. 79 and 154. Also see a map showing the distribution of the Bengali speaking population in greater

Bengal in Joseph E. Schwartzberg (ed), *A Historical Atlas of South Asia* (Chicago: University of Chicago Press, 1978), p. 100.

14. For details see Richard M. Eaton, *The Rise of Islam and the Bengal Frontier, 1204-1760* (Berkeley: University of California Press, 1993) Chapter 1; also see Abdul Momin Chowdhury, *Dynastic History of Bengal, 750-1200* (Dacca: Asiatic Society of Pakistan, 1976). Also his "Islamization in Bengal: Some Aspects of Socio-religious Background", *Dhaka University Studies*, Vol. 47, No. 1, June 1990, pp. 71-79.

15. Nadia is a village about a few kilometers away from Rohanpur railway station in western Rajshahi district.

16. For details see Sirajul Islam (ed), *History of Bengal 1704-1971* (Dhaka: Asiatic Society of Bangladesh, 1998).

17. Rupert Emerson, *From Empire to Nation* (Cambridge, Mass: Harvard University Press, 1960), p. 2. Richard Weekes has sharply articulated the absurdity of Pakistan as one country when he has termed it as a 'double country'. See his *Pakistan: Birth and Growth of a Muslim Nation* (Princeton: Van Nostrand Company, 1964), p. 3.

18. Rounaq Jahan, *Pakistan: Failure in National Integration* (New York: Colombia University Press, 1972), p. 25.

19. Bipattaran Ghosh, "Bangladesh: Factors Contributing to its Emergence" in Verinder Grover (ed), *Bangladesh: Government and Politics* (New Delhi: Deep Deep, 2000), pp. 11-29.

20. Sufia M. Uddin, *Religion, Ethnicity and Language in an Islamic Nation* (New Delhi: Vistaar Publication, 2006), p. 119.

21. For details see Jinnah's speech entitled "National Consolidation" delivered on March 21 and "Farewell Message to East Pakistan" on March 28, 1948 in *Quaid-I-Azam Mohamed Ali Jinnah's Speeches as Governor General 1947-48* (Karachi: Pakistan Publication, nd.). Also see for further details Ratan Lal Chakrabarti, *Bhasha Andolaner Dalilpatra*, (Documents of Language Movement) (Dhaka: Bangla Academy, 2000).

22. Cited in Rangalal Sen, *Political Elites in Bangladesh* (Dhaka: University Publication Limited, 1986), p. 105.

23. Cited in Anisuzzaman, *Creativity, Reality and Identity* (Dhaka: International Center for Bengal Studies, 1993), p. 107.

24. For a detailed narration of the significance of 'Ekushey' see Sufia M. Uddin, *Religion, Ethnicity and Language in an Islamic Nation,* n. 20, pp. 124-136.

25. For details see Asim Roy, *The Islamic Syncretistic Tradition in Bengal* (Princeton: Princeton University Press, 1983).

26. For details on various factors that contributed to the rise of Bengali nationalism in Bangladesh see Talukdar Maniruzzaman, *Group Interests and Political Changes: Studies of Pakistan and Bangladesh* (New Delhi: South Asian Publishers, 1982), pp. 13-17.

27. Urmila Phadnis, *Ethnicity and Nation-building in South Asia* (New Delhi: Sage, 1989), p. 169.

28. Mohammad Ayub Khan, *Friends, Not Masters: A Political Autobiography* (Karachi: Oxford University Press, 1969), p. 275.

29. For details see Rounaq Jahan, *Pakistan: Failure in National Integration,* n. 10, pp. 26-107 and Muhammad A Quddus, *Pakistan: A Case Study of a Plural Society* (Calcutta: Minerva Associates, 1981), p. 113.

30. *Banglapedia,* CD Edition, 2006.

31. For details see Rehman Sobhan, *Bangladesh: The Problems of Governance* (Dhaka: University Press Limited, 1993), pp. 82-108.

32. For a detailed account of the six point charter of demand and widespread arrests of leaders, and implication Sheikh Mujibur Rehman in so called 'Agartala conspiracy' case of January 6, 1968 see Siraj-uddin Ahmed, *Bangabandhu Sheikh Mujibur Rahman* (Dhaka: Bhaskar Prakashini, 2001), Chapters 7 and 8.

33. For a detailed analysis of the rise of Bengali Nationalism that led to the establishment of Bangladesh see Craig Baxter, *Bangladesh: From a Nation to a State* (Boulder: Westview, 1997). Also see Hasan Zaheer, *The Separation of East Pakistan: The Rise and Realization of Bengali Muslim Nationalism* (New York: Oxford University Press, 1994).

34. Richard Sisson and Leo E. Rose, *War and Succession: Pakistan, India, and the Creation of Bangladesh* (Berkeley: University of California Press, 1990).

35. John L. Esposito, *The Oxford Dictionary of Islam* (New York: Oxford University Press, 2003), p.88. Also see Youssef M. Choueiri, *Islamic Fundamentalism* (London: Continuum, 2002), Dilip Hiro, *Islamic Fundamentalism* (London: Paladin Grafton Books, 1988) and Bassam Tibi, *The Challenge of Fundamentalism: Political Islam and the New World Disorder* (Berkeley: University of California Press, 2002).

36. There has been a large number of publications on the Iranian revolution, most notable among them are, John L. Esposito, *Iranian Revolution: Its Global Impact* (Miami: Florida International University Press, 1990); Emmanuel Sivan, *Radical Islam: Medieval Theology and Modern Politics* (New Haven: Yale University Press, 1988).

2

ECONOMY AND POLITY

Lest one should forget, it is pertinent to mention that Bangladesh of today once was under the occupation of the western part of the nation of Pakistan for long 24 years, characterized by a stagnant economy that did not take off at all. But despite sustained domestic and international efforts since its independence to improve the economic conditions and demographic profile, Bangladesh as on date remains a poor, overpopulated and ill-governed nation. The major impediments to growth include frequent cyclones and floods, inefficient state-owned enterprises, inadequate port facilities despite its 580 km long coastline, a rapidly growing labour force that cannot be absorbed by agriculture, a weak industrial base, limited reserves of coal and oil, delays in exploiting some existing energy resources like natural gas, insufficient power supplies and slow implementation of economic reforms. Economic reforms, it is seen, are stalled in many instances by political infighting and instability, and corruption[1] at all levels of government in Bangladesh. Opposition from the bureaucracy, public sector unions and frequent *hartals*[2] has blocked progress in the country. Needless to state that *hartal* has been used to register political protests and stage demonstration by the national parties to paralyze the civic and economic life of the country and also by the student wings to stifle the academic atmosphere on the university campuses.

On the positive side, Bangladesh has made major strides to meet the food needs of its increasing population through increased domestic production and by imports from various countries. The land is devoted mainly to rice and jute cultivation, although wheat production has increased in recent years. The country, today, is to a large extent self-sufficient in rice production. The country's main endowments include its vast human resource base, rich agricultural land, relatively abundant water and substantial reserves of natural gas.

MAINSTREAMING GROWTH*

Synchronizing Savings and Investment

An economy, which had to face deep macro-economic crises in the late 1980s, post transition to a democratic rule in the early 1990s, saw Bangladesh experiencing an economic growth that has been forceful literally. A series of stabilization measures that were introduced into the economy in the mid eighties largely helped in restoring macro-economic stability in the early 1990s. Subsequently, the Bangladesh economy registered an average GDP growth rate of 4.8 per cent in the 1990s, which was higher than that recorded in the previous decade (i.e. 3.8 per cent, 1980s). The later part of 1990s confirmed an even more impressive growth performance (5.21 per cent, 1996-2000) in comparison to that realized in the first half of the said decade (4.4 per cent, 1991-95). The first half of the present decade, in fact, had continued with a rising trend in the average annual growth rate of GDP (5.36 per cent, 2001-05)[3] of the country (Table 2.1).

---

* Scholarly writings of Debapriya Bhattacharya have been used extensively in this chapter.

Table 2.1

Growth Rate of Real GDP, Per Capita GDP and Per Capita Income

Period	*Real GDP (%)*	*Real GDP Per Capita (%)*	*Real Income Per Capita (%)*
1995-96	4.62	2.74	2.67
1996-97	5.39	3.52	3.78
1997-98	5.23	3.40	3.41
1998-99	4.87	3.56	3.75
1999-00	5.94	4.58	4.80
Average Growth Rate (1995-96 to 1999-00)	*5.21*	*3.56*	*3.68*
2000-01	5.27	5.17	5.00
2001-02	4.42	3.06	4.16
2002-03	5.26	3.84	4.75
2003-04	6.27	4.85	4.61
2004-05	5.96	4.57	4.41
Average Growth Rate (2000-01 to 2004-05)	*5.36*	*4.30*	*4.59*
2005-06[P]	6.71	5.33	5.84

Source: Calculated from Table-1 (shown above)

Note: * The term 'real' means constant price (base: 1995-96) figures, P=Provisional.

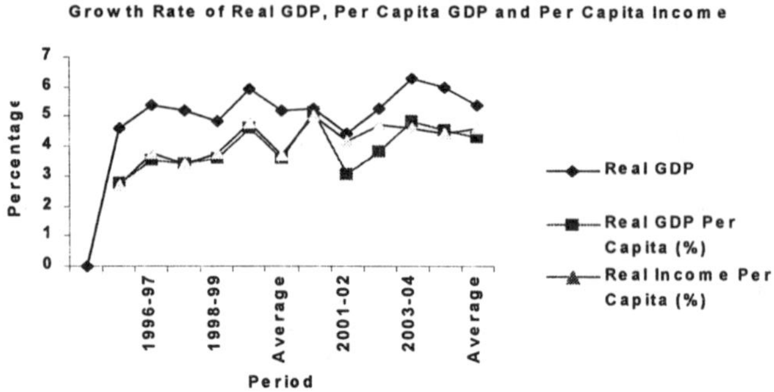

The irony, however is that, despite such impressive growth for more than a decade now, the per capita income of Bangladesh at the beginning of the new century has not only been the lowest among the South Asian countries, but also below the average per capita income of the less-developed countries (LDCs). During the second half (1995-96 to 1999-00) of the 1990s, the average growth in per capita income was 3.68 per cent, which had increased to 4.59 per cent (Table 2.1) in the first half of the new decade of the new century (2000-01 to 2004-05). But a close observation would define that at any rate, a per capita growth rate of 4-5 per cent is impressive, given the infirmities and challenges faced by an LDC like Bangladesh.

A look into the savings and investment scenario in the country could supplement the reasoning behind the growth rate of real GDP in the country. Bangladesh, with one of the lowest domestic savings rate among the developing countries in general, has had a national savings rate that was more or less stagnant in the first half of the 1990s. It was only during the latter half of the 1990s that the saving component showed an increase. Consequent to it, the gross national savings on an average increased from 18.97 per cent of GDP during 1991-95 to 21.79 per cent during 1996-00 and, further to 24.13 per cent of GDP in the first half of the present decade (2001-05) (Table 2.2). On the other hand, the official estimates show that the gross investment as percentage of GDP, on an average, increased from 17.94 during 1991-1995 to 21.51 during 1996-2000, which further increased to 23.64 per cent in the first half of the present decade (2001-2005). On an average, though the public investment rate declined marginally from 6.69 per cent during 1991-1995 to 6.38 during the first half of the new decade (2001-05), private investment, on an average, increased from 11.24 per cent in 1991-1995 to 17.22 per cent of GDP during the first half of the present decade (2001-2005) (Table-2.2).

Table 2.2
Savings and Investments as per cent of GDP (at current market prices)

Indicators	*1991-95*	*1996-00*	*2001-05*
Gross National Savings	18.97	21.79	24.13
Gross Domestic Savings	14.12	16.72	18.78
Gross Investment	17.94	21.51	23.64
Private Investment	11.24	14.52	17.22
Public Investment	6.69	6.79	6.38

Source: *Bangladesh Economy: Macro Economic Performance*, Centre for Policy Dialogue, Dhaka, Bangladesh, 2004 & Bangladesh Bank at http://www.bangladesh-bank.org

Savings and Investments as per cent of GDP (at current market prices)

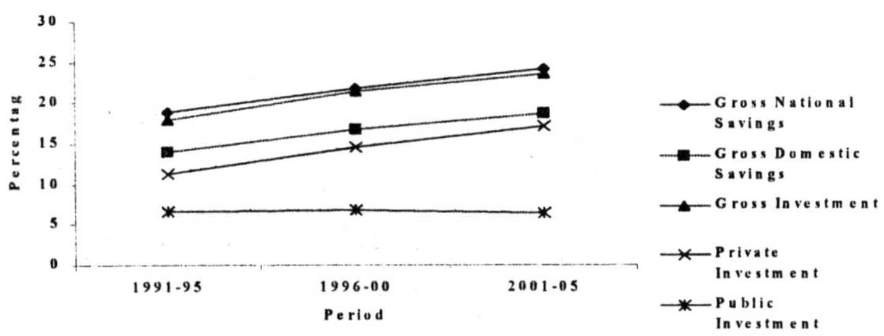

Incremental Growth and Just Distribution in the light of Structural Transformation

A falling share of the agricultural sector with marginal increase in the production of manufactured goods, and a rising contribution of the service sector marks the structural transformation of the Bangladesh economy in recent times. In the years 2001-04, the real economic sector accounted for 39.3 per cent of the GDP, the proportion being 40.98 per cent for the period 1991-95 and 41.25 per cent for 1996-2000. In spite of the marked improved growth rate, the structural transformation is still a far cry in Bangladesh.

The reasoning of incremental growth in Bangladesh in the light of the structural transformation (*de facto*), is, in fact, circumventing. Though within the real economy, a few sectors such as industry demonstrated a stronger growth during the first half of the 1990s, the economy in the subsequent period had again fallen back due to the growth performance of the agricultural sector. The trend continued as it was found that in the financial year of 2005 there was a setback in the agricultural sector due to flood in the previous year for which there was 4% lower agricultural production in the year than the previous year.[4] It is indeed interesting to note that during the second half of the 1990s, the agricultural and industrial sectors yet again emerged as the major sources of GDP growth in comparison to the more pronounced role of the service sector in the earlier half of the decade. But in recent times, it is the service sector, which accounts for the growth of GDP in the country (more than 50 per cent, 2001-2004) (Table 2.3).

Table-2.3

Trends of Sectoral Contribution in GDP growth (% of GDP)

Sectors	*1991-95*	*1996-00*	*2001-04*
Agriculture Sector	20.46	18.05	9.50
Industrial Sector	25.91	33.92	35.54
Service Sector	45.73	42.26	54.67

Source: *Bangladesh Economy: Macro Economic Performance*, Centre for Policy Dialogue, Dhaka, Bangladesh, 2004 and *Human Development Report*, UNDP, 2000

Trends of Sectoral Contribution in GDP growth (% of GDP)

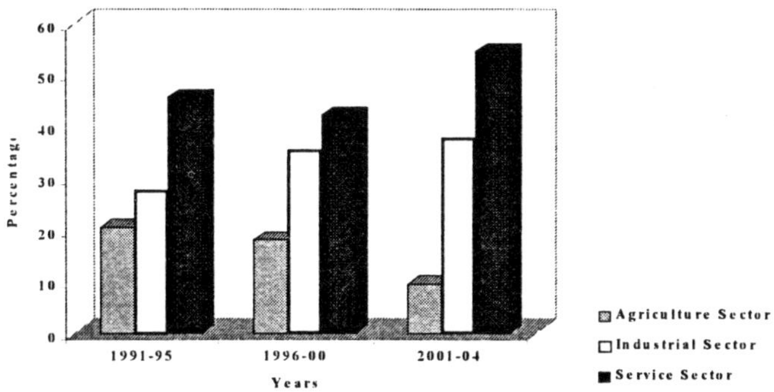

There has been a decline of population below the absolute poverty line from 47.5 per cent in 1992 to 44.33 per cent in 2000 and further to 40.9 per cent in 2004 (Table-2.4). In spite of the improved growth scenario throughout the 1990s, the economy, in general, has recorded a skewed income distribution that deteriorated during the decade coupled with slow pace of poverty alleviation. Between 1992 and 2000, national income attributable to the poorest 10 per cent of the population declined further from a miniscule proportion of 2.58 per cent to 1.84 per cent. Conversely, the control on the national income by the richest 10 per cent of the population increased from 29.23 per cent to 40.72 per cent. One can then conclude that the incremental growth recorded in the economy, is, in fact, a biased one that has resulted in deterioration in the income distribution pattern in the country.

Table 2.4
Trends in Poverty and Inequality of Income

Indicators	*1991/92*	*1995/96*	*2000*	*2004*
Poverty (head count index, % of population)	47.5	47.5	44.3	40.9
National Income to the poorest 10 per cent of Population	2.58	2.24	1.84	–
National Income to the richest 10 per cent of Population	29.23	34.68	40.72	–

Source: *Bangladesh Economy: Macro Economic Performance*, Centre for Policy Dialogue, Dhaka, Bangladesh, 2004 and *Human Development Report*, UNDP, 2000

Trends in Poverty and Inequality of Income (in per cent)

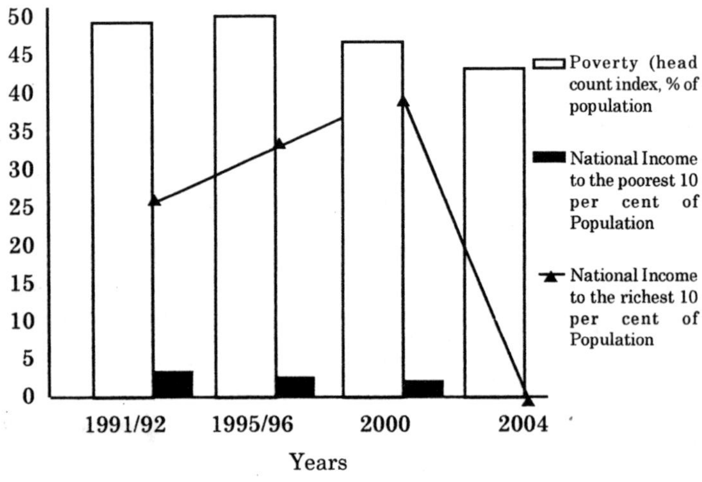

STRUCTURAL CONSTRAINTS: IMPENDING GROWTH IN THE MACRO ECONOMY

Inflation, Deficit and Financing

It is widely held that a low rate of inflation is one of the cornerstones of macroeconomic stability in any economy. Bangladesh has experienced a moderate rate of inflation, below double digit, throughout the 1990s. The increasing trend in inflation rate was corrected in the beginning of the new decade. This sustained low level of inflation in the country has been, more or less, dictated by lower food grain prices ensured by successive good harvests. But the recent inflation rate disturbingly demonstrates an increasing trend; it has increased from 1.94 per cent in 2001 to 6.49 per cent in 2005 (Table 2.5).

Table 2.5

Consumer Price Index and Rate of Inflation- National (Base: 1996=100)

	Twelve-month average basis					
Year	*General*				*Food*	*Non-food*
	Index	*Annual rate of inflation*	*Index*	*Annual rate of inflation*	*Index*	*Annual rate of inflation*
1997	103.96	3.96	103.67	3.67	104.47	4.47
1998	112.96	8.66	114.51	10.46	110.73	5.99
1999	120.94	7.06	125.16	9.30	115.10	3.95
2000	124.31	2.79	128.52	2.68	118.64	3.08
2001	126.72	1.94	130.30	1.38	122.25	3.04
2002	130.26	2.79	132.43	1.63	127.89	4.61
2003	135.97	4.38	137.01	3.46	135.13	5.66
2004	143.90	5.83	146.50	6.93	141.03	4.37
2005	153.24	6.49	158.08	7.90	147.14	4.33

Source: Bangladesh Bank at http://www.bangladesh-bank.org

Annual rate of Inflation (General)

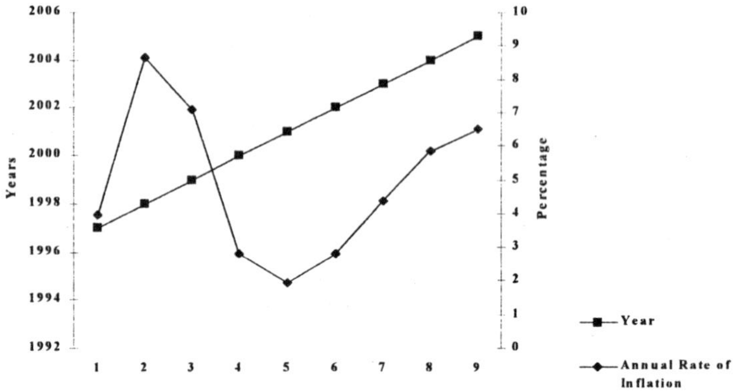

A higher level of the budget deficit as percentage of GDP has been observed in Bangladesh in the early period of the 1990s, although the said share had decreased by the end of the period, from 7.2 per cent in 1991 to 5.8 per cent in 1995. However, with increased demand on expenditure and lower than forecast revenue collection, largely flood related, the overall budget deficit actually increased towards the end of the 1990s (e.g. 7.01 per cent of GDP in 2000). A marginal increase to 7.03 in the relative size of the fiscal deficit had been observed in 2001 (Table-2.6); however its share had been restrained at less than 4.5 per cent during the first half of the present decade.

These deficits, be it budget or fiscal, have been largely financed by foreign resources in the form of official development assistance (ODA). Thus, in 1991, ODA financed 86 per cent of the deficits. The net foreign financing of budget deficit, which had been 4.8 per cent of GDP then, declined to 3.2 per cent in the first half of the 1990s. The incremental share of the budget deficit had been mostly financed by the domestic sources.

Table-2.6
Budget Deficit and Financing

Year	Budget Deficit (in billion Taka)	Budget Deficit (as per cent of GDP)	Financing of Deficit (as per cent of GDP)	
			Net Domestic Financing	Net Foreign Financing
1991	79.5	7.2	2.4	4.8
1995	88.7	5.8	1.97	3.8
1996	81.4	4.9	1.7	3.2
2000	166.1	7.0	3.3	3.7
2001	178.2	7.0	3.5	3.5
2002	118.2	4.3	2.1	2.3
2003	127.8	4.1	1.97	2.1
2004	139.7	4.2	1.8	2.4
2005*	164.3	4.5	2.1	2.4
2006**	186.6	4.5	2.0	2.5

Source: *Bangladesh Economy: Macro Economic Performance*, Centre for Policy Dialogue, Dhaka, Bangladesh, 2004 and Budget documents of Bangladesh 2004-05 & 2005-06 * Revised budget
** Budget Estimate

Budget Deficit and Financing (in percentage)

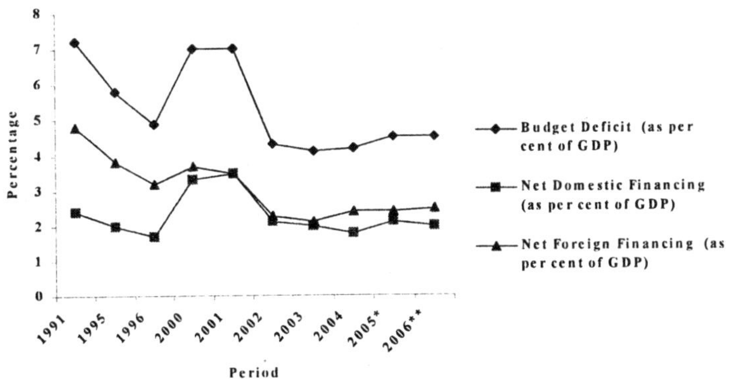

Revenue Receipts and Public Expenditure

Needless to say, the weakness in the domestic resource mobilization has emerged as one of the major structural constraints for the Bangladesh economy since the 1990s. After the success in revenue earnings of the early 1990s, the revenue mobilization process had started showing signs of exhaustion thereafter. The success of the early 1990s had been significantly activated by the introduction of the value added tax (VAT). The VAT has proved to be a bigger source of revenue compared to the taxes it replaced. But the devastating floods of 1998 again led its deteriorating trend, though some recovery had been observed since 2001, when the total revenue collection increased from 9.60 per cent of GDP to 10.6 per cent in 2005. Though the share of revenue (tax and non-tax together) in the GDP increased (from 8.6 per cent during 1991-1995 to 10.2 per cent during 2001-2004) (Table 2.7), the revenue receipts in Bangladesh, as a share of GDP, is still lower than in many developing country.

Table 2.7
Revenue and Expenditures as percentages of GDP

Indicators	*1991-95*	*1996-2000*	*2001-04*	*2005**	*2006***
Total Revenue	8.6	9.2	10.2	10.6	11.0
Total Expenditure	14.0	13.62	14.8	15.1	15.4
Revenue Expenditure	6.7	7.2	8.3	8.6	8.5
ADP Expenditure	6.6	6.1	5.8	5.6	5.9

Source: *Bangladesh Economy: Macro Economic Performance*, Centre for Policy Dialogue, Dhaka, Bangladesh, 2004 and Bangladesh Bank at http://www.bangladesh-bank.org

Note: * Revised Estimates ** Budget estimates

Revenue and Expenditures as percentages of GDP

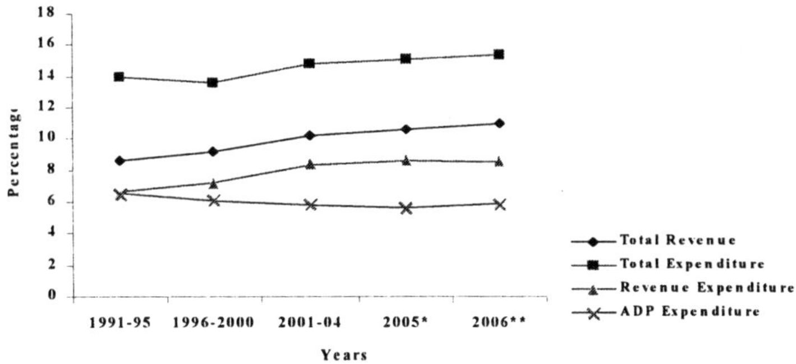

Two distinctive phases in the trend of total public expenditure growth could be discerned in the Bangladesh economy during the 1990s. Public expenditure as a share of GDP experienced a rise in the early 1990s from the benchmark level of 12.91 per cent in 1991 to hover above 14 per cent during the mid 1990s. The said share continued with its increasing trend in the second half of the 1990s, recording its peak in 2000 (14.5 per cent). During 2001-05, the total public expenditure had been stagnant at around 14.8 per cent to 15 per cent of GDP (Table 2.7). Though the revenue expenditure as a share of GDP experienced a rise throughout the 1990s, it was observed that the average growth of revenue expenditure had been lower during the first half of the 1990s compared to the second half. A look at the table shows that a downward trend is observed in the ADP-GDP ratio during the 1990s from 6.6 per cent in 1991-95 to 5.8 per cent in 2001-2004.

DEFINING EXPORT-LED GROWTH: THE EXTERNAL SECTOR

Exports and Imports

Since the mid-1980s and early 1990s, a design in export-led industrialization, export-based diversification and export market consolidation, supported by a conducive policy environment and necessary infrastructure and institutional facilities, has shaped the Bangladesh economy into one that is basically driven by an export oriented growth strategy. The economic reform measures initiated in the mid-1980s set the tone for many important changes in Bangladesh's economic policies, which played a crucial role in introducing competition in the economy and instilling a general policy direction favouring externally orientated actions. The reforms had been crucial for removing anti-export biased policies and integrating Bangladesh with the global economy. As a result, there have been visible shifts in the structure of the economy from the non-tradable to the tradable sectors, and a gradual policy shift away from import-substitution towards export-oriented activities. The structure of trade has also undergone significant changes over the years. There had been a major reallocation of resources from traditional exports such as jute and jute goods, tea and raw leather, towards non-traditional items such as ready-made garments (RMG), frozen foods and shrimps.

Between 1991 and 2005, the export-oriented industries accounted for about one-third of the industrial capacity in Bangladesh. The export sector registered an average growth rate of 14.5 per cent per annum throughout the 1990s. The average growth rate of the export sector (18.34 per cent) during the first half of the 1990s was higher compared to that during the second half (10.7 per cent) (Table 2.8). Almost all export items had experienced an average growth rate in the first half. More specifically, such a moderate growth rate of the export sector was possible due to the encouraging growth of frozen goods, ready-made garments, knitwear, and chemicals. During the second half of the 1990s, the average growth rate of some of these items had drastically fallen. The average annual growth rate of export has shown a downward trend at 8.9 per cent during the first half of the current decade (2001 to 2005) also. Though Bangladesh's export sector has registered commendable growth rate, the export range has not diversified and the country has not been able to translate its comparative advantage of cheap labour into a competitive advantage within the global market. Bangladesh has ranked 98th out of 102 countries in the growth competitiveness index (GCI) and 86th out of 95 in the business competitiveness index (BCI) for the year 2003.

On the other hand, Bangladesh's import sector has registered an average growth rate of about 11.1 per cent throughout the 1990s. During the first half of the decade, liberalization policy decisions taken by the government for swelling imports supported the flow of inputs to export-oriented and domestic industries, and also led to a surge in consumer and non-production related imports. As a result, the total imports have recorded an average growth rate of 14.53 per cent in the said period. The average growth rates of food grain, textile & dairy, and iron & steel sub-sectors have been 39.17 per cent, 25.78 per cent and 23.04 per cent respectively. Imports of oil seeds showed an average growth of 127.55 per cent. During the second half of the 1990s, almost every imported item registered a lower average growth rate compared to that in the previous period. As a result, the average growth rate of total imports in the said period slowed down to 7.7 per cent. The average growth rate of import in the first half of the new decade the 1990s (2001-05) has increased to 9.9 per owing to the increased imports of rice, sugar, fertilizer, POL and capital machinery (Table 2.8).

Table 2.8
Value and Growth Rates of Exports and Imports in Bangladesh

Year	*Exports (US $ mn.)*	*Export Growth (%)*	*Imports (US $ mn.)*	*Import Growth (%)*
1991-95	—	**18.34***	—	**14.53***
1996	3884	11.8	6947	19.1
1997	4427	13.9	7162	3.1
1998	5172	16.8	7524	5.1
1999	5324	2.9	8018	6.6
2000	5752	8.0	8374	4.4
1996-2000	—	**10.7***	—	**7.7***
2001	6467	12.4	9335	11.5
2002	5986	-7.4	8540	-8.5
2003	6548	9.4	9658	13.1
2004	7603	16.1	10903	12.9
2005	8654	13.8	13147	20.6
2001-05	—	**8.9***	—	**9.9***

Note: * indicates average annual growth rate.

Source: http://www.mccibd.org/indicators.html,
http://www.web.worldbank.org,
Economic Trends and Bangladesh Economic Survey, 2005
available at www.fbcci-bd.org

Value of Exports and imports (US $ mn.)

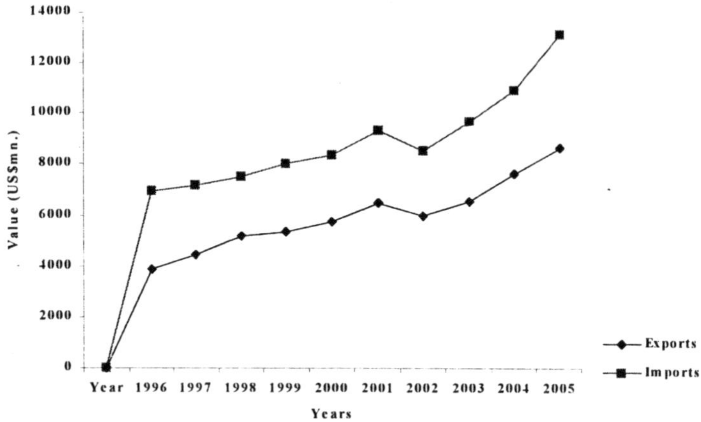

The efforts to improve the situation seemingly continue. Bangladesh has been a signatory to the final document of the Uruguay Round Agreements and is a founding member of the WTO. As the leader of the less developed countries (LDCs) in the WTO, Bangladesh has advocated for the implementation of special and differential treatment in favour of LDCs, emphasising the problems faced by LDCs in the multilateral trading system. Bangladesh plays an active role in the South Asian Association for Regional Cooperation (SAARC), and has been active in the SAARC Preferential Trading Agreement (SAPTA), South Asian Free Trade Area (SAFTA) treaty, and the Bangladesh, India, Myanmar, Sri Lanka and Thailand Economic Cooperation (BIMST-EC) agreement. Bangladesh also has been participating in the Developing Countries-8 (D-8) activities, which includes eight Islamic countries namely Bangladesh, Egypt, Iran, Indonesia, Malaysia, Nigeria, Pakistan, and Turkey. Moreover, Bangladesh has bilateral trade agreements with more than 30 countries, including China, Korea, Egypt, India, Indonesia, Malaysia, the Philippines, Thailand and UAE. Under the generalised system of preference (GSP),

Bangladeshi products currently receive preferential market access to 17 countries. Bangladesh is also a participant in the global system of trade preferences (GSTP) among developing countries, and grants tariff concessions to 47 other signatories on a wide range of products.

Foreign Remittances

The annual flow of remittances received from Bangladeshi migrant workers has showed an encouraging trend since the 1990s rising from US$ 764.0 million in 1991 to US$ 1949.32 million in 2000 and to US$ 3848.29 million in 2005. In the first half of the 1990s, Bangladesh received a total amount of US$ 4844.5 million as foreign remittance with an average growth rate of 9.6 per cent per annum which increased to US$ 14665 million during the period 2001-05 with an average growth rate of 15.2 per cent per annum implying higher earnings by Bangladeshi migrant workers during this period as compared to the previous one. But it is interesting to note here that the annual average growth rate percentage of the number of persons going abroad from Bangladesh has fallen drastically from 18.5, in the said period, to 1.6 in 2001-05.

Table 2.9

Foreign Remittance and Total Number of Workers Abroad

	1991-95	*1996-2000*	*2001-2005*
Total Remittance (million US $)	4844.5	7873	14665
Annual Average Growth of Remittance (in %)	9.6	10.5	15.2
Total No. of Workers Abroad (000)	912	1170	1164
Annual Average Growth Rate (in %)	18.5	5.2	1.6

Source: *Bangladesh Economy: Macro Economic Performance*, Centre for Policy Dialogue, Dhaka, Bangladesh, 2004 and Bangladesh Bank at http://www.bangladesh-bank.org

Foreign Remittance and Total Number of Workers Abroad (in percentage)

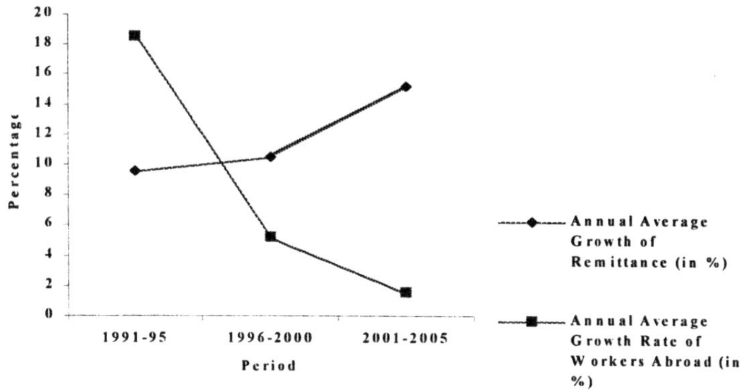

Foreign Aid

During the 1990s, the Bangladesh economy had undergone a historical structural transformation from being an aid-dependent country to a trade-driven entity as a consequence of significant contribution from international trade relative to the aid-flow.

Table 2.10
Foreign Aid and Debt Services

(in million US $)

Year	*Foreign Aid Disbursement*	*Debt Services*	*Outstanding External Debt**	*Outstanding External Debt (as % of GDP)*
	1	2	3	4
1991	1733	317	11934	38.5
1995	1739	468	15947	41.8

(Contd...)

	1	2	3	4
1996	1444	470	14454	35.5
2000	1587	619	15727	33.4
2001	1369	597	14677	31.2
2002	1442	586	—	33.4
2003	1585	608	16953	32.7
2004 (R)	1034	562	17953	31.8
2005 (P)	1491	640	18557	30.9

Source: *Economic Trends, Bangladesh Economic Survey, 2005* available at www.fbcci-bd.org and *Bangladesh Economy: Macro Economic Performance*, Centre for Policy Dialogue, Dhaka, Bangladesh, 2004

Note: R=Revised, P=Provisional
* Excluding IMF loan

Outstanding External Debt (as % of GDP)

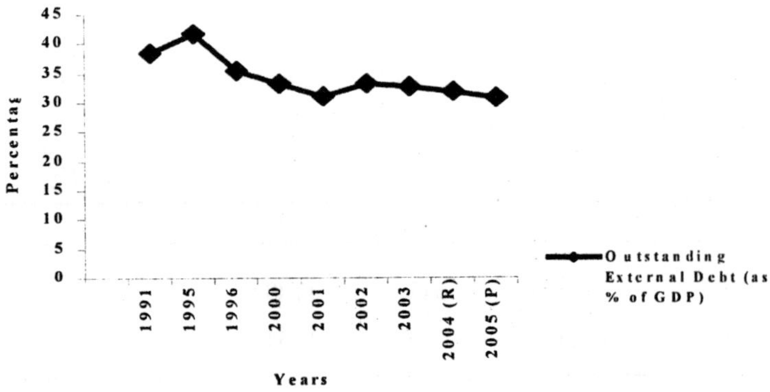

The Table 2.10 provides information about the foreign aid and debt services for the period 1991-2005. As seen, the growth rate of foreign aid disbursement in the first half of the 1990s had indeed been low. But it bounced back with a positive growth in the first three years of the present decade (2001-2003). In post 2003 years, foreign aid disbursement again exhibits a negative growth rate. The total outstanding external debt of Bangladesh as of June 1995 was about US$ 15947 million (41.8 per cent of GDP), which had decreased to 33.4 per cent by the year 2000. In 2001, the amount of total outstanding external debt was 31.2 per cent of GDP, decreased to 30.9 per cent of GDP in 2005. The expectation to have marginal increase in the foreign aid quantum[5], however, is likely to suffer in the backdrop of the current political uncertainty, which is likely to continue at least till the end of the year trend.[6]

It is to be noted that as an LDC, Bangladesh has the inevitable compulsion of facing frequent external pressure. The most glaring example was the US delay in sending food aid during the 1974 famine. Food aid was tagged to Dhaka's cancellation of jute export to Cuba.[7] At any rate Bangladesh has become perpetually dependent on foreign aid. This has retarded its capacity to mobilize internal resources and hence productivity.[8]

Foreign Exchange Reserve

The first half of the 1990s saw the foreign exchange reserve of the country rise from US$ 880 million in 1991 to US$ 3077 million, which has been equivalent to 6.3 months of imports. However, since 1995 the foreign exchange reserve had gradually declined and descended to US$ 1602 million at the end of the second half of 1990s (i.e. in 2000). The decline continued and recorded a low of US$ 1307 million. Since then the foreign exchange reserve, however, has bounced back to US$ 1583 million in 2002 and has continued with its positive trend at the end of 2005 (US$ 2930 million).

Balance of Payments

Though Bangladesh's overall balance of payments (BOP) position has demonstrated a positive trend in 1991-1994, the middle of the 1990s saw a reverse in the BOP due to a significant increase in imports and the outflow for invisible payments. The BOP has shown some improvement thereafter due to high export growth and modest import expansion (Table 2.11).

Table 2.11

Balance of Payments Scenario of Bangladesh (1991-2005)

(in million US$)

Source	2000	2001	2002	2003	2004	2005
Trade Balance	-1865	-2011	-1768	-2215	-2319	-3297
Exports, fob (including EPZ)	5701	6419	5929	6492	7521	8573
Imports, fob (including EPZ)	-7566	-8430	-7697	-8707	-9840	-11870
Current account balance	-418	-1098	157	176	176	-557
Capital account	561	432	410	428	196	163
Financial account	-116	682	391	413	78	760
Error and omissions	152	-297	-550	-202	-279	-299
Overall Balance	**179**	**-281**	**408**	**815**	**171**	**67**

Source: Bangladesh Bank at http://www.bangladesh-bank.org

The current account balance of Bangladesh experienced some amount of diversity throughout the 1990s. It is needs to mention that in 1996 Bangladesh passed through the highest negative trade balance considering the last and a half decade. By the turn of the century, the current account balance though has witnessed some improvements. This facilitated the overall balance of payments to reach a positive amount of US$ 179 million by the end of 2000. In 2002, the current account balance has amounted to a positive sum of US$ 157 million, which increased to US$ 176 million in 2003. As a result, the overall balance of payments increased from US$ 408 million in 2002 to US $ 815 million in 2003. However, this balance has turned negative yet again in 2005 to the tune of (-) US$ 557 million, reducing the overall balance to US$ 67 million.

The Road to a Futuristic Economy: The Most Plausible Turn

More recently, Goldman Sachs has extended the concept of N-11 (Next Eleven)[9]. Through it, Sachs has identified eleven countries including Bangladesh with large and growing populations and hence with the potential to become global economic overweight. Goldman Sachs has developed a Growth Environment Score (GES), a composite measure to evaluate the capacity of each country to realize its growth potential. The GES factors which are divided into five groups, macro economic stability, macro economic conditions, technological capabilities, human capital, and political conditions undoubtedly questions Sachs's inclusion of Bangladesh in N-11. Going by the macro economic indicators, as discussed above, considerable challenges remain open to Bangladesh.

The economic scenario, *per se,* in Bangladesh today is to everyone's understanding, rough and unpredictable, as has been testified to by its inactivity in the fiscal front. It is largely speculated that the government which is likely to emerge out of the current political uncertainty and turmoil in the country is going to adopt an extraordinarily expansionary fiscal stance by increasing its expenditure heads by 16.5 per cent in the financial year 2007-08 (The Economic Intelligence

Table 2.12
Annual Indicators

Indicators	*2002*[a]	*2003*[a]	*2004*[a]	*2005*[a]	*2006*[b]
	1	2	3	4	5
GDP at market prices (Tk bn)[c]	2,732	3,005.8	3,329.7	3,684.8	4,139.1
GDP (US$ BN)[d]	47.6	51.9	56.5	60.0	61.6
Real GDP growth rate (%)[c]	4.4	5.3	6.3	6.0	6.7[a]
Consumer price inflation (av; %)	3,3	5.7	9.2	7.0	6.8
Population (m)	134.0	136.6	139.2	141.8	144.5
Export of goods fob (US$ m)	6,102.4	7,050.1	8,150.7	9,186.2	11,170.4
Import of goods fob (US$ m)	7,780.1	9,492.0	11,157.1	12,291.7	13.766.7
Current account balance (US$ m)	739.5	131.5	-278.5	-131.6	339.0
Foreign exchange reserves excl gold (US$ m)	1,683.2	2,577.9	3,172.4	2,767.2	3,526.0
Total external debt (US$ m)	17.0	18.8	20.3	20.6[b]	22.1
Debt-service ratio, paid (%)	7.4	5.9	5.2	7.1	6.3
Exchange rate (av) Tk: US$	57.88	58.15	59.51	64.33	68.96

Source: Economist Intelligence Unit, *Country Report, Bangladesh*, January 2007

[a]Actual, [b]Estimated by Economist Intelligence Unit, [c]Fiscal years ending June 30, [d]Fiscal year exchange rate used

Unit, *Country Report: Bangladesh*, January 2007). Even a strand of truth in the speculation will certainly lead to an unmitigated inflationary trend in the country causing further deterioration of the economic scenario, consequently, proving it too difficult to achieve the target of generating a revenue of Tk 550.5 billion (US$ 8 billion). In order to cope with the foreseeable crises, there is every chance of the government taking recourse to heavy borrowings from banks. In the light of the fact that the government's borrowings have already increased alarmingly from Tk 7.8 billion in 2005-06 to 32.1 billion in the early part of September end, 2006, the thought of the government borrowing any further is itself questionable. The forecast that the government spending would increase by 10.5 per cent implies that the borrowing spree would undergo a vertical rise and inflation would shoot up to 7 per cent. But if the 'benevolent military backed caretaker government' continues, predictably for some more months, it is hoped that the inflationary trend might be controlled to a satisfactory extent. It would be relevant here to have a look at the annual economic indicators (Table 2.12). These figures, however, present a dismal picture of the Bangladesh economy.

A host of reasons, some of which are extraneous, such as *hartals* (general strikes), political instability, postponement of the general elections scheduled for January 2007, and corruption of grave nature explain this gloomy picture of the country's economy. Some of these are briefly highlighted below while discussing the road to a futuristic economy for the country.

Given the current economic scenario, the new to be elected government of Bangladesh is bound to inherit a poor fiscal situation. The country is invariably going to face post-election political unrest, as the loser partly would dispute the election results and hence challenge the legitimacy of the government. Such a situation accompanied by violence would incapacitate the government in raising revenues and funds from both internal and international sources. There would be *hartals* (general strikes) crippling the economic vitality to a great extent. According to UNDP, the cost of *hartals* to the economy in a normal year without the parliamentary elections is estimated to be between 3-4 per cent of GDP. One can hence easily imagine the cost that the economy will have to bear in the post-election scenario when there would be prolonged spate of disruption of economic activities, adversely affecting the economic development of the country.

The Bangladesh Taka has depreciated gradually against the US Dollar since May 2003. It is owing to rapid rise of merchandise imports and high oil prices that the pace of depreciation against the US Dollar has increased significantly. The Taka's loss of value in 2006 is estimated at 7.3 per cent. On November 13, 2006, when the entire country was under *abarodh* (seize) and *hartal*, the Taka depreciated by 2.6 per cent against the US Dollar to a record low of Tk 71.9: US$; the depreciation from Tk 66: US$ 1, was in fact quite alarming. The Economist Intelligence Unit forecast of a further fall in 2007 and 2008 to Tk 73.4: US$ 1 and Tk 78.5: US$ 1 respectively does not indicate a bright economic picture for the country.

Inflation in Bangladesh has been rising. The annual inflation rate, measured in terms of consumer price index (CPI) rose from 6.9 per cent in September to 7.3 per cent in October 2006. The rate of inflation remained constant at 7 per cent till the end of the year. The inflation is attributed to demand for essential items during the Muslim festival of Eid-ul-Fitr and then Eid-ul-Azha. The inflationary tendency is likely to continue in the current year. Another worrisome trend is that rice production in Bangladesh has declined. The harvest of *aus* rice has come down from 175 million tonnes to 1.51 million tonnes. The fall has been caused by scanty rainfall, shortage of fertilizers and insecticides and higher input prices.

There are also the man-made situations which are causes of concern for the economic performance of Bangladesh. The current political unrest soon after the Caretaker Government took over has led to a political uncertainty that dissuades the foreign investors to invest or in certain cases forces to reconsider new investments in the country. In November 2006, the Board of Investment (BoI) registered FDI proposals worth US$ 13 million only. The media reports suggested that some foreign investors cancelled their visits to Bangladesh for want of security. The BoI estimated on the basis of the progress at the negotiation stage that there would be FDI to the tune of US$ 10.5 billion. But it did not take long to realize that many of the negotiations had been suspended. In view of the current crises in democracy caused by political uncertainty and absence of rule of law created by a highly politicised and biased judiciary, it would be difficult for the country to attract FDI, despite the availability of attractive cheap energy and labour resources in the country. The proposals put forward by a Malaysia-based consortium named Westmont Group for an investment of US$ 5 billion in power and energy sector, three Korean companies named Korean National Oil Corporation, Pohang Iron and Steel Company (POSCO) and Luxon and Thailand Exploration and Production Company for investment in oil and natural gas sectors, and the Tata Group, and Indian conglomerate, to invest a US$ 3 billion in coal, steel, gas and fertilizer production, despite two years of negotiations, are yet to be finally cleared for implementation. It is suggested by the concerned press and academics that the anti-Indian position of the Bangladesh Government stands in the way of clearance of the otherwise highly attractive proposal of the Tata Group. It is reported that discussion on the investment by the Tata Group is still on. It is believed that these investments would generate employment, accelerate economic development in the poor northwest region of the country. It is argued that election-centric economic nationalism would put Bangladesh into more difficulty in properly addressing the countless economic issues faced by a huge poverty stricken populace.

Corruption is another dimension that halts the pace of growth in the country. The UK based Economist Intelligence Unit considers corruption as the single most important barrier to greater investments in Bangladesh.[10] Most of the scholars, political leaders, student and women activists, and media persons with whom I was engaged in intensive discussions in November 2006, believe that corruption at all levels in the country has been hindering economic growth of the country. It is endemic and rampant, and as such, is visible in all fronts. The Berlin-based Corruption Index of Transparency International ranks Bangladesh alongside Chad as the most corrupt country in the world. The World Bank report on Bangladesh economy suggests that the economy of the country would grow by 7-8 per cent, if corruption were chained and transparency were ensured. Corruption and lack of transparency are the most striking factors that have undermined the efforts to attract foreign Direct Investment (FDI).[11] That is why it is believed that the present caretaker government has been taking firm steps to root out corruption and promote the culture of transparency. It has taken harsh measures such as sending known corrupt politicians and bureaucrats to prison. The high ups in politics are also not being spared. But the how long shall these measures continue is the moot question.

With the cloud of political uncertainty hovering over Bangladesh due to the postponement of the general elections, it seems the economy of Bangladesh would suffer to a great extent. No one is certain when an elected representative government would take over. This forecasts a lean or bad economic phase for Bangladesh. A stable political environment is an imperative to restore fiscal discipline, encouraging investment in the manufacturing and service sector and consolidation of growth in agriculture sector. These are the major challenges confronting the economy of Bangladesh.[12]

The Political Scenario: Is Bangladesh a 'Fragile' State?

Bangladesh emerged as an independent member of the international community with high hopes. The popular belief was that it would prove to be a modern democratic and secular country. The national aspiration to present it as a stable and performing state of Bengali Muslims was expected to play the driving role in the nation-building process. Unfortunately, the rise of Islamic fundamentalism has posed a grave threat to the democratic and near secular spirit of the country to a great extent.[13]

Bangladesh has had its enormous problems which were too difficult to be resolved in a short span of time. Its backwardness on all fronts was a telling pressure on the new government headed by Sheikh Mujibur Rehman. The country began to suffer from a crisis of confidence. While the expectation of the masses for a better life was high, the capacity to deliver goods to the level of popular expectation was, unfortunately, dismally and terribly low. Sheikh Mujib depended on his personal charisma rather than on good governance in handling all matters, whether economic or political. The public outburst against his leadership surfaced at the time of the 1974 famine.[14] The crisis, which was not handled properly, led to the death of several thousand people. Mujib's popularity dwindled in the face of the famine, food deficit, rampant corruption at all levels, shortage of foreign currency, and the unwillingness of the international banking institutions to grant soft loans. Further, deterioration of law and order and internal disputes within the ruling Awami League, and failure to muster foreign aid at the time of dire needs alienated Sheikh Mujib from the masses.

In order to tide over the crises on several fronts, Sheikh Mujib tried to initiate economic and administrative reforms, which he termed as the 'second revolution'. Under this, he introduced reforms in the monetary sector, relaxed control on imports, encouraged multi-crop harvest to food production, adopted new strategy on export promotion, liberalized control on industrial sector and formulated open market policy in pricing commodities. Besides, certain administrative reforms were introduced such as appointment of political governors in each district to watch the performance of the administration and to ensure supply of essential commodities so that there would be no starvation.[15] The government took measures to encourage the co-operative institutions to perform better. These measures were taken so that his government could regain the once reposed trust and confidence. But before the initiatives could be fully implemented, he was assassinated along with most of his family members on the night of August 15, 1975 by a group of army officers.

The assassination had a ravaging impact on both domestic and international fronts. It signalled the impending and deepening political crisis, and involvement of the army in political life of Bangladesh. The assassination was followed by two ominous developments – some of the leading Awami League leaders were arrested and put behind bars and at the same time, most of the political prisoners belonging to the Jamaat and pro-China National Awami Party of Maulana Bhasani were released from detention. It marked the beginning of re-emergence of Islamists in Bangladesh. On the international front, Saudi Arabia accorded diplomatic recognition to Bangladesh for showing softness to the Jamaat which was followed by China for showing leniency to the National Awami Party. Simultaneously, the Government of Bangladesh started demonstrating its anti-Indian stance, which continues to dominate Bangladesh's foreign policy till today except, of course, for the period of Shiekh Hasina Wajed

(1996-2001) when some improvement in the relations between the two countries was seen.

Post assassination of Sheikh Mujib, Bangladesh slipped into the hands of military rule, political uncertainty, and politics of assassination for a long period of 16 years. After the killing of Sheikh Mujibur Rehman and overthrowing of his government, the coup leaders made Khondakar Mostaq Ahmad the President and Chief Martial Law Administrator. In three months time, Brigadier Khaled Mosarraf overthrew the Government of Mostaq Ahmad. Being aware of the impending coup, the killers of Sheikh Mujib assassinated four top jailed leaders of Awami League – Syed Nazrul Islam, Tajuddin Ahmed, Mansur Ali and AHM Qamaruzzaman inside the Dhaka Central Jail on November 3, 1975.

Mosarraf was also killed within a week in a counter coup staged by the retired Colonel Abu Taher on November 7, 1975. A quick succession of developments since August 15, 1975 led to the emergence of Major General Ziaur Rahman in the political scene of Bangladesh. He was appointed as the Army Chief soon after the assassination of Mujibur Rahman. Following the coup of November 3, he was arrested by Mosarraf but was freed after the latter was killed in a counter coup. Once freed, Ziaur Rahman staged a meteoric rise to power – from Deputy Martial Law Administrator on November 7, 1975 to President of Bangladesh on April 21, 1977, in an interval of 16 months only.

Ziaur Rahman was successful in enforcing discipline in the army and put down repeated coups. He also integrated the *Rakkhi Bahini* with the military. He paved the way for the reappearance of the condemned religious party, the Jamaat and brought forth the Constitutional Amendment Order, 1977 to drop the word 'secular' and to insert "absolute trust and faith in Almighty Allah" as also invocatory 'Bismillahir Rahmanir Rahim" in the Constitution. These steps were prelude to transform Bangladesh to an Islamic state. His decision to grant general amnesty to all the collaborators with Pakistani forces during the liberation war and to rehabilitate the Jamaat leader Gholam Azam had a far-reaching impact on the ascendancy of political and militant Islam in Bangladesh. In a country plagued with series of political assassinations and judicial murders, Ziaur Rahman too eliminated in the game which had been going on since August 1975. He was killed in a coup at Chittagong on May 30, 1981.

Ziaur Rahman's assassination led to another stint of military rule from March 1982 to December 6, 1990 headed by a military general named Hossain Muhammad Ershad. He too, like Ziaur Rahman, sought the support of the Jamaat and the Islamists in order to consolidate his position. However, his political moves did not work to keep him in power. There was a massive movement against him in which the Jamaat too joined. This compelled him to resign on December 6, 1990.

The sixth general elections of 1991 led to the victory of Bangladesh National Party (BNP), which had been formed by Ziaur Rahman in September 1978. After his death in 1981, his wife Begum Khaleda Zia headed the party and consequently, she became the new Prime Minister and formed the government. Although parliamentary democracy was installed in Bangladesh by the 12th Constitutional Amendment, the elected Government of Khaleda Zia faced serious challenge from the Opposition led by Awami League, more particularly, on the issue of parliamentary by-election held in 1994. It was alleged that the BNP indulged in unfair means to get its candidate elected, and therefore, that the election was a fraud. There were countrywide *hartals* for days together. The Opposition boycotted the parliament. The Awami League demanded a caretaker government to hold the next election. Begum Zia had to succumb to the demand and she tendered resignation and consequently, a caretaker government headed by Chief Justice Habibur Rahman, was installed.

The seventh general election of 1996 led to the formation of the Awami League Government headed by Sheikh Hasina Wajed. During this period India-Bangladesh relations improved to a certain extent. The contentious issues of water sharing, return and rehabilitation of the displaced Chakma people, the insurgent groups from North East India operating from Bangladesh, and balance of trade were negotiated to reach a mutually agreed conclusion. But the table was turned in the 2001 elections when Begum Khaleda Zia regained power.

The second stint for power by Begum Khaleda Zia was marked by the rise of political Islam. The Jamaat forged an alliance with the BNP which eventually led to its sharing of power in the new government. It gave the Jamaat, the party that was once ostracized for collaborating with Pakistan army against the emergence of Bangladesh, a unique opportunity to be the partner of the BNP-led Government. As it would be found in Chapter IV, the rise of political and militant Islam during this period from 2001-2006 has posed a definite threat not only to the minorities but also to the very survival of democracy and intact social fabric.

During the BNP-Jamaat rule, the militant Islam demonstrated its rise by taking recourse to violence against all minorities including the Ahmediyas, Hindus and Buddhists. There was a violent attack on the Awami party workers at the Bangabandhu Avenue on August 21, 2004, killing 22 and injuring 338. The attack was carried out to eliminate Awami League Chief, Sheikh Hasina. A year later, on August 17, 2005, about 500 bomb blasts took place throughout Bangladesh, covering 63 out of 64 districts, and stunningly within a span of half an hour only. The message loudly sent forth was that Islamic law had to be enforces in Bangladesh. The incident testifies to the effective networking and efficient display of integrated efforts that caught the government machinery unaware. Leaving aside a host of related developments, one could safely argue that there has been a steady ascendancy of political and militant Islam in Bangladesh.

A poor, underdeveloped, economically and educationally backward Bangladesh provides a fertile ground for breeding Islamic militancy. The ramification of the trend knows no geographical boundary. As already stated India shares more than 90 per cent of its international borders with Bangladesh. Most of the districts of Bangladesh adjoining the borders of India's North East register low human development indices. For example, the literacy rate of Jamalpur and Sherpur districts close to Meghalaya is only 31 (Census 2001). These are the districts with mushroom growth of unregistered madrassas with no regulated curricula. These private madrassas are known to be the breeding grounds of Muslim militancy, in fact, most of the jihadi cadres are recruited from thereupon.

The recent developments in Bangladesh have been causing grave concern to the international community. As the preparation for holding the 9th general elections are in the fore, the 14-party Opposition alliance led by the Awami League has raised serious doubt about the validity of the electoral register and also the impartiality of the Chief Election Commissioner, M.A. Aziz, who has been known to be close to the BNP Chief Khaleda Zia. Consequently, the attention of the domestic politics and international community has been shifted from the country's economic development to the future of its democratic foundation. Soon after the caretaker government took over and initiated the preparations for the general elections, the Opposition spearheaded a massive movement demanding the resignation or removal of M.A. Aziz and postponement of the elections till a revised and genuine electoral register was prepared. Bangladesh plunged into a major political crisis in November-December,

2006 when the Opposition launched country-wide *hartals* in support of their demands. Close on the heels of these developments, the judicial system of the country came under suspicion as it stayed the proceedings on a petition challenging the duality in the role of President Iajuddin Ahmed as the head of the caretaker government and also as the Chief Adviser to the government, which he had been heading. In the wake of massive agitation and international pressure, the President facilitated the honourable exit of M.A. Aziz and decided to postpone the general elections scheduled for January 2007. He too gave up the office of the Chief Adviser and appointed Fakhruddin Ahmed to this important position. At the same time he deployed the army to enforce law and order. It is noteworthy that the possibility of military intervention has been looming large over Bangladesh ever since President Iajuddin Ahmed taking over the caretaker government. His neutrality is under cloud. The law and order machinery is too fragile to handle a crisis situation which has been created as a result of nation-wide *hartals* and *abarodhs* by the Opposition. November 2006 was a difficult month when the entire country was under seize due to the nation-wide strike. No one was willing to talk and negotiate. This was the height of hostilities demonstrated by the two political alliance groups. It was a testimony to the culture of extreme political positions where political reconciliations for national interest could not be worked out. Both the Awami League and the BNP were not ready to show respect for rule of law, majority verdict and minority opinion.[16] In such a situation entire political process in a democratic country is at stake. It shows the symptoms of political decline in Bangladesh and sets forward the indicators of a fragile state.

While the BNP welcomed the decision to deploy army on the ground that it had saved the country from catastrophe, the Opposition fear that the army would once again take over the government and that even if elections were held, the BNP would 'steal' votes with the help of the army. Impartial observers in Bangladesh and abroad feel that the army has been neutral till now. The administration has not spared anyone in crushing the corrupt system. Even Khaleda Zia and her son had been arrested on corruption charges. There are reports that the Caretaker Government has been pressurizing Khaleda Zia to leave the country and seek asylum in Saudi Arabia as a part of a deal to secure the release of her son. Sheikh Hasina too is in trouble. The government initially had debarred her from entering the country at the end of her foreign trip. A case of murder has been slapped on her making her difficult to return. As she had returned she too was put behind the bar. All this indicate a difficult time for democracy in the country when two chairpersons of the leading political parties are not only at the centre stage of controversy but also facing personal crisis of grave magnitude.

Till now there is no definite move to deal with the problems of non-existent voters, despite the claim of the government that the revised electoral list would be ready by the end of 2007. It is noteworthy that on December 2, 2006 a US-based lobby group named the National Democratic Institute of International Affairs (NDI) reported that it has made an extensive survey of the electoral register and the process of enumeration of voters' name in the electoral list and found that 12.2 million names were "either in error or duplicate". A Dhaka-based election monitoring group, Brotee, also conducted a survey in 30 out of 300 constituencies and has come out with similar findings. So long as corrective measures are not taken, the prospect of holding the 9th general elections in the country seems bleak. This speaks loudly about the future of democracy in Bangladesh.

So long as a truly representative government is not installed through a credible and impartial election process, and unless the army returns to barracks, the thesis advanced by the World Bank Country Director, Christine Wallich that Bangladesh is a 'fragile state' would continue to hold good.[17]

The impact of these developments in a 'fragile' neighbourhood could be as well felt in India in view of the fact that the border is porous and the insurgent groups belonging to the North East are getting logistic support with the connivance of the Government of Bangladesh. It is, therefore, imperative to look at the whole issue of the rise of Islamic fundamentalism in Bangladesh from the perspective of India's national security. The concern among the Indian public at the developments inside Bangladesh, notwithstanding the fact that these fall within the parameters of domestic jurisdiction, is natural and obvious. While the public and the interested section of Indian society often tend to view Bangladesh as a 'fragile' and 'failed' state, the successive governments in India has been adhering to a policy of non-interference in its internal affairs as enshrined in all the formal declaration and agreements with Bangladesh since 1972 and to cultivate fraternal relationship with that country with which India shares common geography, history and culture.

REFERENCES

1. Transparency International's Perceptions Indices put Bangladesh with Chad (rank being 156 out of 163 countries) as one of the most corrupt countries in the world. See http://www. transperancy.org/ policy_research/Surveys_indices/cpi/2006.
2. For an in-depth analysis on the adverse effect of hartals see Akhtar Hossain, "Anatomy of *Hartal* Politics in Bangladesh", *Asian Survey*, Vol. XL, No. 3, May-June, 2000, pp 508-529. Also see Elora Shehabuddin, "Bangladesh in 1999: Desperately Seeking a Responsible Opposition", *Asian Survey*, Vol.XL, January-February 2000, pp. 181-188.

3. *Quarterly Economic Update, Bangladesh, June 2005* of Asian Development Bank records 5.4 per cent GDP growth in the financial year of 2005, which is lower than the preceding year, mainly due to the adverse impact of the flood of July-September 2004.
4. *Quarterly Economic Update, Bangladesh, June 2005.*
5. *State of the Bangladesh Economy in 2004-05 and Outlook for 2005-06* (Dhaka: Centre for Policy Dialogue, 2006), p. 90.
6. *Daily Star*, April 23, 2007.
7. Amartya Sen, *Poverty and Famines: An Essay on Entitlement and Deprivation* (Oxford: English Language Book Society, 1981), pp.135-136.
8. Rehman Sobhan, *The Crisis of External Dependence: The Political Economy of Foreign Aid to Bangladesh* (Dhaka: University Press Limited, 1982), Chapter I, Introduction.
9. For a detailed reading see Goldman Sachs, *Global Economics Paper No. 134,* December 2005.
10. Corruption at all levels not only pulls down the expected economic growth rate but also cripples the governance of the country. The much debated patriot-client relationship between and among various echelon of power structures breeds corruption. For some analysis see Centre for Policy Dialogue, *Crisis of Governance: A Review of Bangladesh's Development* (Dhaka: University Press Limited, 1998).
11. Kochanek, Stanley A., "The Rise of Interest Politics in Bangladesh", *Asian Survey*, Vol. XXXVI, No. 7, July 1996, pp. 706-718
12. Debapriya Bhattacharya, "Bangladesh Economy in FY 2000: Macro Economic Outlook" in Rehamn Sobhan (ed), *Changes and Challenges: A Review of Bangladesh's Development 2000* (Dhaka: Centre for Policy Dialogue and University Press Limited, 2001), Chapter I, pp. 3-30.
13. Bangladesh is no longer a secular country in the true sense of the term after the Eighth Amendment to the Constitution which has made Islam as the state religion. The only façade

of secularism rests on the provision that other religions have the right to profess their own religion. While the Awami League believes in secularism, the BNP has made an electoral alliance with the highly communal Jamaat. Similarly, in the common parlance, the common masses are religious and non-communal but the last Government headed by Begum Khaleda left behind its intolerant image towards non-Muslims.

14. For details of Bangladesh famine of 1974 see, Amartya Sen, *Poverty and Famines: An Essay on Entitlement and Deprivation,* n. 3 Chapter 9 and also M. Alamgir, *et al. Famine 1974: Political Economy of Mass Starvation in Bangladesh* (Dhaka: Bangladesh Institute of Development Studies, 1977).

15. See Rounak Jahan, *Bangladsh Politics: Problems and Issues* (Dhaka: University Press Limited, 1987), p. 119.

16. Gawher Rizvi, "Democracy, Governance and Civil Society in South Asia", *Pakistan Development Review*, Vol. 33, No. 4 1994, pp. 593-624. Also see Elora Shehabuddin, "Bangladesh in 1999: Desperately Seeking a Responsible Opposition", *Asian Survey*, Vol. XVL, No. 1, January/February, 2000, pp. 181-188.

17. Sreeadhara Datta argues: "Despite pessimism, most of these challenges [army rule, rise of Islamists, economic constraints, hartals, weak institutional structures etc.]are not unique to Bangladesh. Compared to other countries in this region, Bangladesh has a better tract record. It is still democratic, changes leaders through ballots, encourages internal debates on serious national issues and is looking forward to prosperity and national cohesion". See author's *Bangladesh: A Fragile Democracy* (New Delhi: Institute for Defence Studies and Analyses, 2004), p. 16.

3

ADVENT OF ISLAM IN BANGLADESH

Bangladesh, as an Islamic nation, throws up a number of inter-connected issues of history, social transformation, religious and political adjustment, conversion and Islamization, conservatism, fundamentalism, secularism, language, culture, and Bengali nationalism. Each one of the issues could generate enough debate to produce a voluminous book. The present Chapter is too small to discuss each and every issue mentioned here and its inter-relations with others. The centrality of the Chapter is the process of transformation of the present Bangladesh into a Muslim nation with 89.6% population of Islamic faith and "the second largest Muslim ethnic population in the world, after the Arabs".[1] The situational context of today's Muslim community in Bangladesh involves a long historical process in which many factors got involved leading to inter-mixture of language, culture and religion. The overlapping of ethnic and religious identities sometimes leads to inherent contradiction that Bangladesh is yet to resolve. While the vast majority of the population prefers to assert its ethnic identity as Bengalis, a driving force that gave the nation-state a distinct international personality at the end of the terrible and violent war of liberation, the religious affiliation brings forth disturbing contradictions of an imagined identity.

A religious community has its own history and socio-territorial base,[2] so also has an ethnic community. While the concept of *umma* (community) brings all the Muslims of the world under one umbrella of Islamic faith and negates the existence of any other linguistic, cultural and social boundaries, ethnicity provides a canopied structure that may shelter all religious and primordial affiliation. It will be seen in Chapter IV how the rise of political and militant Islam flaunts a blanket of pervasive concept, *umma,* to reject all other socio-cultural and territorial boundaries and thus causes a major threat to the security and stability of a given society. Needless to state, the concept of *umma* has little impact even in the Middle East where despite the existence of one Arab culture and language, the *umma* fraternity has not been able to stop unending bloodshed among and between Islamic nations. In a social setting like that of Bangladesh, where Arabic language and culture are least expected to have enduring impact, the argument to negate socio-territorial boundaries is irrelevant and disturbing.

It is difficult to understand the present emergence of Islamic fundamentalism in Bangladesh without attempting at a narration of the advent of Islam in this country. As already stated in Chapter I, Islam arrived in present Bangladesh in the 13th century when Ikhtiaruddin Muhammad Bakhtiar Khilji entered Nadia, the capital city of Lakhnauti ruled by King Lakhmana Sena and conquered it in 1203-04. He created a small principality which gradually started expanded into a Muslim kingdom by the later part of the 14th century. By the next century the whole of Bengal came under the Muslim rulers. The invasion and immigration followed by settlement turned the entire region into a Muslim dominated area.[3]

Prior to the military conquest, legends have it that the Arab traders, who used to dominate the maritime trade, often visited the Bengal coast and then established a small colony of Muslims in the Chittagong region.[4] With the traders, a few Sufis from Mecca, Yemen, Ghazni and Delhi came to Bengal and stayed in the area. It is not out of context that the Sufis belonging to four legal traditions in Sunni Islam – Hanafi, Hanbali, Maliki and Shafi'i – spread to different parts of the world with the missionary zeal of conversion. The Shafi'i Arabs undertook the task of Islamization through commercial contact in the Malabar coastal region of India. The Sufis who reached the Gangetic plain and Bengal, were mostly of the Hanafi tradition.[5] They did exercise tremendous spiritual and charismatic authority on the local inhabitants who appeared to have suffered at the hands of the upper social strata.[6] The Sufis presented an alternative socio-religious paradigm which attracted the peasantry and socially outcast population. However, the massive conversion to Islam did not start till the 14th century when a large number of Sufis from Arabia, Persia, Bukhara and North India came to Bengal to spread Islam. The movement of the Sufis to Bengal remained uninterrupted till the seventeenth century. By 1338 when independent Sultanate was formed in Delhi and its extension reached Bengal, a systematic spread of Islam covering two centuries (1338-1538) had begun through a successful religious campaign spearheaded by Sufis and religious preachers. A steady process of conversion and Islamization induced a vast population to embrace Islam. The process of conversion began in the lower part of Bengal and then engulfed the entire region in just two centuries. It is noteworthy that the countless number of Dargahs (mausoleum of the Sufis) throughout the length and breadth of Bengal testify to their presence and their role in spreading Islam.[7]

That undivided Bengal province experienced a steady but phenomenal rise of the Muslim population to reach a staggering 48 per cent of the total remained unnoticed till the publication of the Census of Bengal, 1872.[8] The census document reported that there had been large concentration of Muslims in the alluvial plains of Bengal. It showed that Chittagong, Noakhali, Pabna and Rajshahi districts had Muslim population of over 70 per cent. The Dhaka district had the lowest figure at 56 percent. It noted that "probably the real explanation of the immense preponderance of the Mussalman religious element in this portion of Delta is to be found in the conversion to Islam of the immense low castes (the Chandals and the Rajbanshis) which occupied it."[9] Reacting to the revelation which stunned the British administration, James Wise, an officer serving in the province of Bengal wrote that "the most interesting fact revealed by the census of 1872 was the enormous host of Muhammadans resident in Lower Bengal – not massed around the old capital, but in the alluvial plains of the Delta...the history of the spread of the Muhammadan faith in Lower and Eastern Bengal is a subject of such vast importance at the present day to merit a careful and minute examination."[10] Although the principality of Bengal was ruled by the Muslims since 1338, as in the case of the rest of India, it was largely inhabited by Hindus. Bengal used to remain insulated over the centuries till it was taken over by the British after the battle of Plassey. As the Muslim conquerors took control of Bengal in 1338, they tried to consolidate their rule by creating an institutional support base. They started building Madrassas, patronized Islamic scholars and Sufi preachers, created endowments to promote Islam, and encouraged immigration.[11] The Sufis played the pivotal role in the process of mass conversion. They cultivated a highly effective relationship with the rural and poor masses. They attracted the people belonging to the lower strata of the Hindu society and also the Buddhist and took no time in starting mass conversion. The process of transformation of a Hindu society into an Islamic religious setting without, of course, altering the folk tradition, culture and linguistic foundation, was not fast; it took two centuries to notice a visible change in the religious demography of Bengal. With this visible transformation, the emergence of a self-conscious Muslim community too was clearly evident.[12] The induction of a new religion, Islam, apparently unified a substantial section of the fragmented but not polarized people under one umbrella in an essentially rural and agricultural society like that of Bengal, despite the existence of minor discordances between the urban dwelling *ashraf*, who were believed to have migrated from the Khyber region and also from North India and largely settled in cities like Gaur, Pandua, Satgaon, Sonargaon and Chittagong and the rural *atraps*, the lower and underprivileged masses, who were spread all over Bengal.[13]

It is noteworthy that while the first generation of Muslim migration that took place in the thirteenth century was from the Arab and Turkish connection due mainly to trade and invasion, the second generation of the Muslim migration was massive and Mughal sponsored. The new immigrants were eventually identified as Urdu speaking *ashraf*. The second phase of the Muslim influx had no definite role in the expansion of Islam as they were basically urban dwellers. The Sufis, the ulema and the mullas, who had been present all through the historical process, played the pivotal role in Islamization of Bengal; their roots were deeply implanted in rural Bengal. As Richard M. Eaton argues:

> By the seventeenth and eighteenth centuries, however, owing to principally to phenomenal levels of agrarian and demographic expansion in East Bengal, the dominant carrier of Islamic civilization in the delta were no longer the urban *ashraf*, but peasant cultivators of the eastern frontier, who in extraordinary ways assimilated Islam to their agrarian world-view."[14]

At any rate, the steady spread of Islam established some contact of the Bengali Muslims with the rest of the Islamic world. The first expression of Muslim solidarity in a larger canvas was evident during the Wahhabi Trials of 1869-1871.[15] The consciousness of the Bengali Muslim as part of Islamic *umma* began to grow since then.

The process of steady Islamization of Bengal as discovered in 1872 that the Muslims constituted more than 50 per cent of the population in three divisions of Bengal and that the phenomenal growth was attributed to widespread conversion sparked off a controversy that descended down the ninetieth century to the last on the origin of the Muslims of Bengal. The explanation for the phenomenal growth led to the formulation of four theories on Islamization – conversion or social liberation, 'sword on the neck', immigration and patronage. The contention of the census of 1872 could be treated as the forerunner of all the theories starting with the conversion theory, which holds the view that the unnatural growth of the Muslim population was due to the large scale conversion of inhabitants to Islam throughout the length and breadth of Bengal. As already stated, the 1872 census figures out the conversion as the principal reason for the unnatural growth of the Muslim population; it however remained silent on whether the conversion was based on force. Henry Beverley's conclusion marked the beginning of the controversy when he wrote that "the existence of Muhammadans in Bengal is not due so much to the introduction of Mughal blood into the country as to the conversion of the former inhabitants for whom a rigid system of caste discipline rendered Hinduism intolerable."[16]

The theory was contested by leading Muslims, the first among them was Abu A. Ghuznavi, who submitted a report to the District Collector of Mymensing, saying that the majority of the 19th century Muslims of Bengal were not the descendents of the low caste Hindus but were of foreign origins. A small fraction might have been converts but all of them were not necessarily low caste Hindus. There were zamindars, diwans and rajputs.[17] Another notable among those who rejected Beverley's thesis was Khondkar Fuzli Rubbee. He argued that the Muslim community in Bengal was formed by the immigrants coming from all over the Muslim world in successive phases, covering more than five and half centuries, starting from the fourteenth. Bengal's fertile land and moderate climate attracted migration of Muslims from other parts of the world and also from India aided by the Mughal patronage. The induction of the Muslims officers and soldiers into the administration and security of the region facilitated the speedy growth of Muslim population in Bengal.[18]

Edward A. Gait report on the Census of India 1901 refuted the contention of Ghuznavi and Rubbee that 90 per cent of the 'Shekhs' (Bengali Muslim cultivators) were of local origin and doubted the validity of the theory that the Bengal Muslims were immigrants from other parts of the country, without, of course, theorizing the rationale behind the local origins of the Muslims.[19] His observation was that the immigrants used to settle down in the peripheries of urban areas and would not migrate to backward and swampy rural areas.

A more recent view too tends to support the explanation that the Muslim population grew in large measure due to massive migration and induction of officials, soldiers, teachers and preachers from all over the Muslim world.[20] However, most of the scholars on the subject do not subscribe to this theory and find conversion as the overriding factor in the phenomenal growth of the Muslim population in Bengal. The logic is that immigration into Bengal did not appear to be so high as to alter its demographic picture. The religious engineering spearheaded through conversion by the Muslim Sufis and preachers had a big role to play.[21] This negates the 'sword on the neck' theory of conversion and Islamization in India, which ascribes the use of military force in spreading

Islam in India and elsewhere. Sir William Muir, a senior British officer serving in India and with a Christian missionary zeal, is one of the forerunners of the theory, which attributed the resurgence of Islam to the use of force.[22] A similar voice is echoed by the noted linguist, Suniti Kumar Chatterji, who wrote:

> The conquest of Bengal by these ruthless foreigners [the Muslims] was a terrible hurricane which swept over the country, when a peace loving people were subjected to all imaginable terrors and torments – wholesale massacre, pillage, abduction and enslavement of men and women, destruction of temples, palaces, images and libraries, and forcible conversion.[23]

A similar narrative could be found in the writings of one of the celebrated historians of Bengal, R.C. Majumdar, who found a closed, mutually hostile and exclusive fortress built by forced conversion that divided the Hindus and the Muslims.[24]

Richard M. Eaton finds it not only overheated rhetoric and imaginary but also argues that it is difficult to subscribe to the normative concept a society could be outrightly and dramatically transformed on religious line by brutal force.[25]

Another theory has been advanced by Aziz Ahmad. His 'political patronage' theory suggests that non-Muslims had been lured to get themselves converted to Islam with the prospect of benefit of tax relief, recruitment in army, and bureaucracy as also to have landed rights[26]. It had contributed enormously to induce the non-Muslims to get them converted. Modern historians with western secular training generally subscribe to such an argument as they believe that religion as an independent variable of a non-religious agency could play a role in the process of conversion.[27] But it cannot hold good the argument that it alone led to massive conversion among millions of rural peasants. The newly converted Muslims did not figure in the process of recruitment in army and bureaucracy. The contesting theory, known as 'social liberation', centres around a putative assumption that the caste ridden Hindu society had alienated many of the lower strata of the society, who eventually preferred to take shelter under Islam. As already stated, the British historians and officers pioneered the theory; and it was eventually rationalized by a host of modern South Asian Muslim scholars, - it suggests that the Hindu caste system and discriminatory treatment to the lower caste propelled the social engineering in the transformation of the rural Bengal towards speedy Islamization. The advent of Islam in Bengal carried the message of social equality and liberation which induced the oppressed castes to escape from discrimination and social humiliation at the hands of the Brahmins. The arrival of the Sufis (mystic and holy men) in rural Bengal provided an escape route to the people of lower order. The oppressed found an egalitarian social space after conversion to Islam. And in this process, the Sufis played a big role to attract the socially persecuted rural masses to Islam.[28] This needs further elucidation.

The expansion of Islam in Bengal was primarily rural-based, egalitarian and reflective of peasant culture and tradition. Bengal in the medieval age, as even today, was preeminently agrarian. The overwhelming population being rural poor, deprived of access to the rest of the world, dependent on primitive mode of production, unified to the local tradition, fatalist, insecure, and religious. They were premodern, prepolitical and vulnerable to a surge of egalitarian invasion that could liberate them from oppression committed by the landlords and the upper caste Brahmins. As Islam emerged in the rural Bengal at the instance of the Sufis, Islam appeared to be more peasant-friendly in nature. With little efforts and preaching about the religious fundamentals such as performance of religious rituals without spending anything in terms of cash or kind, Islam started penetrating deep into the heart of rural Bengal.[29] The introduction of the new religion did not affect the tradition and local practices and beliefs. It became an attractive deal to accept a religion which could offer an equal status and liberate them from social discrimination, and thus, 'peasant Islam' stood before the people of lower strata of Bengal's society as an easy means for their social transformation.[30] Here the Sufis, who were extremely popular in rural Bengal, played the critical and decisive role.

The Sufis of Bengal

As already stated, Sufis are Islamic mystics, who represent Islamic mysticism associated with the "internationalization and intensification of Islamic faith and practice".[31] The Sufis preach about all-pervading and omnipresence of God, and also about the direct divine-human relationship which could be promoted and enriched through prayer and contemplation. They value spiritual development and not legalism, enrichment of soul, emotional imagination and integration with God. Sufism has nothing to do with Sunni-Shia schism, social or class, gender, and territorial divisions, various schools of jurisprudence and family connections. They believe in equality of all human beings.

Sufism does not preach any particular social practice. The Sufis follow all the fundamental principles and practices of Islam, and therefore, Sufism is dear to both popular and conservative Islam. In addition to fundamental Islamic practices, the Sufi rituals include recitation of poems, text of the Qur'an in a melodious tune, and chanting devotional songs (Zikirs) in local language with musical accompaniments. All these carry not only the message of God but also inter-community harmonious relationship and humanity, making Sufism popular among various cross-sections of the society.

The Sufi mystic tradition has been receding slowing in the wake of invasion of so-called modern and materialistic world; it is argued that Sufism is incompatible with modernity. Yet, the Sufi order continues to play a role in expanding Islamic influence in various parts of the world including the West. It has been able to represent a liberal and human face of Islam in the wake of the emergence of revivalist and militant Islam.

As already stated, the Sufis, who represent mystic Islam, played an important part in the massive conversion in Bengal. The common and popular terminology for a Sufi is *Pir*. The Sufis exercise tremendous influence especially among the peasants. They belonged to several mystic orders (*Tariqas*) and used to cultivate a remarkable *Pir-Muridi* (teacher-disciple) relationship. Once a person became a *Murid* of a *Pir*, he had to carry the message of the Islam to the masses and to tell the members of his community to be good Muslims. It is a part of traditional patron-client relationship that got structured and institutionalized owing to the advent of the Sufis in Bengal. The existing patron-client relationship in the *Pir-Murid* form had manifestations in the rural economy of Bengal. It could be seen in the prevalence of zamindari system.[32] It facilitated the speedy process of Islamization in Bengal and sustained the relevance of religion in political domain of present Bangladesh.

The striking point of historiography of Islamization through mass conversion is associated with agrarian rural Bengal. Such a conversion was known to be 'incomplete' in nature because except for induction of the basic principles of Islam, there was no attempt to change the traditional, rural and cultural life of the people. The converts were acquainted with a few fundamental tenets of Islam. They were allowed to retain many of their cultural, traditional, social and even religious beliefs, practices, superstitions and habits. Most of the first generation Sufis was Persian speaking people, but they did not impose their language to disturb the linguistic allegiance. Rather, the Sufis coming from outside made it a point to learn Bengali, preached Islam in Bengali and in this process composed many melodious devotional songs. The second generation of the Sufis turned out to be Bengali by language and culture. When the preachers themselves fully identified as Bengalis by culture and tradition, the converts had no difficulty in retaining their age-long tradition, social practices, food habits and dresses. Later on, however, some practices were considered as *Bed'at* (religious innovations) and *Shirks* (poly-theistic and idolatrous practices), such as worshipping Kali. The Sufis did not make an attempt to draw the converts away from these practices. By the time, some attempt were made in this direction, many of the local practices had become an integral part of Muslim life in Bengal. The converts retained their household names, although formal names were changed to Arabic ones. Eventually, a process of naturalization of names started assimilating the Arabic names, to achieve an exotic dovetailing of Bengalicisation.[33]

As already mentioned the conversion of the locals to Islam had begun slowly, soon after the arrival of the Muslim saints in the ninth century. But the process of the mass conversion started with the arrival of well-known Sufi saints like Shaikh Shah Jalal al-Din Tabrizi in the early part of the thirteenth century. Shaikh Shah Jalal left Baghdad around 1228 and reached Lakhnauti in 1235. It is alleged that Shaikh Jalal indulged in the destruction of a temple in Lakhnauti and started the conversion.[34] That is why such Sufis were known as Ghazis (pious warriors)[35]. Another Sufi saint who arrived in Sylhet in 1345 was Shah Jalal Mujarrad. There were many others who made their mark in the Islamization or peasantization of the region. Prominent among them were Saiyyid Sultan[36], a celebrated poet of the late sixteenth century, expanding his missionary work in the Chittagong region, and Satya Pir[37] of the seventeenth century, who basically worked in rural Bengal. To state precisely, Islam was introduced into a non-Muslim milieu. The new converts lived in a Hindu environment. The neighbours and relatives were Hindus. The social interaction remained unaffected even after conversion. An atmosphere of sister community relationship grew. Except for the matter of principal religious practices, the 'new Muslims' could not be distinguished from the Hindus. Even married women continued to put vermilion on their forehead. Most of the converts had kept Hindu and Bengali names as home and first names. The folk tales and songs depicting the rural and agrarian life of Bengal continued to dominate the cultural life of all the people of Bengal, irrespective of their religious affiliations. All these created an atmosphere of tolerance and brotherhood. Even when over-enthusiastic preachers from north India tried to change some of their old practices, they had to cut a sorry figure. It was the Bengali spirit that governed the minds of the converts. They were enthusiastic about their new religion and a few basic and daily routine practices that a Muslim must follow. This did not clash with the practices they had been accustomed to for generations together.[38] All these factors contributed to creation of an atmosphere conducive to a harmonious interface between Hindus and Muslims[39].

The Sufi *Pirs* had tremendous impact on the process of conversion.[40] They were believed to be divine persons whose initiation was a must to secure salvation and spiritual enlightenment. This led to growth of *Pir-Muridi* (*Pir*-disciple) relationship which might have developed from *Guru*-disciple relationship of Hindu doctrine. In certain cases it exceeded the Hindu manifestation. When alive, the *Pir* is believed to grant solace and boon to the devotees, and to alleviate affliction. They were believed to be immortals in human frame; even after death they could shower boon on devotees. Their souls remain invisible and continue to do good to the people. Therefore, after death the grave of a *Pir* is treated as a *majar* or divine place where devotees come to pray. The graves of *Pirs* are generally transformed into mausoleums (*dargahs*) and are covered by cloths or curtains and are turned into places of worship. Though the practice of *Pir* adoration goes against the tenets of Islam, it is prevalent in most of parts of the Islamic world. *Urs* (celebration of death anniversary) is held in honour of departed *Pirs*. People in thousands flock to the *dargah* at that time. As in the case of other places, the masses in Bangladesh have tremendous respect for *Pirs*. Some of the politicians like Hossain Mohammad Ershad are known to be a *Murid* of a *Pir*. At the same time, the striking point to be noted is that the *Pirs* do not engage themselves in politics. However, they are generally opposed to the Jamaat and Tableeg movement[41] mainly because of the latter's exclusive approach to religion. Inter-community relationship based on humanity constitutes the centrality of Sufism, which is incompatible with the politics of the Jamaat and ideology of the Tableeg.

In Bangladesh there are hundreds of such *dargahs* visited regularly by people of all faiths. It is also interesting to find that Lord Siva is venerated by the Muslims. There is Siva temple in a village named Mahanad in Hughli. Many Muslims of the locality give liberal offerings for fulfillment of their desires. Lakshmi (Goddess of fortune) is another Hindu deity who is much revered by the rural masses. To cite an instance, the Muslim peasants recite chorus seeking her blessings for good harvest and to ward off the insects that are likely to harm the paddy fields. One popular doggerel goes like this:

> Month of Asvin passes, Kartic comes;
> Mother Lakshmi resides in the ear of corn;
> O Mother! Accept our offer of Sudh,
> Away, O pest of paddy! Away from my field.[42]

Similarly, many Muslims in East and North Bengal use to sing devotional songs in praise of Manasa Devi (Snake

Goddess). Manasa cult and the legend of Sati Beula were popular among the Hindus. After conversion they retained the tradition of Manasa cult, at least, in singing songs, if not worshiping the snakes. There are Muslim Ojhas (exorcists) who claim to have cured snake bites. They chant songs which plead with the Hindu Goddesses. Such a song is as follows:

> Hands heal, throat I heal, and the mouth I heal,
> Belly, back and feet I heal, and thorax I do heal.
> Poison from head to feet I heal,
> I remove with the blessings of Manasa,
> Lakhs of venomous shaft can do him no harm.
> Goddess Kamakhya of Kamrup granted me a boon;
> King Bind of Bali says – so and so conquered death.[43]

There are other cults such as Sitala Goddess cult which is followed to ward off occurrence of small pox. When small pox breaks out and takes an epidemic form the Muslims put an earthen pot called Ghot in front of the gate of their houses and hang a black bottle with lime. There was a practice of worshipping Olabibi (Goddess of cholera). In this way the concept of monolithic and omnipotent concept of God according to Islamic faith was to a great extent diluted. The converts continued the practice of exorcism inherited from their earlier faith. No one seemed to oppose or undo this. For generations together the Muslim Ojhas (exorcists) have been practicing the art, which came to be known as an integral part of Bengali tradition.[44]

The practice of elevating *Pirs* and their *dargahs* as places of worship was considered by the orthodox Muslims to be un-Islamic, obviously the result of Hindu influence. Many of Hindu rites and customs such as Rakhi bandhan, celebration of Diwali, and maintenance of *Pir-Murid* relationship were the outcome of enormous Hindu influence on the new Muslims who had been converted to Islam. Even the caste system penetrated deep into the Muslim society. Bengali Muslim religious practices like procession taking out in honour of a

Pir is determined by the folk tradition and not inherited from Arabia. The Shiv worshipping is in urban and Krishna Radha in rural Bengal.[45] These and a host of similar examples inter-community sharing of symbols and observance of traditional practices created a composite society in Bengal.

However, a revivalist movement called the Fariadi movement took place in the nineteenth century to reduce the Hindu influence.[46] Haji Shariatullah (1781-1840) in a village called Shamail in the Faridpur district started the movement in 1818 after returning from Mecca, where he stayed for twelve years. He studied at the Al-Azhar University in Cairo. While in Mecca he established contact with the Wahhabi movement. He started the Fariadi movement to urge upon the Bengali Muslims to adhere to the basic tenets of Islam as preached in the Qur'an. The term Fariadi was derived from an Arabic word 'faraid' which means obligatory duty enjoined by Islam. The movement was continued by his son, named Dudu Miyan (1819-1862). The movement became popular in areas where the Hindu zamindars used to rule the Muslim peasantry. Close on the heels of the Fariadi movement, the Wahhabi movement also tried to instill the puritan culture and tradition of the Arab origins in the Bengali Muslim society. The most important leader of the Wahhabi movement was Maulana Karamat Ali Jaunpuri[47] (1800-1873), who tried to enforce orthodox and puritan Islam in rural Bengal. Both the movements gained some degree of popularity because of their anti-colonial and anti-zamindari positions. However, Karamat Ali changed his anti-colonial position soon after the Sepoy mutiny 'out of pragmatism' and became a supporter of British establishment.[48]

The Fariadi and the Wahhabi movements to alter the socio-religious scenario in Bengal could not register any significant success. However, it seems to have planted the seeds of Islamic fundamentalism which has gained a space in the political process in Bangladesh. Its earliest manifestation could be seen in Bengal politics in 1919 during the Khilafat movement, when the ulema and political Islam rose against the British. The formation of a front called ashraf-ulema-jotedar representing the Bengali Muslim elite, the religious leaders and the peasants was an early promotion to the emergence of political Islam which eventually led to the creation of East Pakistan in 1947. The mobilization of the Muslims in 1919 under a religious umbrella transformed the political scenario in Bengal. It aroused communal passion among the Bengali Muslims forging an intermixture of religion and ethnicity that gave a distinct character of Bengali Muslims.[49] Despite the Sufi influence, communal politics aroused passion for which the bulk of the Muslim population, comprising the elite, the peasants, the middle class, the traders and host of other segments fought for Pakistan. At that point of history, the Muslims were overwhelmed by the religious identity and did not have time or mood to critically examine the question of religion as the foundation of the state. Their emotional attachment to Islam, despite its apparent disappearance in the wake of liberation war against Pakistan, resurfaced in the post-Mujib era, as it could be seen in Chapter IV, to pose a vitally important question as to whether Bangladesh was moving towards Islamization in the rigid sense of the term.

It is striking to note that while the early Sufis concentrated on the conversion of the locals to Islam, the successors accomplished the social engineering to consolidate Islam in rural and peasant society of Bengal retaining its traditional ethos and culture. They did not disturb the Hinduized societal framework. Under the circumstances, they could not afford to be communal. This is the most plausible reason to explain as to why they did not indulge communalization of the Bengal society and nor did they associate themselves in the political process of the country.

The Sufis, like the Deobandis School, did not take part in the movement for Pakistan. It appears that there lied the difference between them and the Jamaat, who were engaged in political Islam and believed exclusiveness.

Development of the Bengali language

One of the striking developments during the Muslim rule in Bengal was that the Bengali language began to flourish due mainly to royal patronage and from an inchoate language it grew into a well developed language, spoken by all the inhabitants irrespective of their religious and other primordial affiliations. There is no denying the fact that the language of the religious scriptures stirs spiritual and emotional attachment to the religion. But Arabic as the language of the scripture could play only a limited role only confined to matters of performing rituals. It could not go beyond the limited role since the common man did not understand the language at all. If religion has to be preached in simple language and its message has to reach the common man, the medium has to be undoubtedly the local language understood by all. The Sufis adopted the Bengali language for the purpose of spreading Islam as it was the primary vehicle of communication. The rulers patronized the language for two distinct purposes – to spread Islam among the common people and to consolidate their rule, despite the fact that Persian was the official language for the administration. The latter was the driving reason for the patronage. The royal support gave birth to the first Bengali Muslim poet named Shah Mohammad Saghir whose creative activities flourished during the reign of Ghias-uddin-Azam Shah (1389-1409). He wrote an epic in Bengali *Yusuf-Zolekha*, which depicted the famous love story known all over the Muslim world. A poet of the mid-fifteenth century named Muzammil composed *Nitisastra* (On Morals) to convey the principles and ideas of Islam to the common people who did not have any knowledge of Arabic. Sheikh Faridullah, Daulat Qadi and Alaul were some of the prominent writers of the 16th and 17th centuries who have left behind rich narratives on common practices and traditions of the Hindus and Muslims that speak of the syncretistic tradition of Bengal[50].

Two striking and distinguishing features in the folk tradition of Bengal deserve attention. One is the development of 'Musalmani Bangla', also known as Dobhashi or Islami Bangla, which is an admixture of Bengali, Persian and Urdu languages spoken by the rural Muslims of today's Bangladesh.[51] It is essentially Bengali language but contains high dose of Persian and Urdu words. It is a highly communicative language developed by the Sufis to transmit the message of Islam to the rural peasants whose mother tongue was Bengali. It was Shah Garibullah, a nineteenth century Sufi who used it extensively in his literary work, mostly his poetry. His poetry was marked by his commitment to cosmopolitanism and his efforts towards blending universal message of Islam with folk tradition of Bengal.

The other is Baul, a unique variety of people common to all religious denominations – Buddhist, Hindus and Muslims. The Bauls may have their own religion by birth but in their social behaviour they cannot be put in the frame of any religious construction. They are basically renouncers. But the Baul songs carry the message of universalism and humanity. To cite a few of such Baul songs:

> I have made the world my home,
> And my home the world,
> I have made others my own people,
> And my own people others.

Another goes like this:

> Hindu, Muslim, Buddhist, Christian,
> You and I, female and male,
> These are not different.
> The problem comes from religion,
> Human beings are one and the same,
> So what is the basis for violence?

Incidentally, this also marked the compositeness of Bengali language and literature.[52]

The Muslim rulers in Bengal extended support to the Bengali language for political reasons to enlist the cooperation of the Hindus in the administration. A great deal of translation works had been accomplished during the Muslim rule in Bengal. Great Sanskrit epics like the *Ramayana* and the *Mahabharata* were translated into Bengal.[53] The Chinese traveler Ma Huan, who visited Bengal in the early part of the fifteenth century (1425-1432), recorded that Bengali was the universal language all over Bengal.[54] The advent of Islam in Bangladesh did not cause any social tension and disharmony. It was mainly because of the adaptation of the new religion in the Hindu environment of Bengal and retention of many of the social and existing religious customs, traditions and practices that the converts used to follow in the pre-Islamic days. It pre-supposes prevalence of a society wherein the hardcore religious fundamentalism has little chance of survival.

The Bengali religious and cultural and linguistic identities created an ethnocentric paradigm – a union of linguistic and traditional Bengal with religion that eventually led to the creation of Bangladesh. It is too difficult to negate it despite the efforts of the political and militant Islam to reverse the century long process of assimilation and accommodation of traditional culture, practices and values, so deeply rooted in the society of Bangladesh.

REFERENCES

1. Richard M. Eaton, *The Rise of Islam and the Bengal Frontier, 1204-1760* (Berkeley: University of California Press, 1993), p. xxii.
2. For some details see Benedict Anderson, *Imagined Communities: Reflection on the Origins and Spread of Nationalism* (London: Verso, 1994), pp. 6-19.

3. Rafiuddin Ahmed (ed), *Islam in Bangladesh: Society, Culture and Politics* (Dhaka: Bangladesh Itihas Samiti, 1983), p. II. Also see his *The Bengal Muslims 1871-1906: A Quest for Identity* (New Delhi: Oxford University Press, 1981), Chapter 1.
4. Arab traders landed on the coastal areas near Chittagong in the first century AD and then started their trade expansion in other parts of Bengal. See Andre Wink, *Al-Hind: The Making of the Indo-Islamic World,* Vol. 1: *Early Medieval India and Expansion of Islam, 7th-11th Centuries* (Leiden: E.J. Brill, 1990), pp. 65-68.
5. For details Francis Robinson, *Atlas of the Islamic World since 1500* (Oxford: Phaidon Press, 1982), p. 29.
6. For some details see U.A.B. Razia Akhtar Banu, *Islam in Bangladesh* (Leiden: E.J. Brill, 1992), Chapter I.
7. G. Saklayen has made a list of 408 Sufis in Bangladesh who started preaching Islam since 13th century through 19th century. For details see his *Bangladesher Sufi Sadhak* (The Sufi Devotees of Bangladesh), (Dhaka: Islamic Foundation, 1982), pp. 157-174.
8. Henry Beverley, *Report on Census of Bengal, 1872* (Calcutta: Secretariat Press, 1872), pp. 12-15.
9. *ibid*, p. 132. also see Rafiuddin Ahmed, *The Bengal Muslims 1871-1907: A Quest for Identity* (New Delhi: Oxford University Press, 1981), p. 2.
10. James Wise, "The Muhammadans of Eastern Bengal", *Journal of Asiatic Society of Bengal,* Vol. 63, 1994, p. 28.
11. Rafiuddin Ahmed (ed), *Understanding the Bengal Muslims: Interpretative Essays* (New Delhi: Oxford, 2001), pp. 11-13.
12. For an elaborate discussion see Asim Roy, *The Islamic Syncretistic Tradition in Bengal* (Princeton: Princeton University Press, 1983), Chapter 1. Also see Richard M. Eaton, *The Rise of Islam and the Bengal Frontier, 1204-1760,* n. 1, Chapter 8.

13. Rana Razzaque Ahsan, "An Introduction to the Trends of Bengali Muslim Thought, 1905-1947", *Journal of Asiatic Society of Bangladesh,* Vol. 43, No. 1, 1998, pp. 37-62.

14. Richard M. Eaton, "Who are the Bengal Muslims? Conversion and Islamization in Bengal" in Rafiuddin Ahmed (ed), *Understanding the Bengal Muslims: Interpretative Essays* n. 11, pp. 26-51, quotation p. 43.

15. For details see Muin-ud-Din Ahmad Khan (ed), *Selections from Bengal Government Record on Wahhabi Trial, 1869-1870* (Dacca: Asiatic Society of Pakistan, 1961), pp. 52-94, 173-186.

16. *Report on the Census of Bengal, 1972,* n. 8, p. 132.

17. For details of the contention of Guzhnavi's report see Richard M. Eaton, *The Rise of Islam and the Bengal Frontier, 1204-1760,* n. 1, Chapter 5.

18. *Census of Bengal, 1872,* p. 132. Also see Rafiuddin Ahmed, *The Bengal Muslims 1871-1906: A Quest for Identity,* n. 9, p.1.

19. Edward A. Gait, "The Muhammadans of Bengal" in *Census of India, 1901,* Vol. 6, *The Lower Province of Bengal and their Feudatories,* Part I, "Report" (Calcutta: Bengal Secretariat Press, 1902), pp. 166-170.

20. Khondaker Fuzli Rubbee, *The Origin of the Musalmans of Bengal* (Calcutta: Thacker, Spink and Co. 1895), p. 1.

21. For details see Richard Eaton, n. 1 and also Muhammad Abdul Karim, *Social History of the Muslims of Bengal* (Dacca: Asiatic Society of Pakistan, 1959) Chapter III and IV.

22. William Muir, *The Caliphate: Its Rise, Decline and Fall,* originally published from London in 1898, Reprint (Beirut: Khayat, 1963), Chapter 2.

23. Suniti Kumar Chatterji, *Languages and Literatures of Modern Bengal* (Calcutta: Bengal Publishers, 1963), pp. 160-161.

24. R.C. Majumdar found it relevant to speak against the much projected communal unity in the struggle for independence to tell a different story of social division caused by forced

conversion. See his *History of Medieval Bengal* (Calcutta: G. Bharadwaj & Co. 1973), pp. vi, 196-197.

25. Richard M. Eaton, *The Rise of Islam and the Bengal Frontier, 1204-1760*, n. 1, Chapter 5.
26. Aziz Ahmad, *Studies in Islamic Culture in the Indian Environment* (London: Oxford University Press, 1964), p. 105.
27. For such an argument on conversion see Peter Hardy, "Modern European and Muslim Explanations of Conversion in South Asia: A Preliminary Survey of the Literature" in Nehemia Levtzion (ed), *Conversion to Islam* (New York: Holmes and Meier, 1979) pp 79-81.
28. Mohammad Enamul Haq, *A History of Sufi-ism in Bengal* (Dhaka: Asiatic Society of Bangladesh, 1975) Chapter XII. For details of the Sufi cult in Islam see J. Spencer Trimingham, *The Sufi Orders in Islam* (London: Oxford University Press, 1971).
29. James J. Scott, *The Moral Economy of the Peasant: Rebellion and Subsistence in Southeast Asia* (New Haven: Yale University Press, 1976) Chapter 1.
30. Asim Roy, *Islamic Syncretistic Tradition in Bengal*, n. 12, Chapter 1.
31. John L. Esposito (ed), *The Oxford Dictionary of Islam* (New York: Oxford University Press, 2003), p.302.
32. For an interesting analysis on patron-client relationship see Stanley A Kochanek, *Patron-Client Politics and Business in Bangladesh* (New Delhi: Sage, 1993) and his "Governance, Patronage Politics and Democratic Transition in Bangladesh" *Asian Survey*, Vol. XL, No. 3, May/June, 2000, pp. 530-550.
33. *ibid*, pp. 319-322.
34. Richard M. Eaton, *The Rise of Islam and the Bengal Frontier, 1204-1760*, n. 1, Chapter 3.
35. Eaton argues that there was no historical record of forced conversion and entitlement of Ghazi. On the other hand contemporary record of Bengal done by Ibn Battuta, a famous

Moroccan traveler, who had spent three days as a guest of Shah Jalal of Sylhet, noted the conversion of local people to Islam but silent about the use of force.

36. In his Nabi Bamsa Saiyyid Sultan depicted Lord Krishna as one of the prophets. For details see France Bhattacharya, 'Hari the Prophet: An Islamic View of a Hindu God in Saiyid Sultan's Nabi Vamsa" in Perveen Hasan and Mufakharul Islam, *Essays in Memory of Momtazur Rahman Tarafdar* (Dhaka: Centre for Advance Research in the Humanities, 1999), pp. 192-208.

37. Satya Pir refers to a cult of five great Pirs. According to Dinesh Chandra Sen Satya Pir was a cult synthesizing Hindu and Muslim approach to religion. The cult is a combination of Sanskrit and Arabic words referring to a Sufi saint who tried to bring a sustainable interface of two communities, see his *History of Bengali Language and Literature* (Calcutta: University of Calcutta, 1954) pp. 676-677. Mohammad Enamul Haq writes that no one is certain who were these five Pirs. Their names vary from place to place. See his *A History of Sufi-ism in Bengal*, n.27, p. 329.

38. For details see S.A.A. Rizvi, *A History of Sufism in India* (Delhi: Munshiram Manoharilal, 1978).

39. For the details of the healthy relations between the Hindus and the Muslims see Jagadish Nararyan Sarkar, *Hindu-Muslim Relations in Bengal: Medieval Period* (Delhi: Idarah-i-Adaiyal-i-Delli, 1985).

40. See Rafiuddin Ahmed (ed), *Islam in Bangladesh: Society, Culture and Politic,* n. 3, p. III.

41. Taj I. Hashmi, "Islamic Resurgence in Bangladesh: Genesis, Dynamics and Implications" in Satu P. Limaye *et al.*, *Religious Radicalism and Security in South Asia* (Honolulu, Hawaii: Asia-Pacific Centre for Security Studies, 2004), p. 40.

42. Cited in Mohammad Enamul Haq, *A History of Sufi-ism in Bengal*, n. 28, p. 349-350.

43. *ibid.* p. 351.

44. For some details see Dinesh Chandra Sen, *The Folk Literature of Bengal* (Calcutta: University of Calcutta, 1920), pp. 86-94.
45. See Rafiuddin, *Understanding Bengal Muslim*, n. 11, pp.53-54.
46. For details see Muin-uddin Ahmed Khan, *History of Fariadi Movement in Bengal* (Dhaka: Islamic Foundation, 1984) and A.I. Shaikh, *Pir Dudu Miyan* (in Bengali), (Dhaka: Islamic Foundation, 1984).
47. Taj I. Hashmi, " Karamat Ali and the Muslims in Bengal, 1880-873", *Dhaka University Studies*, Vol. 23, June 1976.
48. For details how the British administration tactfully enlisted the support of some of the *ulema* in order to create a dependable base in Muslim dominated areas of Bengal, see A.R. Mullick, *British Policy and the Muslims in Bengal, 1757-1856*, 2nd Edition (Dhaka: Bangla Academy, 1977).
49. Rafiuddin Ahmed, *The Bengali Muslim 1871-1906: A Quest for Identity*, n. 9, Chapter I.
50. Asim Roy, *The Islamic Syncretistic Tradition in Bengal*, n. 12.
51. For details see Rajarshi Ghose, "Muslim Bengal in the nineteenth century: Between Shah Garibullah and Sayyied Ahmad Shahid" a seminar paper presented in an international seminar organized by the Indian Council of Historical Research at Shillong in May 2007.
52. Muhammad Enamul Haq, *Muslim Bangla Sahitya* (Muslim Bengali Literature), (Dacca: Pakistan Publication, 1965), p. 59 and 176-177.
53. Amartya Sen, *The Argumentative Indian* (London: Penguin Books, 2005), p. 60. Also see Dinesh Chandra Sen, *History of Bengali Language and Literature* (Calcutta: University of Calcutta, 1954), pp. 10-12.
54. Abdul Karim, *Social History of the Muslims of Bengal (down to A.D. 1538)* (Dacca: Asiatic Society of Pakistan, 1959), pp. 176-177, also see Momtazur Rahman Tarafdar, *Husain Shahi Bengal, 1494-1538: A Socio-Political Study* (Dacca: Asiatic Society of Pakistan, 1965).

4

RISE OF POLITICAL AND MILITANT ISLAM

With the ascendancy of political Islam in Iran in February 1979, when Ayatullah Rohullah Khomeini captured power after overthrowing Reza Shah Pehlavi, Islam as a way of social and political life captured the imagination of the people living in the Muslim-dominated countries. Consequently, it became a focal point of mobilization of people in the Islamic world.[1] Suddenly, a realization that the Islamic world consists of 900 million people spread over 44 Muslim majority countries from Algeria to Indonesia-Malaysia archipelago and that also includes a substantial population in China, Europe, India, Russia, the United States and United Kingdom swept not only the Islamic world but also the West. A wave of resurgence of political and militant Islam engulfed in the Islamic world. This prompted the western scholars to view the world, more particularly after the collapse of the Soviet Union, from a perspective of two mutually hostile camps – the western civilization and the oriental Islamic civilization. It led to an erroneously framed concept called 'clash of civilization'.[2] Islam as a religion and slogans embodying the Islamic faith emerged as rallying points and political symbols not only in Muslim majority countries in the world but also in other societies where a sizeable population belongs to the faith. Consequently, a tendency to use Islam not only for regulation of social life within a hardcore framework of fundamentalism but also to capture political power started to grow, despite the fact that Islam as a religion has nothing to do with fundamentalism which is synonymous with 'Islamic activism' or 'Islamism' nor can it be associated with religio-political ideology.

Islamic fundamentalism is a disputed term used extensively in the West to denote any movement to promote socio-political life in accordance with teaching of the Qur'an, Hadith and Shariah (Islamic law). Some scholars in the Middle East and South Asia would prefer to choose terms such as 'Islamism' and 'Islamicism'. The purpose of this Chapter is not to engage in a discourse to draw the inherent distinction between Islam as a religion and fundamentalism as either militant or political Islam, but to attempt at an analytical narrative of the rise of Islamic fundamentalism understood both in terms of militancy and political tool for capturing power in Bangladesh.

Emergence of Bangladesh as an Islamic state

It is interesting to view the transformation of Muslims of Bengal during the last century in the context three distinct frameworks – Muslim identity in the colonial era, Bengali ethnic community during 1947-1971 and Bengali Muslims since the assassination of Mujibur Rehman. Ever since the rise of self-conscious religious community in colonial Bengal with effect from the Wahhabi Trials of 1869-1871, the Muslim identity grew in a significant manner during the colonial era. The Muslim community gradually started transforming into a 'nation' in order to gain political advantage. Its manifestation could be traced to in the partition of Bengal, followed by formation of the Muslim League and eventually the creation of East Pakistan in 1947. But it did not take long for the gradual disappearance of illusion and confidence of the people of East Pakistan as a part of an Islamic state. The Bengali nationalism became the overriding mobilizing force that eventually inspired the countrymen to face even death and destruction in the pursuit of an independent Bengali nation-state. As already stated, the year 1948 marked the watershed that led to the assertion of the Bengali national identity when M.A. Jinnah insisted on one-language formula in the country and rejected the demand that Bengali could also be a co-language. The twenty three year history of the Bengali Muslims' quest for distinct identity gave birth to the new republic, Bangladesh.

Bangladesh's emergence as an independent, secular and democratic republic in December 1971 did not altogether blur its religious contour.[3] As stated in Chapter III, the seeds of Islamic identity of the Muslims of Bengal had been planted in the nineteenth century with the Fariadi and Wahhabi movements glorifying Islam and preaching a puritan version of the religion. Therefore, it did not take time to find the resurgence of Islam as the overwhelmingly visible face of Bangladesh.[4] The existential question and the foundational issue centering Islam negated the secular credentials that the new nation wanted to promote and to be identified with. But the process of reemergence of Islam as the basis of state's identity encouraged religious forces to attempt at the transformation of Bangladesh into a rigid Islamic state following Shariah laws and ordinances.

In the initial phase of Independence, the Bengali nation-state was the prominently visible identity of the new member of the international community. The father of the nation, Bangabandhu Sheikh Mujibur Rehman, outlined eloquently the rationale behind the secular identity of Bangladesh. Speaking in the Constituent Assembly on November 4, 1972 Sheikh Mujib said:

> Secularism does not mean absence of religion. The 75 million people of Bangladesh will have the right to religion by law. We do not want to ban religion by law.

> We have no intention of that kind. Secularism does not mean absence of religion. Muslims will observe their religion and nobody in this state has the power to prevent that. Hindus will observe their religion and nobody has the power to prevent that. Buddhists and Christians will observe their respective religions and nobody can prevent that. Our only objective is that nobody will be allowed to use religion as a political weapon.[5]

Mujib defended his position to include secularism in the Constitution. He said:

> ...secularism does not mean absence of religion. You are a Mussalman, you perform your religious rites. There is no religiousness on the soil of Bangladesh but there is secularism. This sentence has a meaning and that meaning is that none would be allowed to exploit the people in the name of religion, or create such fascist organizations as the al-Badar, razakars etc. No communal party will be allowed in the country.[6]

The Constitution of Bangladesh (Article 12) also provided the basis for the secular credentials of Bangladesh. Although the new state was predominantly inhabited by Muslims, the foundation of the nation-state was different - it was Bengali ethnicity. Consequently, it gave equal space and share to all communities irrespective of their religious affiliations. The 'vision of a community' on the ethnic nationalism provided a canopied structure under which all the inhabitants could live peacefully. It demonstrated how language and popular ethnic-based life played pivotal role in the formation and construction of Bengali nationalism, despite the fact that Islam has a universal appeal. The idea of 'Islamic nation' remained dormant in an emotionally charged euphoria of a Bengali nation. The emergence of Bangladesh apparently demolished the foundation of the 'two-nation theory', and consequently, the religious identity was sidelined.

Secularism, which came to be considered as synonymous with 'Mujibism', became the cornerstone of political modernization in the newly emerged country. It is also deeply entrenched in the concept of Bengali nationalism, which steered the nation towards independence. By definition Bengali nationalism has a wider cultural framework, which encompassed not only the vast religious majority, the Muslims, but also other religious and social compositions. Nonetheless, the idea of secularism did not crystallize during and after the liberation. It remained an ambiguous and covered with a thick mist of confusion, considering the predominance of the Muslim segment in the religious canvas of Bangladesh. The Bengali term for secularism often used by Sheikh Mujib, 'dharma nirapekshata' (literal English translation, 'neutrality in religion') carried a negative connotation for to the common masses who found it to be either 'religious neutralism' or 'anti-religion'.[7] Secularism, therefore, was misunderstood to be anti-thesis to religion. To the common masses, who were highly religious, it stood as an abnegation of Islam.[8] Therefore, Talukdar Maniruzzam wrote that "secularism in Bangladesh did not reflect in societal spirit and history".[9]

As already stated, Article 12 of the new Constitution envisioned how the state would realize secularism, the state would strive to eliminate communalism of all forms by not granting political status in favour of any religion, end abuse of religion for political purpose, and remove any discrimination against or persecution of any person on the ground of religion. Article 38 is more specific. It banned any communal or other association or union which had a political purpose in the name of or on the basis of religion. They were successful in branding Mujib's measures and constitutionalism as inimical to Islam. It was easy for them to arouse public passion against him. Half of the people are illiterate, as Akhtar Hossain writes, "politically ill-informed, possess unsophisticated character traits, they are vulnerable to manipulation of one form or another by politician".[10] Although Hossain writes in the context of *hartal* which is so common in Bangladesh, as stated in Chapter II, the assertion appears to be valid in other contexts too.

Mujib's secular approach, which laid more emphasis on linguistic nationalism than on religion, could not reach the public in its proper perspective, and consequently, faced severe criticism from various quarters including the academics. Critics felt that he went one step ahead of Jawaharlal Nehru - despite his unblemished secular credentials, Nehru resisted the insertion of the term secularism in Indian Constitution, understandably because of his fear that the inclusion of the term might create misunderstanding among the people. Mujib's secular framework was termed as a "multi religious theocracy".[11] The contesting frontiers of secularism and religious nationalism surfaced during Mujib's life time. His critics took the opportunity to campaign against him, asserting that his secularism had been a manifestation of India's dictates. In order to neutralize such criticism, he starting using religious slogans and symbols on various occasions. Towards the end of his rule, he 'Islamized' his speeches to a considerable extent. He started public speeches with 'bismillahir rahmanir rahim' (in the name of God, the most benevolent and merciful). He used to conclude his speech with khuda hafiz (May God protect you). This replaced his earlier habit of concluding his speech with 'Joy Bangla' (glory to Bengal). Other terms like 'insah Allah' (if God wishes), 'bismillah' (in the name of Allah), 'tawba' (penitence) 'iman' (faith) etc were frequently uttered. A few months before his assassination, he reestablished the already defunct Islamic Academy with a new name, Islamic Foundation, to promote Islam, and strengthened the Madrassa system of education by increasing grants. These steps were taken to prove to the masses that he had an Islamic credential and that he was not a 'munafiq' (religious deviant). But it was 'too late and also too little' to satisfy his detractors who criticized him for his 'secular' and 'pro-Indian' position, despite his desperate efforts to send a message that he was a part of the Islamic 'ummah' and a devout Muslim, while at the same time maintaining that other religious groups had a right to live and co-exist peacefully. It appeared that no one took his secularism seriously, despite his enormous efforts; as Anisuzzaman put it succinctly:

> Mujib himself, his political associates and government functionaries went on explaining ceaselessly that secularism did not mean absence of religion or irreligiosity. Mujib government also helped Madrassahs and elevated the defunct Islamic Academy to the Islamic Foundation.[12]

As already stated, it was difficult for the common masses, mostly illiterate, to comprehend properly the definition of secularism. The opponents took it as an advantage to campaign that secularism was an imposition from India and also repugnant to Islam and that it would reduce the status of Islam as the preponderant religion in Bangladesh. Together with the failure to convey to the masses what his secularism meant, Mujib's failure to handle properly a number of crises such as the 1974 catastrophic flood situation, abject poverty, inflation, deterioration of law and order, corruption and nepotism provided a basis for the religious nationalism to grow as an alternative.[13]

Almost all the opposition parties including the once condemned collaborators of the Pakistani army joined hands to spearhead a massive movement against the Awami League government. Maulana Abdul Hamid Khan Bhasani took the leadership of the movement. His credentials as a peasant leader and an ardent advocate of 'Islamic socialism' appeared to be an attractive rallying point against the Awami League government. He condemned Mujib as to be a highly communal person, who had been using religion to ensure political gains:

> Mujib himself would use every trick of communalism to keep himself in power. In fact, he is the worst communalist this country has ever produced...he was not prepared to drop the prefix 'Muslim' from the name of Awami League.[14]

Close on the heels of these developments, Mujib became intolerant of the movements and tried to suppress the opposition ruthlessly. Many of his opponents were physically eliminated.[15] It appears that Mujib's biggest political blunder was the introduction of single party government in the name of Bangladesh Krishak Sramik Awami League on February 24, 1975 dissolving all other political parties.[16] It not only alienated him from the masses but also gave a scope for the emergence of the army in national politics and simultaneously also Islamic fundamentalism as alternatives to 'so-called' secular and democratic framework that Mujib tried to enforce.[17] Mujibism had its inherent infirmities caused by absence of proper perspective planning, theoretical formulation and well-defined goals.[18] The search for an alternative paved the way for the rise of Islamic fundamentalism in Bangladesh in a surprisingly short time interval.

The assassination of Sheikh Mujibur Rehman made it for the military to occupy the centre stage of governance in Bangladesh spanning a long period of fourteen years. It started with the ascendancy of Major General Ziaur Rahman as the Chief Martial Law Administrator on November 28, 1976 and followed by his occupation of the position of the President of Bangladesh on April 21, 1977. His rule came to an end violently on May 30, 1981, when he was done to death in Chittagong by disgruntled officers.[19] The second stint of military rule commenced on March 24, 1982 when General Hossain Mohammad Ershad took over power and ruled till

December 6, 1990.[20] Soon after the assassination of Sheikh Mujib, the process of Islamization at the behest of the government started. The new rulers at first began to attack the slain leader for neglecting Islam and then started denigrating his secular approach. They tried to demonstrate the preeminent position of Islam in Bangladesh through the mass media. The time allotted to reading the Quran in electronic media was increased from 5 minutes to 15 minutes. The 5 minute time schedule allotted to reading scriptures of other religions remained unchanged. The radio and the TV programmes were customarily closed with readings of Qur'an only. The Islamic face of Bangladesh started appearing prominently. All these facilitated the emergence of fundamentalism in Bangladesh in the subsequent years.[21]

As already stated, soon after the assassination of Sheikh Mujibur Rehman, Khandakar Mostaq Ahmed released the leading functionaries of Jamaat from prison. It was followed by the recognition of Bangladesh as a sovereign country by Saudi Arabia. It uplifted the image of Bangladesh among the Islamic countries. In Bangladesh it was taken as a defining moment reestablishing Bangladesh's image as an Islamic country in the community of Islamic brethren. The suppressed and ostracized Islamists found the development to be squarely rejoiced at.[22]

The emergence of Major General Ziaur Rahman to prominence, soon after the assassination of Sheikh Mujib first as the Chief of the Staff, then as Chief Martial Law Administrator on November 7, 1975 and eventually his ascendancy to the office of President of Bangladesh on April 21, 1977 could be treated as a notable development in the process of turning Bangladesh into a hot bed of militant and political Islam. After making himself the President, General Zia initiated several carefully designed steps to present an Islamic face of the country in anticipation of rich political dividends. Two of such steps had far reaching impact. The first was the amendment that he did to the Constitution of 1972. He incorporated 'Bismillahir Rahmanir Rahim" in the Constitution through an ordinance (Proclamation No. 1 of 1977) and later on it was made a part of the Constitution through the 5th Amendment. Through the same Proclamation, Article 8, Clause 1 containing the principle of secularism was substituted by "the principles of absolute trust and faith in the Almighty, nationalism, democracy and socialism meaning economic and social justice, together with the principles derived from them as set out in this Part, shall constitute the fundamental principles of state policy." The passage of the amendment was put as a precondition to the lifting of Martial Law. In this way he forced the Jatiyo Sangsad to pass the amendment in the teeth of stiff opposition from the Awami League. Several articles of the 1972 Constitution were deleted to present the Islamic denomination of Bangladesh. Article 259(2) was amended to accord preeminence to Islam so as to promote Bangladesh's fraternal relations with Islamic countries. An important casualty due to the efforts towards asserting Islamic identity was secularism as enshrined in Articles 12 and 38, which were dropped. These were far-reaching steps designed to achieve multiple goals, such as, to secure legitimacy, to cultivate closer relations with the oil-rich Arab countries, and thus, to obtain diplomatic mileage and to marginalize the once powerful Awami League. The BNP provided the justification in its manifesto of 1978 for all the changes. While defining Bangladeshi nationalism within the framework of Islam, it asserted: "Religious belief and love for religion are a great and imperishable characteristic of the Bangladeshi nation". It was unequivocal in clarifying what religion it wanted to speak about: 'vast majority of our people are followers of Islam. The fact is well reflected in our stable and liberal national life".[23] Other striking changes followed. On the opening day of the first session of the Jatiyo Sangsad, in clear departure from past practices when recitation from all the holy books had taken place, the session began with the recitation of from the Qur'an only. The Bengali slogan "Joi Bangla", a driving force of the Bengali nationalism, was replaced by an Urduized "Bangladesh Zindabad". Despite his efforts to consolidate his political authority by using the concept of 'Bangladeshi nationalism' in place of Mujibism in domestic and international politics, Ziaur Rahman continued to face formidable challenge from political opponents, bureaucracy and military elite.[24] That eventually led to his assassination on May 30, 1981. Zia's assassination marked the end of one phase of military rule in Bangladesh. But the political decay continued to loom large. In no time, followed another phase of military rule under General Hossain Mohammad Ershad. Initially, Zia put Bangladesh at the crossroads of secularism and sacerdotalism and eventually paved the way for reemergence of Islamists in the politics of Bangladesh.[25]

The second step was taken on the diplomatic front. Close on the heels of the domestic developments, one could notice a major foreign policy shift in Bangladesh. Till the end of the Mujib era, Bangladesh had closer ties with India and the Soviet Union for historic reasons of their support for its liberation and their campaign for international recognition of the new country. Ziaur Rahman brought about a major change in the foreign policy by moving Bangladesh closer to China, Pakistan and Saudi Arabia.[26] It is argued that the shift had been curved due to certain domestic compulsions. He felt that it was in the interest of his Muslim majority country to move closer to Saudi Arabia and Pakistan for their standing in the Islamic world. His pro-China policy was a manifestation of anti-India feelings and suspicions. Both the foreign policy moves pleased the Islamists which eventually helped them to consolidate their ground in domestic politics. He allowed the Pakistan's intelligence service, the Inter-Service Intelligence (ISI) to operate in Bangladesh and work closely with the Bangladeshi counterpart, Directorate General of Forces Intelligence (DGFI), which he formed in 1978.[27] Pakistan, which could not reconcile with its defeat in the Indo-Pak War of 1971 and its dismemberment, was naturally happy to be well placed near India's North East and fish in the troubled water in the region. The ISI operators were now at the door steps of India's North East and could secure an advantage to establish connections with the insurgents belonging to the region.

Later on General Ershad, less known till he made himself the ruler but known for his corruption, amended the Constitution to proclaim Islam as the state religion. It was done to disabuse the doubt among some of the Islamic countries about the Islamic credentials of Bangladesh and to nullify Pakistan's campaign against his country as a non-Islamic state. Article 2A (Eighth Amendment, 1988) was inserted to read "Islam is the state religion. All other religions can be practiced freely in peace and harmony."[28] The idea of Islamic state did not go unopposed. Scholars, judges, media persons dismissed it as gimmick and argued that Islam cannot be the state religion even in a predominantly Muslim majority state. Islam as religion cannot be controlled by the state. The Qur'an is silent about the concept of state religion. The Islamic tenet "Allah is Sovereign" meaning thereby that the state or for that matter the religion cannot be sovereign is to be noted.[29] At any rate, it was a swift implementation of his commitment to the public in a mammoth meeting of the Bangladesh Jamiat-ul-Mudderressin on January 20, 1988 in which he had said that the cultural life of Bangladeshis would be firmly based on Islamic principles for which it would be imperative on his part to declare Islam as the state religion.[30] Among the steps he initiated to woo his fellow Muslims in the country and abroad were introduction of the Zakat Fund to raise poor tax in accordance with the fundamentals of Islam and declaration of Friday as the weekend holiday in place of Sunday. In order to project himself as a devout Muslim he often visited mosques and shrines.[31] Like his predecessor he used the anti-India card on the issue of sharing the Ganges water.[32] It is believed that Ershad did not have commitment to Islam, yet, like Ziaur Rahman, he used the Islamic card to corner the opposition and to legitimize his own rule. Both the Generals had attempted at securing a dependable support base among the Islamists and clerics, besides, of course, the anti-Indian political lobby. But all these failed to impress the Islamists. The Jamaat joined hands with others in a country-wide movement against Ershad and eventually that led to his resignation on December 6, 1990.[33] The Jamaat's association with the anti-Ershad movement gave it some credibility and a scope to emerge as a political force in the near future.

In this way, the successors of Sheikh Mujibur Rehman created a constitutional and political space for the reemergence of the Jamaat to play a role in the governance of the country and simultaneously encouraged, if not directly, the militant Islamists to go ahead with their jehadi politics.

Islamism and its ramifications

As already stated, Islam has emerged dramatically in the political system of Bangladesh drawing global attention. Although the tendency towards providing a distinctive space to Islam as a religion of the vast majority of the people had been visible and the process towards Islamization of the political environment of Bangladesh had begun during the rule of Sheikh Mujib, the resurgence of Islamic movement could be seen prominently during the military rule (1977 to 1990). But sharing of political power by the Jamaat is a matter of only six years, when the BNP forged a pre-election alliance with the Jamaat, the Islamic Oikya Jote (IOJ) and the Jatiyo Party (Naziur) to contest the 2001 elections.[34] The BNP's decision to have a marriage of convenience with the Jamaat and the IOJ to gain political mileage in the election was undoubtedly disturbing, for, both were known for their pronounced anti-democratic and non-secular positions.[35] Although the Jamaat claims that it does not have any links with the militants, its agenda for Islamization and its notorious record during the war of liberation are well known. The IOJ does not hide its colour and is vocal about its support for the Islamist militants, the Taliban and the al-Qaeda. Further, most of the members have direct association with the HuJI. The formation of the four party alliance led by the BNP is undoubtedly a milestone in the history of Islamization of Bangladesh. Consequent upon pre-poll understanding and alliance, the post-poll coalition ministry accommodated two members from the Jamaat, which captured 17 seats, despite the fact that the BNP secured an absolute majority, 193 out of 300 seats in the Jatiyo Sansand.[36] Motiur Rahman Nizami, the Ameer of the Jamaat was given the Agricultural Ministry, one of the most important cabinet berths in country which is essentially agricultural in character. More importantly, the ministry is known to have vital link with the rural population. Later on at the behest of the United States, it is said, Nizami was shifted to the Ministry of Industry, a less important portfolio in an industrially backward country like Bangladesh.[37] Nizami's deputy, Ali Ahsam Muhammad Mujahid, was offered the Ministry of Social Welfare. Naturally, the coalition government had the compulsion to foster Islamization of Bangladesh, leaving enormous scope for the militant Islam to grow rapidly.

The trend of Islamization was intensely felt both inside and outside the country soon after the formation of the government. The Western concern at the rise of the Islamic fundamentalism was focused in a Dhaka based Bengali newspaper which stated that the US Department of State and the foreign donor agencies had been expressing concern at the anti-west and anti-NGO manifestations of the Islamic groups (the anti-NGO movement will be discussed at a relevant context in the Chapter) in the country which might lead to massive human right violations and also affect the economic growth of the country.[38] The publication of an article entitled Bangladesh: A Cocoon of Terror" by Bertil Lintner in *Far Eastern Economic Review* on April 4, 2002[39] was a huge shock. The article highlighted the spectacular rise of the Jamaat in the political scene of Bangladesh by capturing 17 seats in the 300 member parliament and eventually becoming a partner of the BNP-led Government and concluded that the religious intolerance, phenomenal rise of the Islamic militants who had nexus with international terrorism based in Pakistan, Chechnya and some of the countries in South East Asia, mushroom growth of the Islamic seminaries, the middle and lower strata of the population having a strong faith in religion and affiliation to religious symbols were to be taken as the symptoms of impending radicalization of the country, which, if not countered, would foment unmitigated trouble and imperil security in the region. There was a sharp reaction to the contention of the article dismissing the radicalization theory. *Daily Star* took the lead saying that there was some element of truth in the rise of Islamic militancy, nevertheless, the evidence of free elections at regular intervals, participation of women in the electoral process, freedom of expression through print and electronic media and presence of multi-party system testify to the existence of a tolerant and democratic polity in the country.[40]

It did not take long to obtain hard evidence of resurgence of Islamic militancy in Bangladesh. The radicalization of the country became a focused discussion after the publication of a write up by Alex Perry entitled "Deadly Cargo" in the *Time* magazine on October 21, 2002.[41] It flashed a disturbing news item saying that 150 Taliban and al-Qaeda fighters from Afghanistan landed in Bangladesh in December 2001. The article revealed that Ayman al-Zawahiri, a top al-Qaeda leader and trusted deputy of Osama bin Laden entered

Bangladesh through the port of Chittagong and stayed there for several months. He visited Dhaka and stayed in the residence of a local Islamic radical before leaving Bangladesh for Myanmar, with Rohingya rebels. The presence of the foreign militants in Bangladesh clearly suggested the seriousness of the situation which was pregnant with explosive outputs was realized, as Alex Perry reports, when four Yemenis, an Algerian, a Libyan, and Sudanese were nabbed in a house located in Uttara in the Dhaka city. It was revealed by the domestic intelligence agency, the DGFI that the militants were involved in the arm-trafficking and arms training at a madrassa in Dhaka sponsored by a Saudi organization called al-Haramin, which is known to have links with Osama's money distributing infrastructure, operating 37 branches in different parts of Bangladesh. The revelation of the Taliban and al-Qaeda men's presence came from the interrogation of a Rohingya Muslim HuJI fighter named Fazle Karim alias Abu Fuzi, who had been nabbed in Kolkata on October 7, 2002. A veteran of al-Qaeda camp in eastern Afghanistan came from Kashmir and landed in Kolkata, where he disembarked from a train. Perry's article drew an international focus on Bangladesh which could be turned into another hotbed of Islamic militancy.[42] The concern was reinforced by the arrest of four member of JMB and the seizure of a packet of uranium on May 30, 2003; the global angle of international terrorism could no longer be ignored.[43]

Prothom Alo had a scintillating but disturbing report in December 2004 stating that 3000 Bangladeshis fought along with the Taliban fighters in Afghanistan.[44] Among them 2,364 had received training in Afghanistan from the al-Qaeda before returning to Bangladesh. The report confirmed that there were 43 militant Islamic groups operating in the country. Although the police had been successful in nabbing 435 militants from whom the government had been trying to figure out the magnitude of the militants' threat, the volubility of the problems was clear and ominous. Added to it, the problem was compounded by reports of the release of most of the arrested persons on the ground of lack of proper evidence. It was reported that several stage-managed factors, such as, weak First Information Report (FIR), destruction of evidence and absence of coordination among the investigating agencies led to freeing the arrested militants.[45]

It was not unexpected that Bangladesh experienced a series of acts of violence of grave magnitude in the recent years. On August 21, 2004, a bomb attack on an Awami League gathering killed about 22 persons and injured 338.[46] It was allegedly masterminded by Islamists to eliminate Sheikh Hasina Wajed. It was not merely an attack to eliminate the prominent Opposition leader. It could be comprehended in a broader perspective. It was designed to stifle the vocal opposition through terror and intimidation. It also demonstrated how organized the jihadi elements were and how fragile was the security system of the country.[47] On August 17, 2005, there was serial bomb blasts numbering 459 in 63 districts out of 64 triggered by militant Islamists called JMB within a short span of 30 minutes, from 11.00 to 11.30 am, killing one and injuring several others. A message was left behind in each of the bomb sites, "Enforce Islamic Laws".[48] All these point out to the phenomenal rise of militant Islam. It is interesting to note that the BNP leader Asadullah al-Ghalib, who brought Banglabhai to limelight, rebuffed the criticism to the effect that he was responsible for the blasts directly or indirectly saying that it was a conspiracy to defame JMB.[49]

Like Asasullah Ghalib, there are interested quarters which would hurl the blame on India for the bomb blasts. They argue that although the JMB triggered off the blasts, behind the scene the forces inimical to Bangladesh worked. These forces were no other than "RAW and Mossad", trying to destabilize the country, derail its economic growth and defame its image in the world.[50] Although such attempts to divert attention of the public from the problems of Islamic militancy do not work, they reflect the mindset of interested quarters to blame India for whatever crises Bangladesh has to face.

The year 2005 was full of militant activities demonstrating their strength, network and efficient execution of their deadly attacks. Besides the serial bomb blasts of August 17, there were attacks in Chittagong and Gazipur in November and December. These activities finally forced the government to ban the HuJI, the JMJB and the JMB.[51] Despite the ban, the militancy has not ceased to operate.

The trend towards Islamization could be seen with the meteoric rise of Jamaat.[52] It may be mentioned that Maulana Sayyid Abul A'la Mawdudi (1903-1979) founded it in Lahore in 1941.[53] The Jamaat played a significant role in mobilizing people to support the partition of India on religious line. It could not make a significant inroad into the politics of East Pakistan, mainly because of the fact that political issues and movements in this part of Pakistan centered on secular issues such as language and economic development. Therefore, ascription to religious issues was peripheral. Its role in East Pakistan during the period of 23 years of rule under Pakistan was nominal and unknown. In 1947 it had only one unit of *rokn* (primary member). There was only one administrative division of the Jamaat out of 13 divisions in the country. It had only one small office in Dhaka which was looked after by a paid functionary. Whereas, in West Pakistan Jamaat had an effective network through which it continued to accelerate its expanding activities. There had been some attempt to expand its activities, such as, appointment of an *amir* in East Pakistan and active campaign to enlist support of the peasantry. Even then, there was no visible presence of the party in the political scene in this part of the country.[54]

It is interesting to note that the religious leaders like *Pirs* and mullahs did not extend any cooperation and support to the Jamaat, despite the fact the Jamaat had the agenda of strengthening the Islamic values and practices in a Muslim dominated society as of East Pakistan. The religious teachers, the *ulema* and the *Pirs* were not interested in the political overtones of the Jamaat and other organizations such as the Nizam-i-Islami and the Khilafat-i-Rabbani, including the Muslim League. The common man, the intelligentsia and the student groups kept themselves away from all these religious parties. That is why by the mid-1950s most of these organizations became extinct in the wake of resurgence of Bengali nationalism.[55]

The Jamaat earned notoriety by supporting the Pakistan's military regime during the war of liberation. The Government of Bangladesh banned the Jamaat, the al-Badar and the Razakars in 1972. Some of the leaders were killed at the time of liberation. Many were arrested and put behind bars. It appeared that the Jamaat was uprooted from the secular republic of Bangladesh.

As stated in an earlier context, soon after the assassination of Sheikh Mujib, Khondakar Mostaq Ahmed released most of the leaders from prison. This was the starting point of regrouping of the Jamaat. The most significant milestone in its emergence in the politics of Bangladesh is the rehabilitation of Ghulam Azam by the government of Ziaur Rahman.

Rise of Ghulam Azam

It is paradoxical that a totally condemned person, named Ghulam Azam (born 1922),[56] emerged out of ashes to reestablish a party which collaborated with the Pakistani army in heinous crimes of genocide. A unique case of chemistry of contradiction, Professor Ghulam Azam holds an M.A. degree from Dhaka University. He had both secular and sacerdotal education. He studied in a madrassa in his early childhood and later on moved to a regular college. He got himself admitted in the Dhaka University, to study Political Science. Like many a leading political personality in Bangladesh, he also started his political career as a student leader of Dhaka University. He was the General Secretary of Dhaka University Students' Union for two consecutive terms (1947-48 and 1948-49). He shot to prominence as a leader of the language movement. In 1949 he presented a memorandum to the then Prime Minister Liaquat Ali Khan demanding the recognition of Bengali as one of the state official languages of Pakistan along with Urdu. He joined the Government Carmichael College, Rangpur in 1950 as a lecturer. He was arrested in 1952 for his involvement in the language movement. In 1955 the Government dismissed him from the job.

During his short teaching career at Rangpur he started reading the writings of Maulana Mawdudi and developed interest in political Islam. While he was in jail, he joined the Jamaat in 1955 and eventually was elected as its Ameer in East Pakistan in 1969.

Ghulam Azam opposed the independence of Bangladesh and collaborated with the Pakistani army during the freedom struggle. His anti-liberation activities and movements were well-documented in contemporary newspapers, such as, *Protom Alo, Daily Star, Janakantha* and *Bhorer Kagoj*. He was emotionally and politically attached to the idea of united Pakistan, and therefore, collaborated with the Pakistani army's military campaign that resulted in one of the largest genocides known to the contemporary history. He went to Pakistan on November 17, 1971 to attend a meeting of the central committee of the Jamaat. He could not return as the war between India and Pakistan broke out and East Pakistan became an independent republic. From there he went to London where he stayed till July 11, 1978. The Government of Sheikh Mujib cancelled his citizenship along with 39 Pakistani collaborators by a Presidential Order issued on April

18, 1972. His anti-Bangladesh position remained unchanged. He went to several countries in the Middle East to campaign against international recognition of Bangladesh under the slogan "Bangladesh na manzoor" (Bangladesh is unacceptable).

General Ziaur Rahman restored the citizenship of all these 39 former collaborators of Pakistan, including Ghulam Azam. He returned to Bangladesh on July 11, 1978 with a Pakistani passport[57] His application for restoration of Bangladeshi citizenship was rejected by the military government of Ziaur Rahman and H.M. Ershad. But he was allowed to stay in Bangladesh and to continue his political activities behind the scene without holding a formal position. His citizenship was restored in 1994 when the Supreme Court upheld the decision of the Government to it on the ground that he was a Bangladeshi by birth.

Once allowed to stay, Ghulam Azam devoted his time, energy and resources to revitalize the Jamaat. In 1979 he was elected as the amir. As he was not a citizen of Bangladesh he could not function in that capacity. His deputy Ali Khan acted as the amir. In December 1991, the Jamaat formally declared him as the amir on the ground that he was a citizen of Bangladesh by birth. This led to a huge protest by all sections of the people of Bangladesh. In order to avoid any trouble the government arrested him on March 24. The National Coordination Committee for the Elimination of the Killers and Collaborators of 1971 and the Implementation of the Spirit of the Liberation of War organized a massive rally on the Independence Day, March 26, 1992, to try Ghulam Azam in a People's Court (Gana Adalat). The freedom fighters and personalities of the Liberation War under the leadership of retired Colonel Nuruzzam and religious leaders like Ahmed Sharif organized the pubic trial. The hugely attended Gana Adalat found him guilty of genocide and suggested the death penalty.[58]

The Government of Khalida Zia took exception to the verdict of the Gana Adalat and held that he should be tried in a normal court. The Jatiyo Sangsad discussed the issue of Ghulam Azam and held that the matter was sub-judice and that, as such, it could not be debated upon any further. There has been concerted campaign against Ghulam Azam, who in the eyes of most of the people of Bangladesh was a war criminal, a traitor and a rabid communal person.[59] Most of the print media, having liberal and democratic credentials, continued to publish for a long time the stories of his association with the al-Badar, the Razakars and the Pakistani army during the time of liberation war.[60] Nonetheless, he survived all the assault and rebuilt the party from ashes. The resurrection of his party and his survival indicate, in unmistakable terms, that religion as a basis of societal and political interface is fundamentally relevant and sustaining, despite strong and frontal attack on it by a prominently visible section of the populace. The sustained attack by the media and public on the Jamaat explains its feeble performance in the general elections.

At any rate, Ghulam Azam, in a short period of 13 years built up the Jamaat on a considerably solid foundation for which it was able to capture 18 seats of the Parliament and 12.13 per cent votes in the 1991 elections. Besides, it rose to occupy the driver's seat in the formation of the government. The BNP, the largest party in the parliament with 139 seats, was short of 12 members to form a government, and consequently, sought the alliance with the Jamaat. In 2001 the BNP and the Jamaat forged a pre-poll alliance which eventually enabled the BNP to win the elections in a comfortable manner. The alliance continues, despite the fact that the electoral performance of the Jamaat is not quite spectacular as testified to by Table 4.1. But in coalition politics, a small space in the government of a fragile democracy is of enormous and enduring impact and weight on the future political arrangements and alignments.

Table 4.1
Party-wise performance in the general elections in terms of seats and % votes polled

Parties	*1973*	*1979*	*1986*	*1988*	*1991*	*1996*	*2001*
Awami League	293 (73.20)	39(24.55)	76(26.16)	—	100(33.67)	146(37.44)	62(40.18)
BNP	—	207(41.16)	—	—	140(30.81)	116(33.61)	216(47.06)
Jatiyo Party	—	—	153(42.34)	251(68.44)	35(11.92)	32(16.40)	14(7.23)
Jamaat-i-Islami	—	—	10(4.61)	—	18(12.13)	3(8.61)	17(*)

Source: Aminur Rashid and Mostafa Firoz, *Pramany Sangsad* (Dhaka: Tathya Seva, 2002) p.19 and 77, *Percentage of votes poll is not available. It is estimated that Jamaat secured about 8 per cent votes.

The BNP-Jamaat alliance in the power sharing arrangement is a significant development in the political scenario of Bangladesh since 2001.

Ghulam Azam announced his retirement from active politics in 2000. He played the most crucial role in elevating the Jamaat from obscurity to prominence. The phenomenal rise of the Jamaat, besides the personal contribution of Ghulam Azam, underpins a variety of important factors. It has been successful in exploiting the political rehabilitation offered by the military regime of Ziaur Rahman. The popular sentiment that Bangladesh is essentially a Muslim majority state, and therefore, like the Jamaat, Ziaur Rahman too exploited its Islamic identity, in both domestic and international politics. It helped him build his image as an ardent Muslim. There was a mutual dependence syndrome that propelled both Zia and the Jamaat to cooperate with each other without jeopardizing their separate identities.

Ideology and agenda of Jamaat

There are three different categories of Islamic institutions in Bangladesh – the orthodox ulema (theologists), the Jamaat and the Jihadi groups. The ulema (plural form of alim or wise man) are preachers like the Sufis or *Pirs* who preach Islam in traditional and ritualistic terms. They have no political agenda, remain confined to sacerdotal boundaries and propagate the tenets of a simple and pious life. They are not interested in any political campaign, nature or forms of government, types of political parties, and maintain a safe distance from party politics and party ideology. They command respect from all sections of the society including non-Muslims.

The Jamaat is a political party, believes in electoral politics, has a well-articulated political agenda and takes a fundamentalist position on Islam. It draws its political ideology from the political views and beliefs of its founder and ideologue, Maulana Mawdudi. Its political objective is to implement

Islam in letter and spirit in the social and political life of the Muslim community. Paradoxically, at the same time it claims that it is not a religious or political party but an ideological movement for building a truly Islamic society. To quote Maulana Mawdudi:

> The Jamaat is neither simply a political party nor merely a religious organization. It has embraced Islam without any reservation and it considers Islam to be complete and balanced code of conduct. So the Jamaat is both political and religious. It is political to the extent Islam is political, it is neither more nor less political that what Islam wanted to be.[61]

Despite its tall claim to be non-political in ordinary sense of the term, the Jamaat is essentially a political party which has two broad objectives – to spearhead a movement for the establishment of an Islamic society and to organize a truly Islamic party led by indoctrinated leaders, assisted by cadres, capable of transforming Bangladesh into an Islamic state based on the principles of the Qur'an, Hadith and Shariah.[62] The 23-page election manifesto of the Jamaat for the 2001 elections is an interesting document. Being aware of its poor show in the 1996 elections in which it could capture three seats only and secure a mere 8.61 per cent of vote, the Jamaat drafted the electioneering document carefully so as to avoid any promise to impose Shariah Law, which the common masses would have opposed it strongly. The basic thrust of the election promises had been spelt out in eighteen pages wherein it assured that the Jamaat would not go in for chopping of hands of thieves, stoning of persons convicted of adultery, banning of bank interest etc. Its basic focus would be "alleviation of poverty, stopping free mixing of sexes and thus awakening the people to the spirit of Islam and then eventually step by step the Islamic laws would be introduced".[63]

The idea of an Islamic state of Bangladesh conceptualized by the Jamaat is in a complete anti-thesis of secular, tolerant and democratic values that the rest of the world cherishes. It rejects the concept of popular sovereignty and upholds the view that God is sovereign. The holy books of the Qur'an and the Shariah are the only sources of law in an Islamic state. The Muslims derive political power from God, and therefore, the political Muslims are trustees who have to act within well defined limits and boundaries delineated by the holy books. The community has to elect God fearing, pious and honest persons to the national legislature who could pass legislations on issues of social, political and legal nature in complete conformity with Islam, and on all matters not covered by the holy books. The laws in an Islamic state have to enforce Islamic way of life, morality, ethics and good conduct. An Islamic state has to be run by the Muslim community only. In such an Islamic state the non-Muslims (Zimmis) have no place in the government and in its all principal organs including the law making structure. Nonetheless, the Islamic state has to protect their life, property, religion, culture and honour. In other words, the Islamic state, defined by the Jamaat, is no less than a fascist and totalitarian state.

A three-point strategy has been suggested by the Jamaat towards the establishment of an Islamic state. First, Islam has to be preached as a revolutionary ideology. The Islamic thoughts, ideals and practices must reach out to each and every Muslim in order to make every member of the *umma* (community) aware of Islam. Second, those who prepared to join the movement to establish an Islamic state should be organized and trained on the line of Islamic ideology so that they are committed to the Islamic cause and are ready to sacrifice anything in the path of Allah. Third, the trained, disciplined and committed people are to embark upon the realization of the ultimate goal of capturing political power and replacing the existing 'un-Islamic' leadership by a truly

Islamic one capable of establishing an Islamic state of Bangladesh.[64]

The Jamaat is a highly organized and disciplined party having a network of 6,580 administrative units throughout Bangladesh. It has a support base among the upper peasants and lower middle class. Its support base is created through institutional structures in the form of NGOs of its creation, charitable organizations, madrassas and clinics. The Islami Bank is reportedly one institution through which it spreads its wings. The all-pervasive presence of these institutions cultivates the ideology of the Jamaat and operates as an alternative to secular organizations.[65] The members of the party are recruited by a tough selection procedure. The new recruits are granted associate membership for a period of time during which they are imparted lessons in Islamic ideology. Those who succeed in the tests are given full membership. The primary duty of the members of the Jamaat is to convey the message to the community that they are Muslims first and they are to be good 'Mumin' (faithful) dedicated to the path of Allah. The Jamaat, in this way, wants to create a society of faithful Muslims. The duties of the members are manifold, such as, to convey the message of God to the masses, establish individual contacts, distribute Jamaat's publications, build libraries in every branch of the party, and organize lectures and seminars on various aspects of Islam. In this way, the Jamaat believes, it would be possible to transform Bangladesh into a 'truly' Islamic country.[66]

In order to achieve the goal the Jamaat strives to win the masses politically, i.e. through constitutional means and 'democratic' elections. This strategy is undoubtedly at odds with its undemocratic and totalitarian character. It showed its political interests for the first time in 1978 when it extended support to the BNP in the Presidential election and in the next year in the parliamentary elections. In the 1981 Presidential elections it supported the BNP. It contested the parliamentary elections held on May 7, 1986, which was, of course, marred by low turnout of only 4-5 per cent due to the boycott call given by the major political parties and won 10 seats in the 300 member Jatiyo Sangsad. The Jamaat joined hands with the Awami League and the BNP to give a call for boycott of the Presidential election held on October 19, 1986 on the ground that the military ruler would never allow a free and fair election. The voter turnout was low as it had been in the case of parliamentary elections held in May. It opposed the military rule of General Ershad and launched a movement against his government by organizing public rallies, meetings and protest movement against the military coup. It continued such activities relentlessly, sometimes alone and sometimes in close cooperation with the opposition parties. It played a significant role in bringing about the downfall of Ershad in 1990. In this way it showed its political orientation and at the same time, and more importantly, created a political base in the country.

It is interesting to note the social base of the Jamaat. Although the Jamaat could not make any major breakthrough in the political scene of East Pakistan, it could secure 10 per cent of votes in the 1970 elections and emerged as the second largest party after Awami League which secured 75.57 per cent votes in East Pakistan. At that time it had about 40 full-time workers, 425 full members and 40,000 associate members. But after the liberation in 1971 it suffered humiliation and attack for its role during the war of liberation. The party was banned. Many of the leaders were imprisoned. The membership fell dramatically. Soon after Ghulam Azam returned to Bangladesh and became the informal head of the Jamaat; with the Zia's government lifting the ban, the Jamaat membership started increasing. In March 1981 the Jamaat had 650 full members and more than 100,000 associate members. In less than a decade it made a spectacular rise. In 1987 the strength of full members grew to 2000, including 75 women members, and the number of the associate members registered a 100 per cent increase. The growth is reflective of the fact that it could create a support base among the educated and lower middle income group of people.

The rise and rehabilitation of the Jamaat could be attributed to a number of factors. The general aspiration of the Muslims of the Bangladesh to identify themselves as a part of the Islamic world started surfacing even during the time of Sheikh Mujib. This tendency reduced the Bengali nationalism to a great extent. That is why when the process of Islamization initiated by Ziaur Rahman started to pick up, no one, not even the Awami League, tried to halt it. It invariably means that Islam as a religion of Bangladesh had a significant role to play. Second, there was enormous external pressure on Bangladesh from Islamic countries of the Middle East, particularly, Saudi Arabia, to recognize the role of Islam in public affairs. Mujib himself was aware of the pressure. He participated in the summit of the Organization of Islamic Countries (OIC) in February 1974 and there projected the Islamic image of his country. The Saudi Government put the recognition of Islam as a precondition to its liberal aid regime. Third, the Jamaat made its appearance felt for the first time through its association with Islamic United Front led by Maulana Abdur Rahim, as it was a banned organization, and therefore, could not operate openly. Ziaur Rahman's decision to lift the ban in May 1979 in order to containing and if possible crushing the Awami League, known to be a secular party and a rival of his political ambition, made it possible for the Jamaat to function openly and effectively. Just as Ziaur Rahman harvested a handsome dividend in the 'referendum' of 1978 which legitimized his military rule in Bangladesh, Jamaat too exploited the situation to its advantage. Fourth, the Jamaat proved to have an efficient less bureaucratic and less corrupt organizational network which enabled it to have a clean functional face. Fifth, soon the madrassas emerged as the recruiting ground of Jamaat's associate members. This aspect will be further illustrated in a relevant section. Sixth, the Jamaat reportedly started getting substantial funds from Saudi Arabia and Iran during the time of Ziaur Rahman. This gave it an enormous financial strength to expand its activities in a big way. The "Islamic Heritage Society of Kuwait" and "Revival of Islamic Societies" having branches in Saudi Arabia, Kuwait, Qatar and United Arab Emirates are the major source of financial assistance to the Jamaat. An organization named "Revival of Islamic Heritage Foundation" similar to the organization in the Arab world was established in Dhaka, which distributed financial grants to different Islamic organizations, both militant and political. In order words, the Jamaat received government support and financial resources from oil-rich Middle East countries, which enabled it to make an amazing come back in the affairs of Bangladesh. The process of legitimization of Jamaat in the domestic politics of Bangladesh which began since the lifting of the ban on it by Ziaur Rahman was complete with its active participation in the anti-Ershad rallies, demonstrations and movements. Seventh, the anti-Indian passion created by the Islamists and the BNP had provided a ground for the Jamaat to expand its base. Its campaign for an Islamic state in the backdrop of the existence of the most powerful neighbour seems to have worked wonders. Eighth, the lower middle class educated people who suffer from a sense of deprivation and uncertainty were more susceptible to the call of the Jamaat, particularly after the dissolution of the Soviet Union and the creation of some sort of a vacuum in international order in the post Cold War era. The communist parties of Bangladesh started losing their social base among this section of the people; the gainer was the Jamaat. With its vigorous campaign for an Islamic alternative, financial resources and effective networking it could enlist support of the large number of people belonging to the educated lower middle class and to some extent of the peasantry also.

The US-led Gulf War on Iraq in 1991 inflamed the Muslim sentiment in a visible manner. The War coincided with the 5th Parliamentary elections held in February 1991. The entire Muslim community in Bangladesh expressed solidarity with Saddam Hussein. Most of the political parties took a position during electioneering against the invasion. Some of them identified themselves as 'Saddam's candidates'. The Jamaat, however, was against the Iraqi invasion of Kuwait for which it could find a place in the good book of Saudi Arabia and the United States but could not harvest a rich dividend in the elections.[67] Other Islamic forces took the opportunity to mingle with the mass mobilization and demonstration against the Gulf War and for the Iraqi ruler. Although the anti-War emotion did not put any party in an advantageous position, it became a rallying point for all the Muslims in Bangladesh. After the 9/11 incident when the US launched massive attack against the Taliban the public sentiment went against the US Government.[68] It facilitated the Islamists to emerge in the political scene.

The rise of Jamaat could not be understood without a brief narration of its student wing called Islami Chatra Shibir (ICS), despite the fact that it is not officially attached to the Jamaat and it claims to be an independent entity. Founded in 1941 and now headed by Nurul Islam Bulbul and Nazrul Islam as the President and the Secretary respectively, the ICS has six divisions in the country. It is seen as a training ground for the future Islamic political leaders. Many of its former members have become prominent leaders, and some of them have become underground Jihadi activists. Its main agenda is Islamization of the educational system of Bangladesh, at the same time it talks about society and polity based on of the basic tenets of Islam. Like its parent body, it is against modernization, democracy and secularism. It is a member of the International Islamic Federation of Students Organizations and World Assembly of Muslim Youth.[69] It has strongholds in seven universities of Bangladesh, most prominent being the universities at Chittagong, Rajshahi as also the Islami University. The members of the ICS are meticulously recruited and initiated though a training process. The ICS gained most during the time of Ershad, who allowed the foreign funds to penetrate deep into Bangladesh politics. The Jamaat, which received the lion's share, offered by the Dhaka based Islamic Heritage Foundation, provided financial resources to its student wing for expansion. In an atmosphere of political uncertainty and unemployment among the youth, the easy money coming from the oil-rich Arab countries made the ICS an attractive alternative to traditional, democratic and secular student bodies.[70]

The Jamaat has established more than two dozens of trusts in Dhaka and about 70 trusts in other towns and cities to "promote welfare activities in the light of the teachings in Islam and assist other organizations working for the same objectives." It has established more than 200 private schools in different urban centres. These schools are manned by the Jamaat personnel who are paid handsome salaries. They have proved to be profitable organizations. With its known source of income and fund, it is impossible for the Jamaat to expand so dramatically and carry on all the profitable activities.

One striking factor to account for the meteoric rise of the Jamaat is its impeccable clean image of financial management, efficient networking and quick response to public needs. It has an efficient publicity and networking system through which it reaches out to the public. All other parties do not have these credentials.[71] That is why notwithstanding the smallness of its support base Jamaat has a formidable and dependable following which cannot be ignored.

The intolerant face of the Islamists

The Jamaat and other Islamists forces can be put in one broad category in the discourse of militant communalism in Bangladesh. They can be collectively considered as fundamentalists, communal, anti-Hindu and anti-India, anti-secular and anti-democratic, and therefore, intolerant of anything that goes in their parlance against Islam. It will be pertinent to present a few instances of intolerance of extreme form demonstrated by the Islamists over the years; this has generated serious debate on the future of Bangladesh.

(1) Taslima Nasreen's case could be regarded as the turning point, where from Bangladesh has been moving towards intolerance. With the publication of her novel *Lajja* (Shame)[72] in 1993 and for some of her writings and comments on Islam, patriarchy, society and tradition, Taslima Nasreen (born in Mymensingh district in 1962) has come to the limelight; at the same time the extreme intolerant face of the radicals became clearly visible. Soon after the publication of the book and then her comment that the Qur'an "should be revised thoroughly" the death threat has been looming large over her head. At first she went on hiding and in 1994 she escaped from the country. Recently she has been in India and a Muslim organization named All India Ibtehad Council in March 2007 offered an award of Rs. 500,000 for her beheading.

(2) Matir Moina (Clay Bird) is a movie which portrays a vivid account of the madrassa education in Bangladesh. The government banned the movie in May 2002 at the instance of the Jamaat, which believed that it hurts Islamic sentiment.[73] The movie shot to prominence in 2002 when it bagged the International Critic Award in 2002 Canne's Film Festival. The film, made by Tareque Masud, conveys the message of harmony, tolerance and egalitarianism and reflects the personal life of the film-maker whose life was adversely impacted upon by the rigid *dictat* of his unreasonable and orthodox father, who had been very much an Englishman, suddenly turned religious and puritan, imposing his extreme version of Islamic life on other members of his family, compelling his wife to put on purda (veil) and forcing his seven year son to go to madrassa against his will.[74] The movie tells about how Sufism could act as a protective umbrella against Islamic fundamentalism. Naturally, the Jamaat was totally against the movie as it portrayed a negative picture of madrassas and Islamic fundamentalism. It demanded the Government to ban the movie and threatened the cinema theatres of dire consequences, if dared to screen it.

(3) Campaign against the NGOs and the Awami League as India's agents is one of the tactical dynamics of the Islamists to expand their support base. Its attack on the NGOs started in 1993 when the Islamists launched a movement against the BRAC (Bangladesh Rural Advancement Committee), one of the leading and successful showpieces in the NGO sector. Bangladesh has a high concentration of NGOs, about 19,000 in number as estimated in 1996.[75] Out of these, 986 were foreign funded. Most of them are engaged with various issues of children, women health, education and livelihood. They are also known to be gender sensitive and to promote liberal ideas. They have a strong anti-fatwa position. The NGO's position is that a fatwa is an opinion of a cleric or group of clerics, which is not backed by the law of the land, and therefore, cannot be enforced. The Islamists consider fatwa as sacrosanct, for, it is issued by authoritative religious personalities who are supposed to be conversant in Islam, and Islamic tradition and practices. The Islamists have been severely criticizing the NGO sector on a number of the issues. The first and foremost is that NGOs' preference for women to men brings women closer to unrelated men which is un-Islamic. Further, they think that the very effort to bring women to the issue of handling livelihood is a direct hit on patriarchy and is going to affect the family structure. They also argue that many of the NGOs have been promoting Christian missionaries.[76]

The anti-fatwa position of the NGO had been visible for quite some time. The rural women, mostly poor, used to be the easy victims of sexual harassment and rape committed by the influential rich. The fatwas issued by the clerics always used to be biased against women victims. The NGOs used to take up these cases of fatwa victims and try to get justice for them. The cleric would not tolerate such intervention. The turning point came in 2000 when a village woman of Naogaon district in northern Bangladesh committed suicide unable to bear the trauma caused by a fatwa. The NGOs' gave wide publicity to the incident and that eventually led to the historic judgment of the High Court on January 1, 2001 declaring fatwa illegal. The Jamaat, the Ulema Parishad (Council of Clerics) and other Islamic groups immediately condemned the judgment as un-Islamic. On February 2, 2001, Mufti Fazlul Haq Amini and Mufti Azizul Haq, two leading clerics organized a pro-fatwa rally in Dhaka in which they launched attack on the NGOs branding them as "number one enemy of Islam".[77] Other parts of the country too faced the wrath of the Islamists. They were on the rampage in several towns and cities and raised pro-Taliban slogan – "Amra sobai hobo Taliban, Bangladesh hobe Afghanistan" (We all will be Taliban, Bangladesh will be Afghanistan).[78] They attacked the Awami League for its pro-India leaning. Thus started the direct confrontation between the pro-fatwa Islamic clerics and the anti-Fatwa and pro-NGO organization called Sanmilita Nagorik Andolan (United Citizen's Movement), which demanded the government to ban all religiously motivated political parties and organizations.[79] Although the government did not take recourse to an extreme measure, it acted promptly to push the clerics on the defensive by implicating the Ulema Parishad in the murder of a policeman and also in raising funds for jihadi purposes.[80] It is interesting to notice the polarization of opinion on pro and anti-NGO issue; the people are divided in the conflict between the NGO sector and the Ulema. The vertical division is felt everywhere – in urban and rural areas. While the clerics use video and audio devices, full of derogatory and venomous speeches[81], the NGO sector has been penetrating deep inside the rural areas, with their dedicated work meant for development of Bangladesh. The jihadi groups are still continuing their violent campaign against the NGOs. On May 1, 2007, there were three time-device explosions at the railway stations of Dhaka, Chittagong and Sylhet; round aluminum plates covered with newspaper were found in the blast sites in Dhaka and Sylhet with the inscription "The Kadiyanis (Ahmediyas) and the NGOs! Be prepared for death. It is haram (prohibited) to work with NGOs and having relations with the Kadiyanis. All must quit NGO jobs by May 10... if you fail to do so before the aforesaid time, your death is a must".[82]

(4) Attack on minorities, mainly the Hindus and Ahmediyas, is another terrible manifestation, ranging from intimidation, arson, abduction and rape of women, driving the helpless ones to leave the country, to physical extermination. This, for sure, exposes the intolerant face of the Islamists in Bangladesh. As stated in Chapter I, Bangladesh is a Muslim majority country with a huge Muslim population in absolute number. The Muslims do not have any ground to feel insecure nor do they face any threat from a small minority who account for just 11per cent of the total population. The Hindus constitute the largest segment among the minorities, that too with 9.2 per cent. Yet, the Hindus have been the main target of attacks of various nature, such as physical violence which include assault, rape of women and killing and psychological violence in the form of clear discrimination in all matters including employment in the government jobs; further on the economic front, they are at the receiving end of appropriation of properties belonging to them under the notorious Enemy (Vested) Property Act. All these have led to a steady decline in the demographic texture of the Hindus in Bangladesh since 1941 when it was known as East Bengal. The alarming decline is a clear indication of the circumstances forcing them to leave the country. In 1941 the Hindus constituted 28 per cent of the people. At the time of creation of East Pakistan the percentage decreased to 18.5. After the establishment of People's Republic of Bangladesh it came down to 13.5 as many of the Hindus left the country in the wake of Pakistani army targeting them.[83] The 1991 census put them at 10.5% (12.5 million in absolute number). The following Table 4.2 is reflective of the current situation covering a period of six decades.

Table 4.2
Percentage of religious communities in Bangladesh (1941-2001)

Year	*Muslim*	*Hindu*	*Buddhist*	*Christian*	*Others*
1941	70.3	28.0	-	0.1	1.6
1951	76.9	22.0	0.7	0.3	0.1
1961	80.4	18.5	0.7	0.3	0.1
1971	85.4	13.5	0.6	0.3	0.2
1981	86.7	12.1	0.6	0.3	0.3
1991	88.3	10.5	0.6	0.3	0.3
2001	89.6	9.2	0.6	0.3	0.3

Source: Census, 1991 and 2001

Percentage of religious communities in Bangladesh (1941-2002)

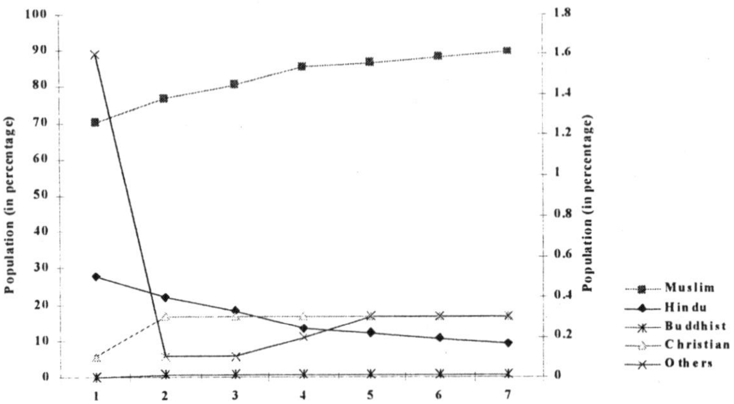

Atrocities committed on the Hindus have compelled them to leave the country and seek shelter in India.[84]

There were two waves of attack on the Hindus on a national scale in the post-liberation period. The first was soon after the demolition of the Babri Mosque on December 6, 1992. The attack was on the premises and properties of the Hindu temples and establishments and the neighbourhood around them.[85] The attack was widespread and affected almost all the Hindu population throughout the country. It was neither sudden nor sporadic or isolated. The BNP Government remained almost inactive in dealing with this nation-wide attack which was followed by out-migration of the Hindus to India.[86]

The second wave of attack on the Hindus took place during the 2001 electioneering and after. Even if the first wave could be considered as a reprisal, soon after the demolition the Babri Mosque, the second was undoubtedly politically motivated. This second phase attack, which continued for several weeks not only before but also after the elections was well planned and devastating. This time some of the Muslim families came under attack for their affiliation to the Awami League.[87] The newspaper reports suggested that the BNP and the Jamaat targeted the Hindus on their assumption that the latter were the vote bank of the Awami League. This seemingly common assumption appears to be faulty. Out of 300 members in the eighth parliament, the minorities hold only 7 seats – 4 belonged to the Awami League and the rest 3 were from the BNP. Even then the BNP activists claim that the Hindus generally vote for the Awami League, and therefore, they were made easy targets.[88]

The Society for Environment and Human Development (SEHD) reports that the intimidation of the minorities had started much before the elections of 2001, on the assumption that they were the dependable vote banks of the Awami League.[89] Almost all the leading newspapers in Bengali and English medium published vivid account of atrocities committed on the Hindu communities.[90] The government connivance of the crimes was palpably visible. The security forces watched the killing, rape and destruction of property silently. Even the Home Minister Altaf Hossain Chowdhury reacted to the newspaper reports as "baseless, exaggerated and politically motivated."[91] The Amnesty International expressed its grave concern at the attack on the Hindus during the elections.[92] It was difficult for the government to cover up the killing of Gopal Krishna Muhuri, the Principal of Nazarihat College in Chittagong, a highly respected citizen in the city, on November 16, 2001.[93] The huge protest against the killing and the wide coverage of the crime compelled the administration to arrest two college teachers who had links with the Jamaat, the very next day of the incident. Added to these dimensions of atrocities committed on the Hindus there were allegation of forceful conversion mostly committed mostly by the ICS.[94]

These are only a few representative instances of violence committed on the Hindu community in 2001. However, they testify to the reign of terror committed during and after the 2001 elections. The atrocities on the tribal communities in the Chittagong Hill Tracts are well-documented and they too vouchsafe for the sordid affairs of the minority situation in Bangladesh. Under the notorious Enemy (Vested) Property Act the government had already appropriated more than 75 per cent of the landed property of Hindus.[95] Abul Barakat estimates that about 2.1 million acres of Hindu land had been disposed of under the Act and "the market price of the land would be about Taka 12,09,600 million (equivalent to 70% of the Gross Domestic Product in the year 2000).[96] Although the Act is kept inoperative in the recent years, it still stands as an instrument of state oppression on the minorities. The Act is one of the issues which has alienated the minorities including the Chakma tribal people from the mainstream politics in Bangladesh.[97]

The attack on the Ahmediyas on regular basis has been going on for a considerable time. It started in the early 1950s in West Pakistan and then, at a later phase, in erstwhile East Pakistan. There are approximately 100,000 Ahmediyas in Bangladesh; most of who live in Dhaka. The attack has been widespread in the recent years, beginning 2001 with the IOJ and the Jamaat allegedly taking the lead. A series of violent incidents took place in October and November 2003 in Dhaka, Jessore, Kusthia and Tejgaon targeting the mosques, the leaders of the community, their houses, and business and other establishments.[98] An anti-Ahmediaya organization called International Khatme Nabuwat Movement Bangladesh (IKNMB) had been leading the systematic attack of the Ahmediyas. On October 31, 2003 Shah Alam, the Imam of a local Ahmediya mosque in a village called Raghanathpur Bak in Jessore district was beaten to death in front of his family by a mob of 90 people.[99] Under the mounting pressure from the Islamists, the Government issued a notification on December 21, 2004 banning Ahmediya publications. However, the High Court stayed the ban, but the anti-Ahmediya groups continued to be active in seizing and destroying the publications with the connivance of the government. On April 18, 2005 the members of IKNMB demanded the government to declare Ahmediyas as non-Muslims and attacked the members of the community in different parts of the country.[100] Reacting to the demand, Mosharef Hossain Shajahan, Minister for Religious Affairs, however, said in a press conference "None less than Allah can do it. As the minister concerned I have no power nor I am entitled to so".[101] The demand accompanied by violence to declare the Ahmediyas as non-Muslim continued till June 2006. On June 23, about 15,000 Islamists and IKNMB activists marched to an Ahmediya mosque in Dhaka to seize and destroy it. However, timely police action frustrated the move.[102]

Although the government has been taking some steps to protect the Ahmediyas, the practice of house arrest and excommunication of the Ahmediyas still continue.[103] The attack on the Ahmediyas, as in the case of the Hindus, has drawn international attention. The Amnesty International, the US Government and other human rights organizations have been raising strong voice of protest against violence committed on the minorities in Bangladesh.[104]

(5) Attempt to rename villages, schools and public institutions is another of the recent dimensions of the Islamists' attempt to change the social and educational face of Bangladesh. A few recent but isolated examples might help understand the dynamics of the trend. *Daily Star* published a news item entitled "Jamaat's 'Islamization' of village names" drew public attention.[105] The Jamaat of Shyamnagar Upazila had issued a fatwa in 2006 to change the name of a school which was established by Hari Charan Roy Chowdhury, the erstwhile Zamindar of Shymanagar at Nakipur in 1899. The school was named after the Zamindar and came to be known as Nakipur Hari Charan High School. Jamaat suddenly discovered a Hindu flavour in the name of the school situated in a Muslim locality and changed it to Nakipur Pilot High School. This was done quietly by the Chairman of the Governing Body of the School without the knowledge of the District Education Officer. This is not an isolated case. The name of Joshoreshwaripur in the Jessore district was changed to Islampur. Another village named Haripur under Noornagar Union was changed to Habibpur. Renaming was prolific: *viz*, Jatindranagar to Zahirnagar, Napitkhali to Niamatkhali, Mendlnagar to Mehdinagar, Gopalpur to Golappur, Gouripur to Garibpur, Kashipur to Kashimpur, Ramchandrapur to Rahmatpur, Shyamnagar to Rupnagar and so on. All these changes have taken place after 2001 when the four party alliance took over power. These moves have not gone unopposed, as each and every name of a village or a school has a history that could not be buried overnight. The Awami League had organized meetings and protest rallies against this process of renaming of the historically important villages and public institutions. But their resistance to the Jamaat's agenda of renaming and rewriting history of the localities remained ineffective as the Jamaat was a coalition partner of the BNP-led government. The Jamaat's retrograde exercise is a reflection of its Islamist agenda and its intolerant attitude that smacks of its lack of history sense.

Foreign fund

The Islamic organizations, reliable sources reveal, secure huge foreign funds coming particularly from the oil-rich Arab countries. The revelation surfaced soon after the nation-wide bomb explosion that took place on August 17, 2005 affecting all but one district. In an article written by Motiur Rahman which appeared in *Prothom Alo*[106] two days after the nerve-racking explosions, it is revcaled that an organization called Benevolence International Foundation Registration was set up in Uttara in Dhaka city in 1992. A report on the activities of the organization had earlier appeared in *Prothom Alo* in June 2003[107]. The existence of the organization had been recorded in the Registration Bureau of Bangladesh. It received funds from Saudi Arabia and established 800 madrassas, a good number of hospitals, mosques and orphanages.[108] Another establishment named "Revival of Islamic Heritage Society" located at Uttara too had been receiving foreign funds but it is not known where do the funds go.[109] The local media gave a wide coverage on its link with al-Qaeda which compelled the Saudi Government to close it down some time in 2004. The quantum of fund the organization received from the Saudi sources is not known.

Although there is no hard data available on the quantum of foreign funds flowing to the militant organizations due to obvious and natural lack of transparency, there are reports of sources of such fund published in the newspapers which go uncontested. It is reported that one Kuwait-based organization named "Islamic Heritage Society of Kuwait" and another "Revival of Islamic Societies" with branches in Saudi Arabia, Kuwait, Qatar and United Arab Emirates are the funding sources from where the Islamic militants secure huge grants to 'promote Islam'.[110] In reality the fund was allegedly used for the promotion of jihadi doctrines, and radical and violent activities including, bomb explosions causing terror and intimidation.

The Jamaat reportedly enjoys the lion's share of the fund. It is believed that other militant groups too get huge fund in the name of promoting the Islamic ideals. The Jamaat has a comfortable financial position, according to one of its functionaries. The fund comes from four sources: (1) regular contributions of the members and the associate members, (2)

Zakat (religious tax that the Muslims have to pay), (3) donations and (4) profit from sale proceeds of its literatures. It is reported that in 1960 the Jamaat had an annual budget of Rs.4.5 lakh.[111] It is not known officially what its recent annual budget is. Reliable sources reveal that it has an annual budget of several hundred crore Taka. Such a huge budget cannot be conceived with the sources stated above. The most dependable and regular source of fund is said to be oil-rich Arab countries. It is reported in the media that the Islamic Heritage Society located in Kuwait sends a huge amount to all the Islamic political and militant groups in Bangladesh. During the time of Ziaur Rahman, a branch of the named Islamic Heritage Foundation was established in Dhaka. Arab money used to be funneled through this branch to reach all such organizations. Under pressure from domestic and international fronts, the government recently closed down the Dhaka office of the Islamic Heritage Foundation of Bangladesh. However, another source of funds is active - it is the Zakat fund of the Arab oil-rich countries. It is known as a common pool of all zakat money in the region. A huge amount is said to be distributed to different countries in the world. Bangladesh, known as a LDC, is a notable beneficiary of the fund. The fund comes through informal channels and hence could not be identified. The government turns a deaf ear to reports of such inflow of foreign funds. It maintains a discreet silence on the issue in order to encourage foreign inflow ostensibly to strengthen the economy of the country. In the process, the political and militant Islamic groups get indirect support to expand their activities.

The financial affluence of the Jamaat has provoked strong criticism of it as an agent of the "imperialists and their petro-dollar-rich lackeys, particularly, Saudi Arabia".[112] The allegation were brought by Maulana Abdul Jabar, an influential member of the Jamaat, who tried an abortive split in the Jamaat in October 1983. The Jamaat dismisses such allegations but admits that some of the non-governmental institutions and organizations such as Rabat-i-Alama al Islami of Saudi Arabia extends financial help to it and facilitate employment of Bangladeshi workers in the Middle East. The jehadi organizations remain silent about their financial resources, leaving enormous scope for legitimate doubts about its financial links with other terrorist groups around the world.

A well-researched article entitled "Fundamentalist Economy in Bangladesh" by a Dhaka University Professor Abul Barakat which appeared in *Daily Inqilab* and his book in Bengali entitled *Bangladeshe Maulobader Orthaniti* brought to focus the entire spectrum as to how profitable fundamentalism is in economic terms.[113] He argues that as commonly perceived, the fundamentalist political parties are being financed from outside the country. But it is also a fact that eight powerful business houses and sectors in the country too offer part of their profit to the Islamists to run their organizational activities. To quote him "the net profit from fundamentalist economy in Bangladesh is approximately Taka 1200 crore." [114] To put estimates of Taka 1200 in a tabular form (Table 4.3):

Table 4.3
Breakup of Taka 1200 earned by fundamentalists from eight sectors

Business houses and sector	% of share
1. Banks and insurance companies etc	27.0
2. Non-governmental organization	20.8
3. Commercial organization	10.8
4. Hospitals, healthcare, pharmaceuticals	10.4
5. Educational institutions	9.2
6. Real estate business	8.3
7. Transport sector	7.5
8. Media and information technology	5.8

Leaving aside details as to how the fundamentalist economy is tailored to operate the activities of the Islamists, Barakat claims that it is "possible to engage 5 lakh party members for full time if only 10 per cent of the annual net profit of fundamentalist Taka 1200 crore can be used in organizational activities. This is what they (fundamentalist) do and give cross-subsidy in other sectors".[115] This is a conservative estimate. If one takes into account the hidden foreign sources a larger dimension of the money flow to the Islamists would emerge. But the entire money laundering involving several hundred crore dedicated to Islamic militancy makes it easy for the jihadis to flourish. It will be seen in a relevant section how much an Islamic militant cadre earns in a month. It will be indicative of the fact the militancy has become an industry, a profitable and lucrative sector in an economically backward country like Bangladesh.

Militant groups

As already stated that with the publication of the sensational article of Alex Perry in *Time* magazine entitle "Deadly Cargo" on October 21, 2002, the steady rise of militant Islam in Bangladesh became a matter of great concern in Bangladesh and elsewhere. There are a number of militant Islamic groups; some of the prominent among them deserve attention.

Islamic Oikya Jote (Islamic Unity Front)

The Islamic Oikya Jote (IOJ) is one of the most secret jihadi groups in Bangladesh.[116] It is not clear when and where it was formed. It is led by Mufti Fazlul Haq Aminee, the ameer allama of the organization and Azizul Haq, the Sheikh-ul-Hadith. It is essentially a rural based organization and uses the madrassas to build up its support and mobilization. Unlike the Jamaat which appears to be sophisticated, the IOJ is an intolerant fanatic organization. It believes in hate campaign against all minorities including the Ahmediyas.

It is known to be an ardent supporter of Taliban and al-Qaeda. It is alleged that it facilitated the movement and shelter of the 150 Taliban and al-Qaeda men in Bangladesh. In 2001 it fought the general elections and secured only 2 seats. It extended support to the BNP-led government.

There is no authentic data on the support base and strength of the IOJ because of its strict secrecy.

Jamaat ul Mujahideen Bangladesh (JMB)

Established in 1998 in Jamalpur district adjoining India's Dhubri district, Jamaat ul Mujahideen Bangladesh (JMB), drew the attention of domestic and international media after the serial bombing of August 17, 2005 in 63 out of 64 districts. *Prothom Alo* reported three days before the bomb blasts that police recovered huge amount of weapons which included 143 AK 47 rifles, 43 M-16 and 727 rounds of ammunitions from the JMB and revealed that it had an effective network in 36 districts of Bangladesh.[117] It claimed responsibility for the explosions of August 17. It left leaflets at the all the explosion sites, as already stated, numbering around 459, conveying the message "Enforce Islamic Laws". The explosions rocked the country. The intelligence agencies were left dumb-founded by the incident. The JMB demonstrated its effective network and execution capacity. There was no doubt in any quarters that the country-wide explosion was JMB's handiwork. It wanted to transform Bangladesh into an Islamic state by enforcing Shariah laws, strict Islamic code of conduct for women, banning music and cinema. The outfit has an agenda against the United States and the United Kingdom. It believes in violence as a tool to establish an Islamic state of Bangladesh.

The JMB earned notoriety for its terror tactics of intimination, extortion and killing spree. There was a strong pressure on the government to nail it with a heavy hand. Consequently on February 23, 2005 the government banned the organization and arrested Asadullah al-Galib along with some others. Its leaders are Maulana Abdur Rahman, Siddiqur Rahman (better known as Bangla Bhai), and Asadullah al-Galib, a former lecturer at Rajshahi University. As already stated in Chapter I, Abdur Rahman and Bangla Bhai along with four others were sentenced to death by the High Court. The Supreme Court confirmed the sentences. The President rejected their petition for mercy, and therefore, all the six condemned men were executed on midnight of March 30, 2007 on charges of murdering 64 persons, including two judges.[118] Bangla Bhai was known as the key operational leader and expert in bomb making. He was instrumental in establishing a network of mosques, madrassas, and militant training camps in 57 districts, where members were given training in arms along with bomb making and explosion techniques. It was active in Chittagong, Dinajpur, Joypurhat and Jamalpur.

The JMB has a strength of 10,000 highly trained full-time jihadi members and around 100,000 part-time members drawn from all levels of the society. It has also a sound financial strength as it reportedly spends about Taka 8,000 on each full-time cadre every month. Most of the recruits are drawn from madrassas all over the country.

The JMB received a moral boost after Begum Khaleda Zia came to power for the second time in 2001. The law enforcing agencies appeared to have taken an appeasement policy toward the outfit, allowing its cadres to carry on militant activities. Many of the cadres were the members of ICJ and have links with the Jamaat which is a partner of the coalition government.

It receives fund from philanthropic private organizations based on oil-rich Arab countries, such as Saudi Arabia, Kuwait, Bahrain and Libya

Jagrata Muslim Janata Bangladesh (JMJB)

The Jagrata Muslim Janata Bangladesh (JMJB) was formed in 1998 by Maulana Abdur Rahman, the Ameer (Chief) of the outfit. The Maulana studied in Madina Islamic University where he came into contact with the Wahhabi movement. He worked in the Saudi Embassy for five years (1985-1990). The outfit is regarded as the student or youth wing of the JMB. Its long term goal is to transform Bangladesh into an Islamic state based on the principles of the Qur'an and the Hadith through jihad. The leaders of the JMB, Maulana Abdur Rahman, Siddiqur Rahman (Bangla Bhai) and Asadullah al-Galib were also its leaders. Bangla Bhai was the commander of the organization. He was originally a leader of the ICS which he left in 1995 as a protest to a decision to admit girls as members. They became a symbol of terror and got involved in a series of killings.[119] The JMJB has its headquarters in Dhaka but its operational headquarter is in Jamalpur near India's Dhubri district. It has 57 training camps most of which are located in Jamalpur, Rajshahi and Naogaon districts.

There are reports which say that the JMJB is an offshoot of Harkat-ul-Jihad-al-Islami; others say it is an outgrowth of the JMB. It means that it has a network with the two militant organizations. It has 300,000 activists and 10,000 full members. The cadres are recruited from madrassas. Each cadre is paid a salary of Taka 7000 every month. The centre of its recruitment and training is Al-Madina Islamic Cadet Madrassa established by Maulana Abdur Rahman with Saudi money. The cadres are given military training including bomb making and explosion training. It is believed that some of its cadres were trained in Afghanistan. It is reported that it distributes audio-tapes of Osama bin-Laden with Bengali translation. The JMJB had indulged in kidnapping and extortion and in enforcing their version of Islamic way of life. The *Daily Star* reported on May 5, 2004 that the BNP sought and got the assistance of the outfit to crush the left wing parties and their cadres.

Harkat-ul-Jihad-al-Islami (Movement for Islamic Jihad)

This organization, known widely by its acronym HuJI, was formed in 1980 to fight against the Soviet forces in Afghanistan.[120] At the end of the Soviet withdrawal from Afghanistan in 1987, the returnees estimated to be around 5000 became active in Bangladesh with enormous funds provided by Osama bin-Laden.[121] The group, led by Showkat Osman, alias Sheikh Farid as the chairman and Imtiaz Quddus as the general secretary, is known to be a dreaded militant Islamist group in the country, because of its financial and organizational strength, possession of fire arms and training in Afghanistan. Another important leader, an ideologue named Mufti Abdul Hannan, who had happened to be a madrassa teacher, was trained in Gourhardanga Madrassa in Pakistan. Later on he enrolled himself at Aligarh University and obtained MA degree in Islamic Studies in 1987.[122] It engaged 25 Taliban to train its cadres in different camps. It has operational links with the ISI and the ULFA. It is a signatory to the International Islamic Front of 1998 which declared war on the United States. Osama bin-Laden is the one of top signatories of the document of the Front. It enjoys the patronage of the Jamaat and the BNP. It receives funds from Afghanistan, Pakistan and Saudi Arabia. Some Bangladeshi NGOs too are believed to have extended financial support to it.

The principal agenda of HuJI is to establish Islamic rule in Bangladesh through a violent jihad. It follows the ideology of the Wahhabi movement and the Taliban tradition of extreme conservatism. It is totally against all secular and democratic parties and practices, and therefore, vows to eliminate them by violent means. Like Taliban it wants to ban music, cinema, dances and all cultural festivals. It is thoroughly against India and the West on purely religious grounds.

The HuJI draws recruits mainly from madrassas. It has an estimated 20,000 hard core well trained cadres. It has six training camps mostly located near Cox Bazar in south east of Bangladesh adjoining Myanmar. Some of the cadres belong to the displaced Rohingya community of Myanmar, who are trained in these camps. About 251,000 Rohingya Muslims are taking shelter in Bangladesh. The HuJI's dreaded image and activities invited the US Government to designate it as a terrorist organization in 2002. It has several camps in Kurigram and Rangpur which are near India's border. The North East militants are trained in these camps. It is an extremely intolerant fascist organization. It stabbed to death a Bangladeshi journalist in November 2000 for making a documentary on the plight of Hindus. On July 20, 2000 it attempted to assassinate Prime Minister Sheikh Hasina Wajed.[123] It made an attempt on the life of a noted poet Shamsur Rahman, who had been campaigning against the Islamists, on January 18, 1999.[124] It attacked the American Center at Kolkata on January 22, 2002. It sent its cadres to Afghanistan to fight against the US-led coalition forces. It provided shelter and support to the Taliban and al-Qaeda escapees from Afghanistan. It provides support to the Kashmiri and North-East militants. It has links with other terrorist outfits such as Jaish-e-Muhammad and Laskar-e-Toiba. The government of Bangladesh banned it on October 17, 2005.[125]

The caretaker government has taken firm measures in curbing the activities of all the jihadi groups. The government's firmness has been seen in the quick implementation of the High Court's judgment awarding death sentences to six militants. It is noteworthy that Bangladesh did not experience any visible demonstration against the quick execution of the militants. The families received the bodies and quietly performed the last rites. It testifies to the absence of public support for them. As a result of the harsh measures taken by the government against the jihadis, they are presently maintaining a low profile. It is difficult to conclude that they are finished once and for all in view of the fact that they could be funded, organized and armed by foreign powers. They have a domestic support base which may not be formidable, but has the potentiality to foment trouble. There are reports to suggest that they are regrouping and trying to resurface, after the crackdown in the recent months.[126] It is also difficult to foretell what policy the next government would take toward the Islamists after the general elections.

The madrassas

As already stated there has been a steady growth of madrassas in Bangladesh. This increase surpasses the growth of state funded and private general schools in the country. The data presented in Table 4.4 reveals the ground reality, which is undoubtedly worrisome. It reflects the growing trend towards Islamization.

Table 4.4
Growth of madrassas and general schools in percentage (2001-2005)

	Madrassas	*General schools*
Number of institutions	22.22	9.74
Teachers	16.52	12.27
Enrolment	10.12	8.64

Source: *Bangladesh Economic Review, 2006.*

There are 9000 registered madrassas (official figure is 7373 as in 2002) which follow regulated curriculum. But there are equal numbers of unregistered madrassas which do not have uniform and regulated curriculum. Unofficial reports put a much higher figure to the stunning tune of

64,000.[127] The private madrassas, which are under Bangladesh Qawami Madrassa Education Board, are registered and they follow a regulated curriculum. But there are several thousand more of the other variety which are neither registered nor following a regulated curriculum. These are reportedly the breeding grounds of the jihadi groups in Bangladesh. As already stated in the previous section all the militant organizations recruit their cadres from these private madrassas. In other words, there is a nexus between the private madrassas and the Islamic extremist outfits.

There are four types of madrassas in Bangladesh – (i) registered madrassas under the Madrassa Education Board, (ii) Hafizia or Furqania, (iii) Qawmi and (iv) Madrassas under Tanjimul Ummah Foundation. Besides, there is a pre-madrassa set up called Maktabs.[128]

The registered madrassas are government regulated and are under the Madrassa Education Board. They receive government grants. They are known as Aliya madrassa.[129] Like any other schools under general education, these madrassas have four levels of education – Dakhil (primary), Alim (secondary), Fazil (higher secondary) and Kamil (college/university). Table 4.3 bears the statistics of these madrassas.

Table 4.5
Number of Madrassas, teachers and students under the Madrassa Education Board, 2002

Levels	*No. of Madrassas*	*No. Teachers*	*Enrolment*
Dakhil (primary level)	5077	67894	2,088,000
Alim (secondary)	1100	18440	528,000
Fazil (higher secondary)	1041	21376	602,000
Kamil (Graduate/above)	155	3788	93,000
Total	**7373**	**111498**	**3,311,000**

Source: *Bangladesh Bureau of Statistics, 2004.*

These madrassas follow a curriculum developed by the Madrassa Education Board which includes Bengali language and literature, English, social studies, science and mathematics, principles of economic, civics, history and the environment imparted at various levels. These are like any other general schools. The degrees conferred at the Kamil level are recognized as equivalent to those of the university degrees. These madrassas are in a position to compete with other schools. The product of these madrassas becomes eligible for employment in government service and in the private sector.[130]

The other variety, known as Deobandi madrassa includes Hafizia madrassas also called Furqania or Qur'ani madrassas offer pre-primary education in which the children are acquainted with Arabic alphabets and then are taught how to memorize the Qur'an and to learn the basic tenets of Islam. It may take several years to completely memorize the Qur'an. These traditional madrassas have Islam-oriented courses and the students are taught Arabic, which is important from the theological point of view, and also Urdu, which, however, is not a language of Bangladesh, The products, known as Hafiz, eventually become Imams in mosques and lead namaz there. They are often engaged as private tutors teaching children the basics of Islam and the religious rituals and also how to read the Qur'an. They are also considered unemployable products, academically too weak to take up any mainstream professional means of livelihood. They could be easily lured by the Islamic militant groups to become jihadis and to indulge in acts of assassination, bomb explosion, communal riots and anti-government demonstrations.[131]

The Maktabs also offer pre-primary education in which the children are taught the basics of Islam and how to read the Qur'and perform namaz. The annexies of local mosques are used as Maktabs. The children are taken to the Maktab in the early hours between 6-8 o'clock, before going to the general and regular schools. There is no fee for attending these Maktabs. The community organizes the sessions and engages a teacher to look after the Maktabs.

The Qawmi madrassas are privately run institutions. They have a complete course from primary to secondary education. Here the students are generally taught the Qur'an and Tafsir (interpretation), the basics of Islam, theology and Islamic history. These are the minimum course content of this type of madrassas. Most of them do not teach English, science, mathematics and social studies; besides, they do not have a uniform curriculum. It may be mentioned that the BNP Government, before the completion of its tenure, passed an order on August 21, 2006 making the degrees of Qawmi madrassas equivalent to the university degrees.[132] This was done to make the Islamists happy, ahead of the general elections. Although the Jamaat and other Islamists were jubilant over the government decision[133], the media expressed anxieties at the far-reaching consequences of the decision affecting Bangladesh's "economy, politics, culture, society, civil administration and law and order with one tunnel vision – to win votes in the upcoming elections".[134] However, mere announcement would not serve the purpose. It would be the onus on the part of the next elected government to implement it. For the time being, it was just a populist attempt of the BNP to catch vote.

Tanjimul Ummah Cadet Madrassas are newly set up institutions which are run by Tanjimul Ummah Foundation established in 1999. The Foundation has set up its schools in six districts of Bangladesh. These are private madrassas in the mould of modern Christian missionary schools. These madrassas have pre-primary, primary, secondary and higher secondary level courses. The courses are taught both in Bengali and English. Science, mathematics, social sciences are taught in these madrassas. Computer education is a compulsory subject. Besides, physical drill, cultural activities, games and sports are co-curricular activities in these madrassas. The fee structure of these schools is higher than general schools. Only well-to-do families can afford to send their children to this type of school. In an interview the Principal of the Dhaka branch of the Cadet Madrassa and the Chairman of the Foundation said that their madrassas had shown an alternative model of the madrassa education system so that children could not only learn the centrality of Islam but also would be able to become a complete and capable citizen of the country. Their products could compete with any students of general schools. If the efforts of the Foundation work, it is expected that these madrassas could position themselves as a viable alternative to the traditional and outdated private madrassas.

The international dimension

The political and the militant Islam in Bangladesh found a ready and catchy issue to take recourse to for mass mobilization in 1991 – the invasion of Iraq by the US led allied forces to eject the Iraqis out of Kuwait. As stated in Chapter I, the Muslims of Bangladesh are mostly Sunnis and as such look forward to find some kind of affiliation to the Sunni world. Although Iraq is not pre-eminently a Sunni dominated state, its ruler Saddam Hussein was a Sunni. To most of the Sunnis he was a symbol of inspiration and pride. Despite the fact that the Islamic world did not approve the Iraqi invasion of Kuwait which is also a Sunni dominated country, which helped Saddam Hussein during his war against Iran, the Muslim world felt that an amicable solution could have been found at the instance of IOC or the Arab world. The US-led invasion to resolve the crisis was viewed as an invasion of the Islamic world by the West. There was widespread rally organized by the Jamaat to protest against the invasion. The Jamaat took it as a unique opportunity to penetrate into the masses. It tried to prove that it was a party which defended the cause of the Islamic ummah against the conspiracy of the Christian West. Almost all parties joined the anti-West rallies and demonstrations throughout the country. The US-led attack to topple the Taliban government in Afghanistan added fuel to the anti-West sentiments in Bangladesh.[135] The second war against Iraq further inflamed the anti-US and anti-West sentiment of the people of Bangladesh. This time the Jamaat was a partner of the coalition government. It had the greater advantage in mobilizing the public to rise against the West. The jihadi groups too found a rallying point to muster support. The Jamaat and the militant Islamists took the opportunity to consolidate their support base among the urban and the rural masses. This time around, the entire nation came forward to raise a voice of protest against the US-led invasion. The jihadi groups vowed publicly to attack the US interests wherever possible; subsequently, the HuJI cadres attacked the American Center at Kolkata in January 2002.

Opposition to Jihadis and Jamaat

Despite the fact that Bangladesh has a relatively homogenous society because of its religious and linguistic composition, free from social cleavages and division that plague other societies[136], it suffers from certain institutional weaknesses. It has a weak parliamentary system. The Government is not accommodative to demands of the opposition even if the opposition is moving a bill or resolution in the best interest of the country. The two main political parties do not like to listen to each other and do not find a common platform to interact. The two leaders of the Awami League and the BNP do not meet each other to start dialogue on issues of national interests. Consequently, the parliament remains nonfunctional most of the time. The opposition parties often call for boycott of the parliament, and therefore, the highest law making body remains practically inactive through out the year.[137] Although it is easy to declare a *hartal* which virtually paralyses the civic life, or to bring out a procession in which thousands participate, or to organize street corner meetings in cities of Bangladesh, the fight for reestablishment of democracy and to make the parliament function, despite the popular urge, is not easy because of non-elected authoritarian rule.[138] The Jatiyo Sangsad, it is reported, hardly discussed the issue of fundamentalism despite the fact that there had been a series of jihadi attacks on secular and democratic parties since 2001.

The 14-party alliance led by the Awami League appeared to be active and strong so far as opposing the ruling BNP led alliance. But when it came to raising a strong voice of protest against the Islamists, it was found lacking. The left wing parties are organizationally too weak to fight against religious fanaticism, despite their commitment to secularism and democracy. Consequently, a brave fight against the Islamists is yet to be initiated.

It would be wrong to assume that all the people of Bangladesh allow the political and militant Islam to operate unopposed. In fact, the opposition to Islamic fundamentalism has been always active and formidable.[139] The print media has always been vocal in raising a concern at the attack on the minorities. It is difficult for the political parties, including the Awami League, to negate the preponderance of Islam in a staunchly religious society as of Bangladesh. However, the Awami League has been raising a voice of concern against the atrocities committed on the minorities. The Convention on Crimes against Humanity backed by the Awami League has been campaigning against the alleged "systematic persecution" of religious minorities and has been demanding punitive action against the perpetrators of such crimes against humanity. These steps yielded results. In September 2003 a speedy trial he court in Barisal sentenced two of the accused to life imprisonment. A month later the Speedy Trial Court sentenced six others to life imprisonment for raping a Hindu woman, after the 2001 elections. These are rare cases, for, in most of the instances the criminals were not booked, and therefore, were not punished.

The campaign against the atrocities on Hindus had been going on despite repressive measures adopted by the BNP-led government. The arrest of Shahriar Kabir, a noted journalist and writer drew the attention of the Amnesty International. His 'offence' was that he went to West Bengal to meet the Hindus who had left Bangladesh in the wake of violence against them soon after the 2001 elections. He was arrested at the Dhaka international airport on November 22, 2001 on his return from India. Police seized his passport, five video cassettes, 13 audio cassettes, 3 CDs and several unprocessed films and his camera.[140]

There are a number of instances when intellectuals and media persons came under attack for their criticism of Islamic fundamentalism. One such incident took place on the Dhaka University campus on February 27, 2004, when Professor Humayun Azad was stabbed by Islamic fundamentalists. Azad survived in the attack but later on died in Germany on August 13, 2004.[141] Poet Shamsur Rahman was attacked on January 18, 1999; he survived, but he was attacked again and killed on July 16, 2000 in Jessore. A plan to eliminate National Professor Kabir Chowdhury and Director General of Islamic Foundation Maulana Abdul Awal was foiled. On January 27, 2005 Shah A.A.M.S. Kabira, former Finance Minister and opposition member of parliament was killed soon after a public address in Habiganj.[142] He was killed for his strong public campaign against the fundamentalists. There are many more who suffered at the hands of either the BNP led government or the Islamists for taking up minority and human rights issues, and for fighting against communalism.

Religious slogans and symbols are part of the Bangladeshi life; wall writings and banners in support of Islamic fundamentalism do appear in cities and urban centres. It is, however, not a reflection of popular support for fundamentalism. The majority of the people are not fanatic and blind followers of the Jamaat and the jihadi groups. This is proved by the outcome of all the general elections shown in Table 4.1. But a conservative estimate of around 10 per cent of Jamaat's support base in a highly populated country of more than 14 crore along with a couple of lakh jihadi supporters could unleash havoc in a geographically small country like Bangladesh. The realization of the ground reality after the August 17, 2005 bomb blasts has compelled the conscious elite, democratic and liberal forces to oppose political and militant Islam. There has been rallies and public meeting against these deadly activities. Some of the press, both vernacular and English, have been publishing accounts of militant groups as a part of awareness campaign against them. A section of the intelligentsia has even risked life to combat the jihadis. They have suffered harassment at the hands of both the militants and the government.

The political Islam in Bangladesh has the advantage of securing the support or connivance of the Government. The Jamaat was a partner of the coalition led by the BNP. Hence, it had government backing. So was the case with the jihadi groups. The government arrested some of the key jihadi leaders and put them in prison. A few of them have been awarded death sentences. But no visible steps have been taken to clamp down on their activities, such as recruitment, extortion, acquisition of arms and training infrastructures. The foreign fund is allowed to flow in aid of the militants. Although the government of Bangladesh has banned all the militant outfits, the underground activities are reportedly going on. The Jamaat's activities towards Islamization and its hate campaign, which speak of its intolerant and anti-democratic face, are not restrained, not to speak of banning. The government inaction gives it a leverage to expand its network and activities besides giving other militant outfits an indirect encouragement to go ahead with their jihadi agenda.

The democratic and secular political elite, the media, the intelligentsia, the student community in general are aware of the rise of Islamic fundamentalism and its consequent impact on the political and civic scenario of Bangladesh. For example, there was a robust resistance to a determined move in the parliament in April 2002 when G.M. Qader, brother of Hossain Mohammad Ershad tabled a bill to make it compulsory for every Bangladeshi Muslim to offer five times namaz daily, non-compliance leading to jail term or heavy fine.[143] The left wing students union named Bangladesh Chatra Union claims that in close cooperation with the Bangladesh Chatra League, the Awami student wing, of Dhaka University, it has been able to keep the campus free from Islami Chatra Shibir. The women forums appear to be worried about its ascendancy. They would invariably be the soft target of the repressive and rabid patriarchic fundamentalists on gender issues. They have been fighting for their rights for a considerable period of time despite occasional threats and harassments. The liberal section of the society in Bangladesh has been trying to create a strong public opinion against fundamentalism in and outside the country. Besides Taslima Nasreen, Salam Azad and Shahriar Kabir a number of leading personalities have been raising a strong voice of protest against fundamentalism, which has been trying to subvert secularism, democracy and liberal values in the country. A noted playwright Mamunur Rashid, while participating in a drama festival in New Delhi in January 2006, blamed the Jamaat and the BNP for pushing the country into the hands of obscurantist forces. He believes that the majority of the people "are very secular. They will never go to any extreme action. They will never take any extreme position like Afghanistan because this 14 crore people do not want them."[144] Like him many of the people belonging to the different sections of the society argue that the people as a whole are tolerant and democratic. It is rather sad that the vast majority becomes ineffective in the face of the highly organized, motivated, financially strong, well trained armed Islamists backed by government appeasement policy. The majority of the people is unorganized and without resources required to face a motivated and violent section of the society. The strength of the Islamists in terms of percentage of population is not significant. Therefore, it is unlikely that the political table shall be turned to the advantage of the Islamists.[145] The Jamaat secured only 4.29 per cent votes in the parliamentary elections, 2001.[146] Nonetheless, in absolute number the supporters of the Jamaat could be around 2.5 million, which is definitely a sizeable figure, considering the territorial contour of the country. The Islamists are significant, powerful and ominous. This demands attention of the concerned people.

Fundamentalism: How visible in Bangladesh?

All the people of Bangladesh are not fundamentalists. At the same time it could be a disturbing factor to find that a conservative estimate of 2.5 million may have been following the footsteps of religious fundamentalism. The common masses are religious and devout Muslims. That could not be taken as an indication of the massive influence of fundamentalism. Even then one could find certain indices of the surge of religious fundamentalism in the rural and urban areas of Bangladesh. The sermons of some of the Imams in the mosque on the Friday *Jumma* prayer, the public address of the Jamaat leaders, the environment around some of the private madrassas, the Islamic slogans written on the walls and the body of auto- rickshaws (such as "Namaz kayem korun" i.e. perform namaz[147]), the rise in the number of burqa-clad women[148] in cities, the clandestine circulation of audio tapes and CDs containing inflammatory, communal of the fascists speeches of the fundamentalists, the steady increase of private and unregistered madrassas and the activities of the ICS on university campuses suggest the visibility of Islamic fundamentalism in Bangladesh.

The *modus operandi* of Islamic militants is secretive. It is difficult to find their presence in the normal civic life of Bangladesh. The recruitment and training centres are located in remote areas and are not easily accessible. Their presence is felt only through violent activities.

Role of the media

Bangladesh has 26 daily newspapers, mostly published from Dhaka and 16 TV channels, out of which 2 are government run and others are private. The print and electronic media play a role in the political process of the country. A thorough study on the role of the media might reveal its approach to militant Islam in Bangladesh.[149] A quick survey of the newspaper reports on the violence committed in 2001 before and after the elections reveals that the print media had played a considerably laudable role in drawing nation-wide attention of all concerned forcing the government to take steps to stop it. The pre-election violent campaign against minorities started in the mid-September which was first brought to light by *Sangbad,* giving a detailed narration of the attacks committed in Khulna, Firojpur and Feni.[150] Thereafter other dailies such as *Prothom Alo, Daily Star, Ittefaq* started publishing the reports of violence committed on the Hindus. The attack was mounted to terrorize the minorities, who were known to be strong supporters of the Awami League, so that they refrain from voting.[151] The media reported that in the pre-election violence, 163 lost their lives and 6000 others were wounded severely.[152] Print media brought out the magnitude of horrors and suffering unleashed by the terrorists on the minorities after the election, for which several thousand people were compelled to leave the country to seek shelter in India. The newspaper reports carried vivid description of the intimidation, assault, rape of women, destruction of property and places of worship and of killings. All this created an awareness among the public about the atrocities. This forced the individuals, writers, artists, NGOs, civil societies to organize protests against the violence allegedly let loose by the BNP-Jamaat cadres in different parts of the country. It is argued that the print media played a commendable role in highlighting the atrocities committed on the Hindus. But at the same time, it failed to address the basic issue that had plagued Bangladesh – communalism sponsored and promoted by the Islamists which led to the widespread violence against the Hindus.[153] Like the print media, the private electronic media too telecast the trail of destruction, killing and atrocities committed in September and October 2001. The Government run TV channels however remained almost silent.[154] There had been processions, meetings, demonstrations and discussions against the 2001 communal attack on the minorities. The striking point to be noted is that the 2001 violence was engineered by the BNP and Jamaat cadres. Therefore, the coalition government of Khaleda Zia did not take any firm measure to stop it. Thus, it became the worst violence since the atrocities committed by the Pakistani army during the time of the liberation war.[155]

The media has been giving adequate coverage on the concern of the public and the civil society about the rise of militant Islam. Almost every incidence of violence committed by the militants is reported in the leading newspapers with critical comments and condemnation. The liberal section of the society raises a strong voice of opposition to terrorism perpetuated in the name of religion. Almost all the dailies published from Dhaka and elsewhere have taken a position to prevent the apparent surge of religious fanaticism. The lead role has been taken by *Daily Star, Prothom Alo, Ittefaq,*

Sangbad, Jugantar and *Janakanta*. The message is loud and clear; Bangladesh cannot afford to be a hotbed of Islamic fundamentalism. It would be a suicidal to follow the course of religious fanaticism.[156]

The recent press coverage, lauding the firm measures against the Islamic jihadis and the appreciation of the quick dispensation of justice in respect of six jihadis soon after the execution on March 30, 2007 is a sign of media's campaign against fundamentalism. One finds a clear distinction made by the media between religiosity within the framework of Islam and political Islam which is based on fundamentalism, hate and intimidation. The media is in favour of the Islamic flavour of the country, but it concurrently believes in equality and fraternity among all religions, as also justice and respect for human rights.

It is noteworthy that the media has been playing a considerably commendable role in combating communalism and Islamic fundamentalism. Had the media secured the due support from the government to retain and promote the values for which Bangladesh was born in 1971, the country would have been free from hatred and violence to a considerable extent.

REFERENCES

1. For details of Islamic resurgence see John L. Esposito, *Iranian Revolution: Its Global Impact* (Miami: Florida International University Press, 1990), Emmanuel Sivan, *Radical Islam: Medieval Theology and Modern Politics* (New Haven: Yale University Press, 1988).

2. The concept of 'clash of civilization' was authored by Samuel P. Huntington and was published in *Foreign Affairs*, Summer, 1993. The concept was fully developed and published in the form of a book entitled *The Clash of Civilization and the Remaking of the World Order* (New York: Simon & Schuster, 1996).

3. Talukdar Maniruzzaman, "Bangladesh Politics: Secular and Islamic Trends" in Rafiuddin Ahmed (ed), *Islam in Bangladesh: Society, Culture and Politics* (Dhaka: Bangladesh Itihas Samiti,1983), pp. 185-219.

4. Basant Chatterjee argues that the emergence of Bangladesh did not destroy the validity of two nation theory. Had it been so Bangladesh could have been a part of the Indian Union. See his *Inside Bangladesh Today: An Eye-witness Account* (New Delhi: S. Chand & Co. 1979), p. 155.

5. For the full text of the speech delivered in Bengali see Khandakar Mohammad Ilias (ed), *Bangladesher Samaj Biplobe Bangabandhur Darshan* (Bangabandu's Philosophy for Social Revolution), (Dhaka: Bangladesh Parishad, 1979) p. 118. An English version was published in *Bangladesh Observer*, November 5, 1972.

6. Government of the People's Republic of Bangladesh, *Speeches of Sheikh Mujib*, (Dhaka: External Publicity Division, Ministry of Foreign Affairs, 1972), pp.16-17.

7. The campaign against secularism is still strong and pervasive. There are publications at the behest of the Jamaat, to condemn the concept of secularism as anti-Islam. One of such recently published and highly circulated booklets is Al Mehedi, *Dharmaniropekshotar Fanchi Sai* (Hang Secularism) (Dhaka: Al Amin Prakashan, 2006).

8. Muhammad Ghulam Kabir, *Changing Face of Nationalism: The Case of Bangladesh* (New Delhi: South Asian Publishers, 1994), p. 201.

9. Talukdar Maniruzzaman, "Bangladesh Politics: Secular and Islamic Trends" in Rafiuddin Ahmed (ed), *Islam in Bangladesh: Society, Culture and Politics,* n. 3, pp. 192. He concluded, "Sheikh Mujib was clearly advocating the negative, non-discriminatory, Indian type secularism", p. 192.

10. Akhtar Hossain, "Anatomy of *Hartal* Politics in Bangladesh", *Asian Survey*, Vol. XL, No. 3, May-June, 2000, pp 508-529.

11. Talukdar Maniruzzaman, "Bangladesh Politics: Secular and Islamic Trends" in Rafiuddin Ahmed (ed), *Islam in*

Bangladesh: Society, Culture and Politics, n. 3, pp. 192-193.

12. Anisuzzaman, "Religion and Politics in Bangladesh", in S.R. Chakravarty (ed), *Society, Polity and Economy of Bangladesh* (New Delhi: Har-Anand Publications, 1994), p. 43.

13. Badruddin Umar, *Juddhotor Bangladesh* (Post-War Bangladesh) (Dhaka: Muktadhara, 1975), pp. 15-16. There are several works which reflected the putative fear of the anti-Mujib faction, which exploited the situation to their advantage and spread the rumour that Hindus would dominate Bangladesh's politics. See Iftekharuzzaman and Mahbubur Rahman, "Nation Building in Bangladesh: Perceptions, Problems and Approach" in M. Abdul Hafiz and Rob Khan (eds), *Nation Building in Bangladesh: Retrospect and Prospect* (Dhaka: BISS, 1982), Taj I Hashmi, "Islamic Resurgence in Bangladesh: Genesis, Dynamics and Implications' in Satu P. Limaye *et al. Religious Radicalism and Security in South Asia* (Honolulu, Hawaii: Asia-Pacific Center for Security Studies, 2004), pp. 45-46, Basant Chatterjee, *Inside Bangladesh Today: An Eye-witness Account,* n.4, pp. 68-70.

14. Basant Chatterjee, *Inside Bangladesh Today, ibid,* pp. 86.

15. Ashraf Kaisar, *Bangladeshe Rajnaitik Hatyakanda* (Political Killings in Bangladesh) (Dhaka: Mawla Brothers, 1998), pp. 34-65. One of the most tantalizing killing was that of Sirajul Haq Sikdar popularly known as Siraj Sikdar of Jatiyo Samajtantrik Dal (JSD). Mujib's infamous rhetoric "Kothai aj Siraj Sikdar" (Where is Siraj Sikdar today?) in the Parliament on January 25, 1975, 22 days after the killing in police custody left ample scope to point an accusing finger at Mujib complicity in the crime.

16. For an analysis of the collapse of the popular base of Sheikh Mujibur Rehman see U.A.B. Razia Akhter Banu, "The Fall of the Sheikh Mujib Regime: An Analysis", *Indian Political Science Review,* Vol. XV, No. 1, January 1981, pp 1-19.

17. For details see Zillur R. Khan, *Marital Law to Martial Law:*

Leadership Crises in Bangladesh (Dhaka: University Press Limited, 1984), Chapter 4.

18. Lawrence Ziring, *Bangladesh: From Mujib to Ershad: An Interpretative Study* (Dhaka: University Press Limited, 1992) Chapter V.

19. For details of Zia's ascendancy to power see Golam Hossain, *General Ziaur Rahman and the BNP: Political Transformation of a Military Regime* (Dhaka: University Press Limited, 1988).

20. Samina Ahmed, "Politics in Bangladesh: The Paradox of Military Intervention" in Virender Grover (ed), *Bangladesh: Government and Politics* (New Delhi: Deep and Deep Publications, 2000), pp.97-129 also see Emajuddin Ahamed, *Military Rule and the Myth of Democracy* (Dhaka: University Press Limited, 1988). Also see Lawrence Ziring, *Bangladesh: From Mujib to Ershad: An Interpretive Study, ibid,* Chapter VIII.

21. Talukdar Maniruzzaman, "Bangladesh Politics: Secular and Islamic Trends", n. 3, pp. 197-198.

22. Derived from my interaction with a Jamaat functionary at his office on November 29, 2006. He suggested that "Saudi Arabia is the nerve-centre of the Islamic world. Its delayed recognition carried a message to the general people of the country. The Mujib regime actually did not deserve recognition of the Islamic world."

23. Bangladesh National Party, *Ghoshanpatra* (Manifesto) (Dhaka, 1978), p. 1.

24. Marcus Franda, "Ziaur Rahman and Bangladeshi Nationalism", *Economic and Political Weekly*, Annual Number, March 1981, pp. 357-380. Also see Golam Hossain, *General Ziaur Rahman and the BNP: Political Transformation of a Military Regime,* n. 19.

25. For an interpretative study on the issue see Tazneen M. Murshid, *The Sacred and the Secular: Bengal Muslim Discourses, 1871-1977* (Calcutta: Oxford University Press, 1995).

26. Muhammad Ghulam Kabir, *Changing Face of Nationalism: The Case of Bangladesh,* n. 8, pp. 196-197, also see Mohammad Abdul Halim and Kamal Uddin Ahmed, "Foreign Affairs: Safeguarding National Interest" in Habib Zafarullah (ed) *The Zia Episode in Bangladesh Politics* (New Delhi: South Asia Publishers, 1996) pp. 125-139 and Ali Riaz, "Bangladesh in 2005: Standing at a Crossroads," *Asian Survey,* Vol. XL VI, No. 1, January/February 2006, pp. 107-113 also his *God Willing: The Politics of Islamism in Bangladesh* (New York: Rowman and Littlefield, 2004).

27. Bertil Lintner, "Religious Extremism and Nationalism in Bangladesh" in Satu P. Limaye *et al.* (eds), *Religious Radicalism and Security in South Asia* (Honolulu, Hawaii: Asia Pacific Center for Security Studies, 2004), p.430. Also see, Bibhuti Bhusan Nandy, "DGFI: State Within a State" in Jaideep Saikia (ed), *Bangladesh: Treading the Taliban Trail* (New Delhi: Vision Books, 2006), pp.173-187.

28. For details of the passage of the Amendment adopted on June 7, 1988 see *Daily Star* and *Prothom Alo* and other newspapers, June 8, 1988.

29. For a collected essays dealing with this issue see Muhammad Delwar Hussain (ed), *Bangladesher Rajnitite Dharma O Dharma Niropekshata* (Religion and Secularism in the Politics of Bangladesh), (Dhaka: Prerona Prokashan, 1993).

30. For details of speech see *Prothom Alo* and *Daily Star,* January 1988.

31. For an in-depth analysis on the Generals taking the shelter of Islam to legitimize their dictatorial rule see Emajuddin Ahamed and D.R.J.A. Nazneen, "Islam in Bangladesh: Revivalism or Power Politics?", *Asian Survey,* Vol. XXX, No. 8, August, 1990, pp. 795-808. Also see Peter Custers, "Islamisation and More Aid for the Generals", *Economic and Political Weekly,* June 25, 1988, pp. 1317-1318.

32. Talukdar Maniruzzaman, "Bangladesh Politics: Secular and Islamic Trend" in S.R. Chakravarty and Virendra Narain (eds), *Bangladesh: History and Culture,* Vol. I, (New Delhi: South Asia Publishers, 1986), pp. 114-116.

33. Talukdar Maniruzzaman, "The Fall of the Military Dictator: 1991 Elections and the Prospect of Civilian Rule in Bangladesh", *Pacific Affairs*, Vol. 65, No. 2, Summer, 1992 pp. 203-224.

34. The Jatiyo Party (Naziur) got 4 seats out of 11 seats contested and the Islamic Oikya Jote captured only 2 seat out of 7 contested. Compared with the Jamaat these two parties do not have any significant support base.

35. For a general concern at the alliance see the newspaper reports appearing in *Prothom Alo* and *Daily Star*, October 3-5, 2001.For an analytical discourse on the fall out of the 2001 elections results which provided a secured platform to the Islamists see Ali Riaz, *God Willing: The Politics of Islamism in Bangladesh* (New York: Rowman and Littlefield, 2004).

36. Aminur Rashid and Mustafa Firoze (eds), *Pramanya Sangsad* (Approved Parliament) (Dhaka: Tathyasewa, 2002) pp. 12-14. The coalition partners got 216 seats, Jamaat 17, Islami Okyajot 2 and Jatiyo Party (Naziur) 4.

37. Based on my discussion with a number of media persons and scholars in Dhaka in the month of November 2006.

38. *Dainik Dinkal*, February 28, 2001.

39. Bertil Lintner, "Bangladesh: A Cocoon of Terror", *Far Eastern Economic Review*, April 4, 2002.

40. For the criticism of Lintner's article see *Daily Star*, April 5, 14 and 16, 2002.

41. Alex Perry, "Deadly Cargo", *Time*, October 21, 2002, pp. 22-25. The cargo ship carried 150 Taliban fighters and consignment of arms and ammunition bore the name 'Mecca'.

42. For a passionate argument on this line see Hiranmay Karlekar, *Bangladesh: The Next Afghanistan* (New Delhi: Sage, 2005). The US intelligence does not consider Bangladesh as a "real hot account" of Islamic militancy despite the appearance of posters and wall writing saying "Amra sobai hobo Taliban, Bangladesh hobe Afghanistan" (We will all be Taliban and Bangladesh will be Afghanistan), see Alex Perry, "Deadly Cargo", *ibid.*

43. See *Daily Star*, May 31, 2003 and also Alex Perry, "A Very Dirty Plot", *Time*, June 9, 2003.

44. For details seen *Prothom Alo*, December 22 and 23, 2004.

45. *ibid*, August 21, 2006.

46. For the details of the attack planned to kill Sheikh Hasina in a party rally see, *Prathom Alo* and *Daily Star*, August 18-20, 2004.

47. For an analytical insight see Aravind Adiga, "A Democracy is Shaken", *Time*, September 6, 2004, pp 38-40.

48. For details of the bomb blasts that rocked Bangladesh see *Prothom Alo* and *Daily Star*, August 22-23, 2005. Other newspapers too published details of the blasts in which not much damage had been done. There was a report of the death of two persons.

49. *Daily Star*, August 18, 2005.

50. For such a representative view see Sahidul Islam, *Jongider Nepothey 'RAW'-Mossad* (In the Background of the Militants 'RAW'-Mossad) (Dhaka: Professor's Publications, 2006).

51. For an analysis of the militants' activities see Ali Riaz, "Bangladesh in 2005: Standing at a Crossroads", n. 26.

52. A number of noteworthy studies on the Jamaat highlight its phenomenal rise in the politics of Bangladesh. Some of these are: U.A.B.Razia Akhter Banu, "Jamaat-i-Islami in Bangladesh: Challenges and Prospects" and Taj ul Islam Hashmi, "Islam In Bangladesh Politics" in Hussin Mutalib and Taj ul-Islam Hashmi (eds), *Islam, Muslims and the Modern State* (London: Macmillan, 1996) pp. 80-99 and 100-138, Enayetur Rahim, "Bangladeshe Jamate Islamer Utthan" (Rise of Jamaat-i-Islami in Bangladesh) in Mohammad Jafar Iqbal (ed), *Bish Bachar Pore* (Twenty Years After) (Dhaka: Mohana Pradasani, 1993) also his "Bengali Muslims and Islamic Fundamentalism: The Jama't-i-Islami in Bangladesh" in Rafiuddin Ahmed, *Understanding Bengali Muslims: Interpretative Essays* ((New Delhi: Oxford University Press, 2001), pp. 236-261, B.M. Monoar Kair,

"The Politics of Religion: The Jamaat-i-Islami in Bangladesh" in Rafiuddin Ahmed (ed), *Religion, Nationalism and Politics in Bangladesh* (New Delhi: Oxford University Press, 1990) pp. 124-125, Hasan Mohammad, *Jamaat-i-Islami Bangladesh: Netritto, Sangathan, Adarsha* (Jamaat-i-Islami of Bangladesh: Leadership, Organization, Ideology) (Dhaka: Academic Publishers, 1993). Some others are Partha S. Ghosh, "Bangladesh at the Crossroads: Religion and Politics", *Asian Survey*, August 1990, pp. 795-808 and Emajuddin Ahamed and D.R.J.A. Nazeen, "Islam in Bangladesh or Power Politics?" *Asian Survey*, n. 31, pp. 395-408. For a highly critical assessment of Maulana Mawdudi see Maulana Mansurul Haq (ed), *Mr Mawdudir New Islam* (Mr. Mawdudi's New Islam((Dhaka: Lalbag, Jamia Quraniya Arabia, 1985) and Jatiyo Ulema Parishad, *Jamaat Unmasked: The True Colour of a Fundamentalist Party* (Dhaka: Council for National Religious Scholars, 2001).

53. For details of political biography of Maulana Sayyid Abul A'la Mawdudi, see Seyyed Vali Reza Nasr, " Mawdudi and the Jama'at-i-Islami: The Origins, Theory, and Practice of Islamic Revivalism" in Ali Rehana (ed), *Pioneers of Islamic Revival* (New York: Zed Publication, 1994) pp. 98-124, his *Mawdudi and the Making of Islamic Revolution* (New York: Oxford University Press, 1996).

54. Enayetur Rahim, "Bengali Muslims and Islamic Fundamentalism" in *Understanding Bengali Muslims: Interpretative Essays* (New Delhi: Oxford University Press, 2001), pp. 236-237.

55. *ibid*, p. 238.

56. For a detailed profile of Ghulam Azam see Muhammad Qamruzzaman, *Adhyapak Ghulam Azamer Sangrami Jibon* (The Struggled Life of Professor Ghulam Azam), (Dhaka: Al Falah Printer, 1989), and see a recent publication Istiaq Hossain and Noore Alam Sidiquee, *Islam in Bangladesh Politics: The Role of Ghulam Azam* (London: Routledge, 2004) also for his own writings see Ghulam Azam, *A Guide to the Islamic Movement* (Dhaka: Oriental Press, 1968).

57. There had been widespread protest against his landing on the soil of Bangladesh. Almost all the newspapers carried news and views against his arrival and demanded his trial for war crimes.

58. Almost all the newspapers carried the news of the public trial which created a strong public opinion against the Jamaat and its leaders, particularly against Ghulam Azam. News items and letters to the editor carried public emotions against the Jamaat.

59. In my interaction with scholars, media personalities, non-Jamaati political leaders and businessmen the role of Ghulam Azam surfaced. Without any exception, all consider him anti-Hindu, anti-India, anti-democratic and responsible for the genocide committed during the Bangladesh liberation war.

60. A large number of publications appeared soon after Ghulam Azam was accorded political rehabilitation. Some of these were highly critical of Ghulam Azam and his party. See Aman-ud-Daula, *Ghulam Azamer Nagarikatta Mamla* (About Ghulam Azam's Citizenship) (Dhaka: Dibya Prakash, 1993), Ahmed Sharif *et al.* (eds), *Ekattarer Ghatok O Dalalra Ke Kothay* (Where are the Killers of 71 and Collaborators) (Dhaka: Mukti Juddho Chetona Bikash Kendra, 1987), Shahriar Kabir (ed), *Ekattarer Ghatok Jamaat-i-Islami: Atit O Bartaman* (The Killers of 71 Jamaat-i-Islami: Past and Present (Muktijuddha Chetona Bikas Kendra, 1989), Maulana Abdul Awwal, *Jamaater Asal Chehara* (The True Portrait of the Jamaat), (Dhaka: Agami Prakashini, 1993), Borhanuddin Khan Jahangir, *Bangladeshe Jatiyotabad Ebong Moulabad* (Nationalism and Fundamentalism in Bangladesh) (Dhaka: Agami Prakashini, 1993).

61. Quoted in Ghulam Azam, *A Guide to the Islamic Movement* (Dhaka: Azam Publications, 1968), pp. 61-62.

62. Jamaat has not openly said that it has a political agenda. While defining the objectives of Jamaat Ghulam Azam writes "To achieve victory of Allah's religion is the objective of the Jamaat-i-Islami". See his *Jamaate Islamir Karmaniti* (Policies of the Jamaat-i-Islami), (Dhaka: Publication

Division of Jamaat-i-Islami, 1990), p. 16. The introductory note on Jamaat states "In the accepted terminology Jamaat-i-Islami is not a religious, political, social or cultural party. Just as Islam is present in all aspects of personal and collective life of an individual, Jamaat-i-Islami is also all pervasive." See *Parisiti* (Introduction) (Dhaka: Jamaat-i-Islami Bangladesh, 2006), p. 1.

63. *The Reporter's Guide Handbook on Election Reporting* (Dhaka: Society for Environment and Human Development, 2001), p. 101.

64. Most of the publications of the Jamaat are in Bengali in which the ideology of the party is clearly stated. Some of such are Motiur Rahman Nizami, *Islami Andolong O Sangathan* (Islamic Movement and Organization) (Dhaka: Prakashana Bibhag, Jamaate Islami Bangladesh, 2006), Mohammad Eusuf Ali, *Islami Biplob Sadhone Sangathan* (Organization in Accomplishing Islamic Revolution) (Dhaka: Prakashana Bibhag, Jamaate Islami Bangladesh, 1995), *Jamaate Islamir Karyabibaroni*, Vol. I and II (Activities of Jamaat-I-Islami), (Dhaka: Prakashana Bibhag, Jamaate Islami Bangladesh, 2005).

65. In a lengthy conversation with one of the functionaries of the Jamaat, who after initial hesitation agreed to speak considering my religious background and proficiency in Bengali on the condition that he would stand anonymous, on November 29, 2006 at his residence in Dhaka, revealed that the Jamaat was inspired by the success of the efforts made by the Islamic Brotherhood of Egypt (founded in 1924 by Sayyid Qutb) after the death of President Gamal Abdel Nasser, who suppressed it with a heavy hand.

66. For some details see U.A.B. Razia Akhtar Banu, "Jamaat-i-Islami in Bangladesh: Challenges and Prospects", n. 52, pp. 80-99.

67. Taj ul-Islam Hashmi, "Islam in Bangladesh Politics" n. 52. Jamaat could capture only 18 seats out of 222 seats contested and secure 12.13% votes. See Aminur Rashid and Mostafa Firoz, *Pramany Sangsad*, n. 36, pp. 29 and 33.

68. Meghna Guha Thakurta, "The Nature of the Bangladesh State," unpublished article.

69. For details of its action programme and ideology, see some of its publications, mostly in Bengali such as *Karmapadhhati* (Action Procedure) (Dhaka: Bangladesh Islami Chatra Sibir, 2001), *Amra Ki Sai Keno Sai Kibhabe Sai* (What Do We Want Why Want and How Want) (Dhaka: Bangladesh Islami Chatra Sibir, 20002), , *Ganatantra* (Democracy) (Dhaka: Bangladesh Islami Chatra Sibir, 2006).

70. For details of ICS's programme action see *Karmapodhoti* (Functional Procedure) (Dhaka: Bangladesh Islami Chatrasibir (Dhaka: Bangladesh Chattra Sibir, 2001).

71. I personally visited the Jamaat office in Dhaka city in search of its publications. The person in charge of the publicity division was kind and courteous and handed over to me one copy each of most of its publications. None of the other party offices in the city was efficient and cared about its publication division.

72. Taslima Nasreen, *Lajja* (Bengali) (Dhaka: Pearl Publishers, 1993); the English translation *Lajja: Shame* (London: Penguin Books, 1994).

73. See Afsan Chowdhury, "Is 'Islam in danger' Slogan Back on Circulation?", *Daily Star*, May 21, 2002.

74. For a critical appreciation of the movie see " 'Matir Moina', a film conveying message of egalitarianism, *The Hindu*, January 26, 2006.

75. For details see The World Bank, *Pursuing Common Goals: Strengthening Relations between Government and Development NGOs* (Dhaka: University Press Limited, 1996) Chapter 1.

76. Based on my interactions with a number of functionaries including the BRAC.

77. For details of the rally see *Prothom Alo*, February 3, 2001 in which the most critical portions of the Muftis' speeches were reproduced.

78. For details of news coverage on the February 2, 2001 demonstration see *Prothom Alo* and *Daily Star*, February 3 and 4, 2001. One might find walls writings raising this slogan in different cities in Bangladesh including Dhaka.

79. *Prothom Alo*, February 9, 2001.

80. Most of the newspapers published stories on the nexus between the jihadis and the Ulema, and measures by the government to corner them firmly. See *Protom Alo* and *Daily Star*, February 3-10, 2001.

81. In the heart of Dhaka city such audio and video tapes and devices are available which indicates that there are listeners to such speeches. It is difficult to assess, without an empirical study, what appeal these speeches carry to the masses.

82. *Daily Star*, May 3, 2007.

83. The figures are drawn from various sources such as Bureau of Statistics, Muhammad Ghulam Kabir, *Minority Politics in Bangladesh* (Dhaka: New Delhi: Vikas, 1980), Chapter I and internet sources.

84. One of the well documented book on the atrocities committed on the Hindus is Salam Azad, *Hindu Somprodai Keno Bangladesh Tyag Koreshe* (Why are Hindu Community Leaving Bangladesh) (Kolkata: Punosho, 2001) also his "Status of Minorities in Bangladesh" in Jaideep Saikia (ed), *Bangladesh: Treading The Taliban Trail*, n. 27, pp. 107 and 114; and for some more details see *Nirjatoner Dalil – 2001* (Document on Atrocities), (Dhaka: Sanmilita Samajik Andololon, 2002).

85. Sultana Nahar, *A Comparative Study of Communalism in Bangladesh and India* (Dhaka: Dhaka Prokashon, 1994) pp. 260-273. Nahar provides a detailed account of the nature and places of attack. For a detailed analysis on marginalization of the minorities see Partha S. Ghosh, "Conservative Ascendancy in Bangladesh", *South Asian Survey*, Vol. 12, No. 2, 2005, pp. 247-265, especially, pp.253-257.

86. Based on my discussion with student leaders, media persons,

scholars and a few political activists belonging to the Awami League.

87. Rounaq Jahan, "Bangladesh in 2002: Imperiled Democracy", *Asian Survey*, Vo. XLIII, No. 1, January/February, 2003, pp. 222-229.

88. For some details see Ruchira Joshi, "Islamic Fundamentalism in Bangladesh and its Impact on Minorities" in Dipankar Sengupta and Sudhir Kumar Singh (eds), *Minorities and Human Rights in Bangladesh* (New Delhi: Spandan, 2003), pp. 89-114.

89. Society for Environment and Human Development, *Eighth Parliamentary Elections 2001* (Dhaka: 2001), p. 161. Also for details of pre and post elections violence committed on the minorities see Sanmilita Samajik Andolon, *Nirjatoner Dalil – 2001* (Document of Atrocities) (Dhaka: 2002).

90. For details see the Dhaka based newspapers published during the period from October 10 to 25, 2001.

91. *Prothom Alo*, October 16, 2001. Ten days later he, however, admitted that atrocities had been committed on the Hindu community. But he refrained from giving details of the crimes committed. For details see *Prothom Alo*, October 27, 2001.

92. Amnesty International, *Bangladesh: Attack on Members of the Hindu Community*, December 2001). Also see Bibhuranjan Sarkar, *Cleansing of Religious Minorities in Bangladesh* (Dhaka: Citizens' Voice, 2002) and Dipankar Sengupta and Sudhir Kumar Singh, *Minorities and Human Rights in Bangladesh* (New Delhi: Authorspress and SPANDAN, 2003).

93. *Prothom Alo*, November 17 and 18, 2001.

94. For some narrative and well documental account see Salam Azad, "State of Minorities in Bangladesh: From Secular to Islamic Hegemony", a paper presented at Regional Consultation on Minority Rights in South Asia held at Kathmandu in August 2004, http://www.mukto-mona.com/Articles/Saleem/secular_to_islamic.htm

95. See N.C. Bhowmick, "Repeal Enemy (Vested) Property Act for National Interest", *Daily Star*, November 29, 1998.
96. Abul Barakat (ed), *An Inquiry into Causes and Consequences of Deprivation of Hindu Minorities in Bangladesh through Vested Property Act* (Dhaka: Prip Trust, 2000), p. 63.
97. For a perspective understanding on the problems of minorities see Khan Md. Lutfor Rahman, "Minorities of Bangladesh and their Alienation", *Journal of Asiatic Society of Bangladesh*, Vol. 41. No. 2, December 1996, pp 299-314.
98. US Department of State, *Bangladesh: International Religious Freedom Report 2005,* http;//www.state.gov/g/drl/irf/2005.
99. *Prothom Alo*, November 1, 2003.
100. For the details see *Protom Alo* and *Daily Star*, April 19, 2005.
101. *Daily Star*, December 9, 2005.
102. For details see *Prothom Alo* and *Daily Star*, June 24, 2006.
103. For some details see *Human Rights News*, "Bangladesh: Government Fails to Act against Religious Violence", June 17, 2005.
104. Amnesty International Press Release, June 22, 2006, http://web.amnesty.org/library/index and n. 78.
105. For details see *Daily Star*, November 25, 2006.
106. Motiur Rahman, "Sarkar Akhon Ki Korese? (What the Government is doing now?)*Prothom Alo*, August 19, 2005.
107. For details of the news see *ibid*, June 23, 2003.
108. *ibid*, July 29, 2004.
109. *Sangbad*, April 9, 2005.
110. *ibid*, "Jongira Taka Pai Kothai?" (Where from the militants get money?), August 20, 2005.
111. Based on my interaction with a Jamaat functionary on November 29, 2006. Also see Talukdar Maniruzzaman, *The Bangladesh Revolution and Its Aftermath* (Dhaka:

University Press Limited, 1988) pp 32-33 and Ghulam Azam, *A Guide to the Islamic Movement*, n. 45, pp. 46-47.

112. B.M. Monoar Kabir, The Politics of Religion: The Case of Jamaat-e-Islami" a mimeographed article, 1986.

113. Abul Barakat, "Fundamentalist Economy in Bangladesh", *Daily Inqilab*, April 27, 2005 and his *Bangladeshe Maulobader Orthaniti* (Fundamentalist Economy in Bangladesh), (Dhaka: Mukti Bhawan, 2005).

114. *ibid*, p. 17.

115. *ibid*, p. 20.

116. For details of the prominent Islamic militant groups see http:/ /www.satp. org/satportp/_countries /bangladesh/ terroristoutfits 3/19/2007. Also see Bertil Lintner, "Religious Extremism and nationalism in Bangladesh" in Satu P. Limaye *et al.*, (eds), *Religious Radicalism and Security in South Asia* (Honolulu, Hawaii: Asia Pacific Centre for Security Studies, 2004) Appendix 1, pp. 435-436.

117. *Prothom Alo*, August 14, 2005.

118. For details see *Daily Star*, March 31, 2007. The other four of the executed persons were Abdul Awal of JMB, Ataur Rahman, a brother of Abdur Rahman, suicide bomber Iftekhar Hasan Mamun and Khaled Saifullah of JMB.

119. For details see "Tyrant Bangla Bhai finally captured", *Daily Star*, March 7, 2006 reported the details of the capture of dreaded Bangla Bhai in Mymensingh district after a brief skirmish on March 6, 2006. The text of report is an unequivocal expression of the magnitude of hate the liberal section of the society had borne against him.

120. For some details see *Prothom Alo*, December 22 and 23, 2004.

121. See http://www.satp.org/satportp/countries/bangladesh/terroristoutfits/huji.htm.3/19/2007. This website states that HuJI was established in 1992 reportedly with the assistance from Osama bin Laden's International Islamic Front.

122. For details of the confessional statement of Mufti Abdul Hannan and HuJI's strategies as revealed by him see *Daily Star*, November 22, 2006.

123. *Prothom Alo*, July 21, 2000 reported that the during its routine check the police recovered explosive devices in Gopalganj district near the venue where the Prime Minister was scheduled to make a public address. The police suspected that the plot to blow up Shiekh Hasina was engineered by Mufti Abdul Hannan.

124. *Daily Star*, January 19, 1999. 18 months after Shamsur Rahman was killed in Jessore on July 16, 2000. For details see *Prothom Alo*, and *Daily Star*, July 19, 2000.

125. *Prothom Alo*, October 18, 2005.

126. *Assam Tribune*, May 28, 2007.

127. Bertil Lintner, "Religious Extremism and Nationalism in Bangladesh" in Satu P. Limaye *et.al.* (eds), *Religious Radicalism and Security in South Asia*, n. 116, p.418, for details of relevant discussion on the rise of Islamic militancy see pp. 413-466.

128. For a brief note on Madrassa education in Bangladesh with a comparative perspective see Mumtaz Ahmad, "Madrassa Education in Pakistan and Bangladesh" in Satu P. Limaye *et.al., ibid*, pp. 101-107

129. For details of madrassa education in Bangladesh see A.K.M. Azharul Islam and Shah Muhammad Habibur Rahman, *Bangladesh School O Madrassa Sikshaniti O Pathyakram* (School and Madrassa Education and Curriculum in Bangladesh (Dhaka: Islamic Academy, 2003).

130. Salahuddin Babar, "Rise of the Right", *Probe Newsmagazine* (Dhaka), March 1-15, 2002.

131. *ibid.*

132. *Daily Star*, August 22, 2006.

133. In my interaction with the Chairman of Tamjmul Ummah Foundation, Habibullah Muhammad Iqbal, on November 23, 2006, he expressed happiness about the decision, for, his

variety of modern madrassa called Tanjimul Ummah Cadet Madrassa, could be equated with any other modern educational establishment run by the government. At the same time he also expressed doubt as to the standard of other Qawmi madrassas.

134. For an analytical criticism on the issue see Inam Ahmed and Zayadul Ahsan, "Islam being used for political gains, again", *Daily Star*, August 24, 2006.

135. Meghna Guhathakurta, n. 68.

136. Marcus Franda, *Bangladesh: The First Decade* (New Delhi: South Asia Publishers, 1982) p. 332.

137. The Left opposition is too fragile to fight against the Islamist. The Awami League was in grave crisis during the military rule from 1977 to 1990. It was in opposition during 1991-1996 and again during 2001-2006. The BNP was in the opposition during 1996-2001. While the BNP is a close ally of the Jamaat and has soft corner for the Islamist as testified to by the statements of BNP leaders from time to time. For a classic statement of one of the functionaries of the BNP in defence of Bangla Bhai see *Protom Alo*, August 22, 2005. For a detailed study on the opposition see Al Masud Hasanuzzaman, *Role of Opposition in Bangladesh Politics* (Dhaka: University Press Limited, 1998). Also see Badaruddin Umar, "Problems of Left Unity in Bangladesh", *Economic and Political Weekly*, July 21, 1990, pp.1576-1577.

138. Moudud Ahmed, *Democracy and Challenge of Development: A Study of Political and Military Interventions in Bangladesh* (Dhaka: University Press Limited, 1995).

139. Shahriar Kabir, *Resist Fundamentalism: Focus on Bangladesh* (Dhaka: Central Committee for Resisting Killers and Collaborators of Bangladesh Liberation War of 1971, 1999).

140. *Daily Star*, November 23 and December 2, 2001.

141. *Daily Star*, February 28 and August 14, 2004.

142. For details of the news of Kabira's assassination see *Daily Star* and *Protom Alo*, January 28, 2005.

143. *Daily Star*, March 7, 2002.

144. India News, http://www.newkerala.com/news dated 2/17/2006.

145. M. Rashiduzzaman, "Bangladesh in 2001: The Election and a New Political Reality", *Asian Survey*, Vol. XLII. No. 1, January/February 2002, pp.188-189.

146. There is no official data on the percentage of votes secured by the Jamaat. However, the study conducted by the Democracy Watch suggests that it secured 4.29 per cent votes. See *Jai Jai Din*, October 23, 2001.

147. I was told that the beneficiaries of the Islami Bank are reportedly told to put this kind of slogans on their auto-rickshaws, adhere to conservative religio-social life forcing women to put on burqa and men to grow beard.

148. It is important to note that the poor and rural women do not put burqa. They cannot afford to put it purely for two economic reasons. A burqa is more expensive than a sari. A burqa clad women can work neither in an agricultural field nor in a garment factory because of its cumbersome size and style. The rich simply would hardly use it because of its uniform and uni-colour style. It remains confined to middle class women who do not do physical labour and who can afford to purchase.

149. One notable study had been done by Rajarshi Dasgupta entitled "Representations of Communalism: A Study on Recent Print Media Reports in Bangladesh", *Asian Studies*, Vol. XXII, January-December, 2004, pp. 39-63. It covers only print media.

150. For details see *Sangbad*, September 19, 2001. The newspaper give a coverage of the BNP-led attack on Awami League offices and supporters in Kachua on September 14. See *Sangbad*, September 15, 2001.

151. Rajarshi Dasgupta, "Representations of Communalism: A Study on Recent Print Media Reports in Bangladesh", n. 146, and *Nirjatoner Dalil*, n. 72.

152. *Sangbad*, October 1, 2001.

153. Rajarshi Dasgupta, "Representations of Communalism: A Study on Recent Print Media Reports in Bangladesh", n. 146, p. 52.

154. Drawn from my interaction with a few leading media personalities such as Aminur Rashid.

155. *Ajker Kagoj*, October 16, 2001. Even Muslim families known to be the supporters of the Awami League were not spared from assault, rape, killing and destruction of property, although the number may be few compared to the Hindus.

156. For a representative public voice against terrorism see A.M.M. Shawkat Ali, *Faces of Terrorism* (Dhaka: University Press Limited, 2006).

5

IMPACT ON INDIA

As already stated, Bangladesh has a common border with India, 4,053 km long, which accounts for more than 95 per cent of its international boundary. Any development in that country is bound to have impact on India, more so when the border is mostly porous and is afflicted by weak security arrangement. Its border adjoining India's North East has been an easy route for the Bangladeshi migrants to enter India.[1] The mighty river Brahmaputra cuts across the international border with Bangladesh making it too difficult to demarcate and manage it. The river islands (Chars) appear and disappear frequently – sometimes within the territorial jurisdiction of India and sometimes on the other side. Who the inhabitants of the Chars are is a problematic question to reply. The porous border provides escape routes to the North East rebels to enter Bangladesh, where they have established many camps with the active support of the jihadi groups and with the connivance of the Government of Bangladesh.[2] There is a marriage of convenience between the jihadi groups in Bangladesh and the North East insurgents including the Muslim militants. There are reliable reports to the effect that the nexus among all the jihadi and insurgents groups of India and Bangladesh is mutually rewarding, and therefore, has been working for a considerable period of time. A chemistry of terrorism is prepared in this way at the active support of the ISI of Pakistan and the DGFI of Bangladesh.[3] A common agenda unite them facilitating workable coordination and thus makes them effective in operational tactics.

There is a South Asian perspective of Islamic fundamentalism of militant nature. All the jihadi groups have effective networks covering the entire South Asia. The Islamic militant organizations in Bangladesh and India reportedly maintain active relations with Pakistan-based militant groups, such as Harkatul Mujahidin and Jaish-e-Muhammad.[4] All these groups have a common anti-India agenda, which makes it easy for them to have a meeting ground. The political Islam in Bangladesh has been trying to exploit this commonality to its advantage. The Bangladesh government led by the BNP had been adopting an anti-India position all through since the time of Ziaur Rahman. In its common rhetoric, it has been trying to arouse popular sentiment against India. In their public addresses, Ziaur Rahman and his successor Khaleda Zia used the anti-India bogey to convince that India had been playing a 'big brother' role in South Asia; points stressed were: the Government of India had a military and territorial ambition to capture Chittagong area, a lot of injustice had been done to Bangladesh by depriving it of its legitimate share of the Ganges water, the imbalance of trade at India's instance has affected the economic development of Bangladesh and the Chakma rebels had been aided and abetted by New Delhi to create troubles in the Chittagong Hill Tract.[5] The jihadi groups too have almost similar anti-Indian campaigns and slogans, centering, however, around the broad agenda of Islamization in the region. In the pursuit of their agenda they have used terror tactics on Indian soil.

As already stated in the preceding Chapter, the HuJI had launched deadly attack on the American Center, Kolkata in January 2002. There were reports about its involvement in number of terrorist activities in India. To name a few are

– it triggered off blast in Delhi-bound Shramjeevi Express near Jaunpur in Uttar Pradesh on July 28, 2005 in which 14 persons were killed and 79 were injured; it exploded bombs inside the Sankat Mochan temple and cantonment railway station in Varanasi on March 7, 2006 in which 20 persons were killed and 100 persons injured; and its latest act of terrorism was inside the Mecca Mosque, Hyderabad, on May 19, 2007 killing 16 persons and injuring 50 others and two more blasts in the city on August 24, 2007 killing 40 and injuring 70. The media reports and the police assertion of HuJI's involvement in all these terrorist attacks have been confirmed recently, when two HuJI terrorists, nabbed on June 23, 2007 in Lucknow with arms and explosives, confessed their involvement in all these terror attacks on Indian soil.[6] The two terrorists are the HuJI's agents in India, while the kingpin of the August 25 blasts having HuJI affiliation had been held in Bangladesh on September 3, 2007. Their deadly activities throw an ominous signal as to how the Bangladeshi jihadi outfits are spreading their wings to unleash terror in the region.

To arouse public passion among the common masses is an easy task in an economically and educationally backward country. As stated in Chapter I, Bangladesh is a poor and backward country. The backwardness is prominently reflected in its economic performance and in other relevant indices, more pronounced is the backwardness in the field of education. A poor country which has literacy rate of less than 50 per cent is susceptible to misinformation and to catchy fanatical slogans. Bangladesh does not stand out as an exception. The audio tapes, public speeches by the political and militant leaders inimical to India and the sermons of the jihadi-oriented Imams in the mosques could arouse mass hysteria.[7] The government of Bangladesh under Khaleda Zia reportedly had a hidden agenda to encourage, indirectly through inaction, all the anti-India militants operating from its soil. It has a well-planned diplomatic objective also to facilitate Bangladesh in coming closer to China and Pakistan.[8]

Anti-Indian position

The India-Bangladesh relations traverse through a strenuous and difficult path. From an apogee of cordial and mutually appreciated relations since March 1971, the scenario suddenly turned to mutual distrust and suspicion after the assassination of Sheikh Mujibur Rehman in August 1975. Although India's tremendous humanitarian, moral, diplomatic, and more importantly, military assistance to the people of Bangladesh during the war of Independence is well recognized[9], with the change of government in the post-1975 era when military generals took over, a visible tendency to fix India on certain contentious issues plummeted the relationship to a considerable low. Dhaka's perception was that India earned a strategic advantage in South Asia by liberating Bangladesh[10] and that the influential sections in New Delhi wanted Bangladesh to be eternally grateful.[11] Among the issues that plagued the relationship, the most prominent are:

(i) The Treaty of Friendship, Cooperation and Peace signed between the two countries during the visit of Prime Minister Indira Gandhi on March 19, 1972 at the instance of Sheikh Mujibur Rehman who had felt "uncomfortable with the international environment"[12] The opponents to Sheikh Muijb and the successive post-Mujib regimes considered it to be discriminatory and heavily advantageous to India's interests.[13]

(ii) There had been an allegation that "some of the Indian soldiers" conducted themselves in a disgraceful manner in looting or forcibly taking away "foreign made cars and other consumer goods as 'booty' from Bangladesh"...A majority of Bangladeshi people who had earlier greeted Indian soldiers was disappointed by the reckless and unchecked behaviour of some of the Indian soldiers".[14] At the same time, however, the fact that such army personnel were arrested and quickly put up for trial in military courts[15] did not receive due attention of the media in Bangladesh.[16]

(iii) The sharing of the Ganges waters in accordance with the April 1975 limited agreement to enhance the upper limit of India's withdrawal of water from 11,000 to 16,000 cusecs which underwent a substantial change after August 1975 had been a source of tension.[17] The issue dominated the domestic politics and used to remain a major source of irritation in the relations between the two countries for a considerably long period of time till the conclusion of the treaty on sharing Ganga waters at Farakka on December 12, 1996 between H.D. Deve Gowda and Sheikh Hasina, which provided for a larger volume of water "in accordance with the principles of equity, fair play and no harm to either party".[18] However, in recent years the volume of water released at the Farakka point sometimes exceeds the expected figure.[19]

(iv) The Tin Bigha corridor is one of the contentious issues. India and Bangladesh inherited some territorial problems in the form of enclaves in the territories of both the countries. A small patch of Indian land measuring an acre known as Tin Bigha Corridor separates two enclaves of Bangladesh, named Dahagram and Panbari. The connectivity of the two enclaves could not be resolved during before the independence of Bangladesh. However, the Indo-Bangladesh Land Boundary Agreement signed on May 16, 1974 provided a solution to the problem. Under the Agreement India agreed in principle to lease in perpetuity the Tin Bigha Corridor measuring about 178x85 metres to Bangladesh to provide access to and from the two Bangladesh territories in lieu of Berubari. Bangladesh's complaint was that while India secured the possession of Berubari, Tin Bigha Corridor had not been handed over. However, on June 26, 1992, the corridor was actually handed over to Bangladesh.[20] The delay due to a case filed challenging the agreement to lease in perpetuity, caused irritation between the two countries.[21]

(v) Return and rehabilitation of the Chakmas in the CHT, during the Awami League rule from 1996-2001, had been considered by the Jamaat and the BNP to be a result of India's pressure. There were about 60,000 Chakma refugees camped in Tripura, who took refuge in India due to absence of security in their normal habitat. The Chakmas formed a group named Shanti Bahini to protect themselves against any attack by Bangladeshi nationals. Bangladesh used to level charges that India had been providing sanctuary, training and arms to the Shanti Bahini.[22]

The deterioration in the relationship between the two countries had begun on the very day of Independence of Bangladesh. The surrender ceremony of the Pakistan forces on December 16, 1971 was the starting point. It was alleged that the entire ceremony of Pakistani surrender was an all-India show. The Mukti Bahini which played an important role in the liberation of the country was not given an equal status. The Instrument of surrender was signed by Lieutenant General Jagit Singh Aurora and General Amir Abdullah Khan Niazi. General A.M.G. Osmany abstained from attending the function, in anticipation of a secondary role awaiting him there. Two of his junior officers represented the Mukti Bahini. The mute expression of unhappiness at the structured arrangement on the historic day was the starting point of deterioration of relationship between the two countries. Amena Mohsin writes:

> Seeds of anti-Indianism were shown in the nascent army of Bangladesh right at the time of independence. The *Mukti Bahini* resented the way the surrender ceremony of Pakistan Army was handled. It was the *Mukti Bahini* which had fought the war for eight long months; yet the Indian army which had come at the eleventh hour stole the thunder. The Pakistani army was to surrender to the joint command of Indo-Bangladesh Forces. During the surrender ceremony on 16 December 1971 Colonel Osmani, the Commander of Bangladesh liberation forces, was absent from the ceremony.[23]

There are issues of trade imbalance between India and Bangladesh which tends to cause tension. Bangladesh holds the provisions of Indo-Bangladesh Trade Agreement signed on March 28, 1972 responsible for this.[24]

There is a striking correlation between the anti-Indian feeling and the rise of Islamists in Bangladesh. India played the most crucial role in the liberation of Bangladesh. Naturally it was expected that the relations between the two neighbours would be cordial and mutually beneficial. It appeared to be so till the assassination of Sheikh Mujib. In the post-Mujib era the relations started deteriorating. There are many people in Bangladesh, at all levels of the society, who believe that without the active help and the military intervention of India, it surely would have been impossible for the people of Bangladesh to become a free nation. At the same time there are people who believe that the Government of India behaved like a 'big brother' which led to the deterioration of the relations.[25] Their arguments, besides the points already enumerated in this section, could be summarized as follows:[26]

An unusual situation cropped up with the deployment of Indian bureaucrats in newly liberated Bangladesh. It was alleged that the Indian bureaucrats had the 'big brother' and overtly arrogant attitude and hence injured the pride and sentiment of the Bangladeshi officers, who had considerable experience in administration. They divulged the matter to the local press which took no time to flash it in the print media. The publication of such news of the dissatisfaction of Bangladeshi officers caused bitter feeling in the minds of people.[27]

The general public appeared to be unhappy at the way the Pakistani forces were allowed to return home, without any trial for their war-crimes. A huge number totaling 93,000 Pakistani soldiers surrendered to the Indian forces on December 16, 1971. The people of Bangladesh expected that a proper court would be instituted to try many of the men and officers and that some degree of punishment would be awarded to the guilty, at the least to 195 army officers and soldiers who were identified as war criminals. It was commonly held that India had the key to put them on trial. The Bangladeshi side expresses dissatisfaction at the Indian decision to free all the prisoners, without any trial, for by doing so India deprived Bangladesh of a strong leverage with Pakistan in negotiating certain outstanding issues.[28]

There other irritants such as Bangladesh harbouring the North-East militants, the problems of displaced Chakma population and the influx of Bangladeshi nationals into India have been sources of tension between the two countries.

Bangladesh complains that there has been imbalance of trade between India and Bangladesh. Bangladesh's import from India stood at a staggering Taka 6973 crore in 2002-03 while its export to India is considerably lower. Table 5.1 presents a balance sheet of trade relations of Bangladesh with some major countries.

Table 5.1

Trade relations of Bangladesh in million Taka

Countries	Export					Import				
	98-99	99-00	00-01	01-02	02-03	98-99	99-00	00-01	01-02	02-03
USA	96244	99385	119395	126595	113851	11670	17187	15503	23742	16079
UK	19964	20600	26989	-	35629	8189	7325	8070	7643	7948
JAPAN	3834	4100	5508	4781	6342	27057	28119	31848	32477	34310
KUWAIT	25	17	140	56	170	2223	3234	620	827	2725
SAUDI ARAB	240	201	729	433	594	5550	10807	11415	6486	5358
INDIA	390	869	1325	1238	1867	59278	24763	47571	60454	69739
PAKISTAN	2249	2306	1756	1571	1872	4690	5223	5666	6258	5429
TOTAL*	245620	247415	487049	254660	337885	341017	372077	443698	542629	506200

*Total volume of trade with all countries of the world.

Source: *Statistical Yearbook of Bangladesh, 2004.*

Trade relations of Bangladesh in million Taka

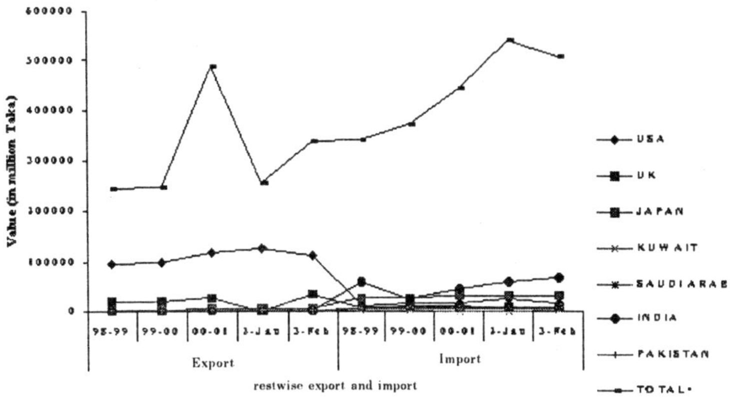

Indian source suggest similar imbalance in Indo-Bangladesh trade Table 5.2.

Table 5.2
Indo-Bangladesh trade figures in million dollars

Year	*India's export*	*India's import*	*Trade balance*	*Total trade*
2000-01	872.98	73.87	799.11	946.78
2001-02	1002.18	59.12	943.06	1061.30
2002-03	1176.00	62.05	1113.95	1238.24
2003-04	1740.75	77.63	1663.12	1818.38
2004-05	1586.18	54.88	1531.30	1641.06

Source: Directorate General of Commercial Intelligence and Statistics, India

Indo-Bangladesh trade figures in million dollars

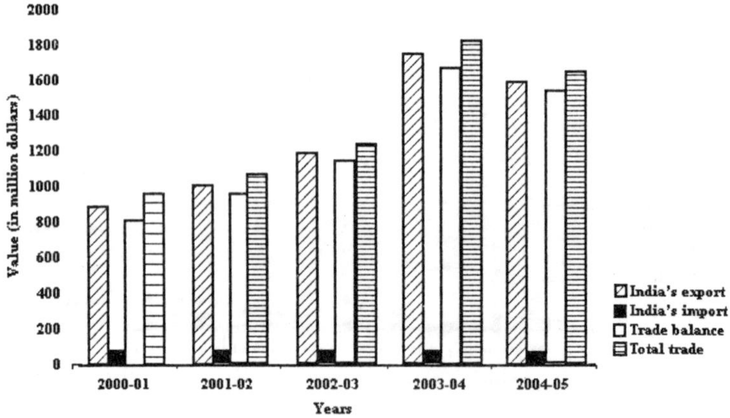

The issue of trade imbalance is dependent on how fast the economy of the two countries opened up on reciprocal basis. It is stressed that too much importance should not be attached to the question of trade deficit in view of the fact that "nearly 60 per cent of Bangladesh's official imports from India (including fabric and yarn) were in the nature of inputs, primarily meant for export production. Such imports strengthened Bangladesh's export processing (value addition) capacity in readymade garments."[29] The problems of trade imbalance is, as pointed out by Prime Minister Manmohan Singh in an interview with *Daily Star* and *Prothom Alo*, is not 'one sided'. He recognized that there was a problem which could be dealt with by means of removing quantitative restriction on reciprocal basis.[30]

Despite the fact that Bangladesh has trade deficit with its South Asian neighbours, its trade deficit with India becomes an explosive issue in its domestic politics. In order to disabuse the suspicion and apprehensions of Bangladesh, Manmohan Singh, while representing the country in a

SAARC conference held in Dhaka in 1994 made a statement that deserves attention: He said:

> If you have normal transit routes you will find that Bangladesh's balance of trade with India will increase dramatically. If our trade regime becomes liberal, in the long run Chittagong can become a better place for joint venture production for supply of goods to North-Eastern states than shipping them from Bombay. All have a vision that transit route and liberalisation of trade policies will offer vast opportunities of industrialisation for Bangladesh helping the North-Eastern states of India also to flourish.[31]

Recognizing the prevalence of the existing trade deficit, it is argued that the issue could well be looked after by certain concrete steps such as "free flow of FDI and joint ventures between India and Bangladesh based on natural resources and factor abundance".[32] It is argued that certain factors such as non-tariff barriers, marketing, technology upgradation, product diversification and changes in commodity composition of exports especially in favour of high value-added products could eventually reduce the trade deficit to a considerable extent. The prospect of rail and road connectivity between India's North East and Bangladesh would integrate the markets of the region.[33] Unfortunately, Bangladesh government is yet to show its willingness to facilitate the process of connectivity.

To achieve a mutually beneficial target what is needed is building of confidence between the two governments and mutual appreciation of each others points of view, and diplomatic exercises towards confidence building. It is argued that the negative position taken by Bangladesh on the issue of gas pipeline by linking it with its demand for a free trade corridor to Nepal regates the prospect of reducing the trade deficit.[34] Bangladesh's insistence on the use of its containers only for shipment and transportation of goods to and from

Nepal has complicated the whole issue of creating a free trade corridor.

It is relevant to point out here that India's economic assistance to Bangladesh in 1972-73 was Rs.133 crore. Bangladesh received the lion's share of the total assistance of Rs.150 crore offered to all the South Asian countries.[35] However, there was dramatic decline in the quantum of assistance during the post Mujib era, mainly because of the anti-Indian position taken by the successors of Sheikh Mujib.[36] The general plea among the media persons in Bangladesh is that India could easily double its import bill from Bangladesh in return for latter's huge imports.[37] The trade relations are dovetailed with other important issues such as transit and trans-shipment of goods, and upgradation of border trade infrastructure which could be mutually beneficial. These are complex issues involving spillover problems, such as migration, drug and human trafficking, transmission of HIV and insurgency. However, there is an enormous prospect of international connectivity through the proposed Asian Highway, which is expected to link Bangladesh to India's North East; at the same time, there are advantages of sharing of energy resources, communication network, technological knowledge, besides water and limestone resources, which need to be emphasized.

Despite the inherent differences, Bangladesh has to value its trade relations with India. That is why Rehman Sobhan writes: "Bangladesh's ongoing search for greater access to the Indian market is therefore not just an issue of commercial relations. The political economy of Indo-Bangladesh relations has its own special features which merits separate discussion."[38]

At any rate, the deterioration of relations between the two countries is always exploited by Islamic fundamentalists to raise the Indian bogey to further their campaign against

India. It becomes easier for them to exploit the anti-Indian (anti-Hindu) sentiment for mobilizing their support base to their advantage. It is easier for the parties like the BNP and the Jamaat to use its anti-Indian card as a vote catching device; in fact the same device has been used extensively by the jihadi groups to mobilize support.

Jihadi groups in North East India

India's North East has a large number of militant groups some of which are secessionist and others are taking a militant course in order to get their political demands fulfilled through violence and intimidation. The most feared militant groups are the NSCN (both the IM and the Khaplang factions), the ULFA, the TNV and the NDFB. While both the factions of the NSCN have training camps in mostly in Myanmar, the rest have bases in Bangladesh. There are a few jihadi groups in Assam[39], the most prominent among them is the MULTA, which reportedly operates from a river island called Shialmari Char in the Barpeta district. It was founded in 1994 by an Imam of a mosque named Muslim Ali in the wake of the Bodo's attack on Muslim areas in the district and a massacre at a relief camp in Barpeta by the Bodo militants.[40] It was formed with the objectives to provide armed safeguard to Muslims in lower Assam. Muslim Ali later on surrendered and decided to abandon the course of militancy and returned to his mosque as Imam. The police sources state that with the surrender of Muslim Ali and some of his cadres, the outfit suffered a blow and those who are still in the fading organization have become extortionists and criminals. They do not have a specific cause to pursue.

The MULTA's areas of operation are the chars of the Brahmaputra River in Goalpara, Dhubri, Barpeta, Darrang, Nalbari, Sonitpur and Nagaon districts.[41] The most notable the Shialmari Char in the district of Barpeta, where the outfit had a strong base. However, it is reported that there had been erosion in the support base after the surrender of its top leaders including Muslim Ali. It was a big blow to the outfit when in two years time as many as 130 members had surrendered. The security forces have arrested 39 cadres. One of its leaders named Akram Master who hails from Dhubri and received training in Bangladesh, eventually established links with Jaish-e-Muhammad. He is reportedly settled in Pakistan. Maulana Fakhruddin, who hails from Jogighopa in Goalpara, and a product of Deoband madrassa, was another notable leader. He too surrendered. It has been found that most of the leaders of Muslim militant groups are products of private madrassas.

The surrendered MULTA cadres revealed in interrogations that most of them crossed over to Bangladesh and took military training there, mostly in the premises of private madrassas, imparted by "tall, sturdy and Urdu speaking" men who appeared to be Pakistanis. The trainers used to be rough in behaviour and often ill-treated the "weak and soft-spoken" insurgents. They disdainfully used to dismiss the MULTA cadres as "good for nothing".[42] The training camps were located in three adjoining districts of Bangladesh, Kurigram, Jamalpur and Sherpur, very close to Meghalaya, and Cox Bazar.[43] The latest information revealed that the MULTA had organized a training camp in Bangladesh in November 2004. In a meeting of its general body held on May 25, 2006 it decided to organize another training session before December 2006 in order to revamp the organizational structure. It failed to do so owing to the end of the tenure of the BNP-led government as also tough measures taken by the caretaker government in dealing with jihadi groups in Bangladesh. It may be noted that the JMJB, the JMB and the HuJI were either founded in or are operating from some districts close to India such as Dinajpur, Sherpur or Jamalpur. These districts are known to be backward economically and educationally. These districts have high concentration of unregistered private madrassas, which are known to be the breeding grounds for Islamic fundamentalism. The Intelligence sources indicate that the ULFA has a number of training camps in Sherpur. Naturally the MULTA has been maintaining its links with most of the Islamic militant groups in Bangladesh including the HuJI, the JMB and the JMJB, as also with the ULFA. Newspaper reports and government sources suggest that it has links with the ISI.[44]

The MULTA's approximate strength is 250. However, the number of active cadre is not more than 50. It is dependent on "contribution and donations" offered by its sympathizers, rich Muslims and local contractors. There are a few instances of extortion but there is no record of kidnapping and killing.

There are a few Muslim militant outfits which have come into being with more or less similar objectives, such as, to protect and defend the community from any possible assault by any organization, to instill and strengthen the ideals of Islam in the mind of the community, to make people lead a puritan life based on Qur'an and Hadith and to establish an 'Islamic state' comprising the Muslim dominated areas in Assam. Most notable amongst these are :

- Muslim United Liberation Front of Assam (MULFA) formed in Nagaon district in 1990 as a fallout of massacre of Muslims in Nellie in the district of Marigaon in February 1983. Its strength is not known. It is reported that some of its cadres have undergone arms training in Bangladesh in close cooperation with the jihadi outfits in Bangladesh. There is no report of extortion, kidnapping and killing by the outfit. It is believed that the by now almost defunct MULFA used to depend on the funds provided by businessmen and contractors.

- United Muslim Liberation Front of Assam (UMLFA) was established in February 1997 at Chowranghee

Hillock under the Katgorah police station in the Cachar district of Assam. It was reported that the UMLFA was formed as a result of the merger of the MULTA, MULFA and MLA (Muslim Liberation Army, which is said to be defunct). It was formed as an umbrella organization. Subsequently, it could not hold the unity of the three outfits due to leadership and personality clashes.

- People's United Liberation Front (PULF) is basically a Manipur based Muslim militant group formed in1994-95. It has reportedly some hold in the localities of the Cachar district of Assam bordering Manipur. Its activities came to light when one of its activists, Salauddin Kazi was arrested along with two others on April 19, 2006 in Lakhipur sub-division in Cachar. Its activities such as fund raising, arms training and meetings in secret places were confined to just two Imphal districts. Its cadres reportedly receive training in Bangladesh.

Three striking points deserve attention. First, all the Muslim militant organizations send their cadres to Bangladesh for arms training. They consider Bangladesh to be the last destination for shelter, training and arms. The reason is simple and understandable. It is easy to cross over to Bangladesh due to the existence of porous international border between India and Bangladesh. In common parlance of insurgency Bangladesh has been a safe haven for the insurgents of North East India because of the 'non-friendly' attitude of its successive governments towards India[45], the logistics offered by the Islamic militants of Bangladesh and the training imparted by the ISI personnel.

Second, they advance tumultuous arguments rationalizing the formation of their organizations. Some of these are - (i) 'recent attacks on the Muslims' compelled them to have their own militant outfits to "protect and defend" the community against any future attack; (ii) they want to be a part of Islamic resurgence in terms of armed preparation; (iii) they have wider design to create an independent political space for the Muslims; and (iv) they want to prove that "sounds of gun could be heard from a distance". It appears that none of the leaders have debated about the chimerical foundation of their organizations.

Third, unlike the Bangladeshi militant outfits the North East jihadis do not appear to have an agenda to force the Muslim society to follow the puritan ways of life as dictated by the mullahs and fundamentalists.

Closely related is the issue of arms and drug smuggling. The gravity of the arms trafficking was unmasked on April 2, 2004 when Bangladesh police, army and coast guards confiscated a huge cache of arms. It was reported that the security personnel took ten hours to count the different variety of arms seized from the Chittagong Urea Fertilizer jetty.[46] The quantity of arms captured exceeded all earlier records[47], which indicated in clear terms the magnitude of the illegal arms trafficking that had been going on in Bangladesh in which jihadi outfits of North East might have a share.

Madrassas in Assam[48]

The Muslim population in Assam is about 30 per cent which is next to Lakshadeep and Jammu and Kashmir. While a line of demarcation between the Hindus and the Muslims living in Upper Assam in terms of education and economic development could not be drawn because of the social setting, the Muslims living in the Lower Assam, most of who are immigrants from Bangladesh, are generally backward economically and educationally. The poor and backward Muslims in Lower and Central Assam, a substantial number (estimated to be 12,18,509) of whom live in the river islands called Chars[49], find it difficult to send their children to general schools run by the state. They generally send their children to the private madrassas, which are unregistered and which do not have a uniform and regulated curriculum.

There are four different types of madrassas in Assam.[50] These are as follows:

(i) the government run madrassas, which follow the curriculum prepared by the State Board of Secondary Education, Assam, which include science, mathematics, social studies besides Arabic and theological courses. These are maintained with a regular state grant and are like any other general schools.

(ii) the madrassas under the Madrassa Education Board, which follow a regulated curriculum that includes science, mathematics and social studies, with higher emphasis on the Arabic language , Qur'an and its interpretation and theology. They have graded levels such as primary, secondary, higher secondary and graduate courses.

(iii) Hafizia and Kharizia madrassas, purely private and follow an unregulated curriculum. The Hafizia madrassas teach how to memorize the Qur'an recited in a particular tone. Some ideas of Islam and interpretation of the Qur'an are also imparted. The products of these madrassas are called Hafiz (one who knows). The Kharizia madrassas teach how to memorize only a few chapters or Suras of the Qur'an. They teach other theological matters. Their products are called Kari. These madrassas do not teach any science, mathematics or social studies.

(iv) Private madrassas which follow the curriculum prepared by the Bhaskhandi Madrassa, Cachar. The students studying in this variety are taught the Qur'an, Islamic theology, history of Islam and elements of arithmetic.

The Hafizia and Kharizia private madrassas are not registered madrassas. There is no official statistics about them. They depend on donation from individuals and private agencies. It is difficult to ascertain their sources of income. They impart free education and maintain hostels where the boarders are not charged any fee. It is believed that these private madrassas get funds from some 'corrupt' politicians and government officers, and foreign sources, mainly oil-rich Arab countries and funneled through informal channels. As in the case of Bangladesh, Islamic Heritage Society of Kuwait and other Revival of Islamic Societies with branches in Saudi Arabia, Kuwait, Qatar and United Arab Emirates are the funding sources for the madrassas, ostensibly to promote Islamic education. The madrassas collect fund form individuals during the month of Ramdan. Lack of transparency about the sources of funds put the madrassas under cloud of suspicion.

Some of these Hafizia and Kharizia madrassas indulge in false glorification of Islam and hate campaign against other religious communities. To cite one example, the Mufti of one of such a madrassa in the congregation of students recited the following in an emotional way:

What is the total Muslim population of the world?

Ten thousand crore.

Who built the pyramids?

The Muslims.

Who built the great China wall?

Changiz Khan, a Muslim.

Who built Tajmahal?

Emperor Shahjahan.

Who constructed the hanging garden in Persia?

Abu Saad Nazar, a Muslim.[51]

The innocent and uneducated children value these misinformation and misinterpretation of history as almost divine words. These students after finishing their education become mullas and imams in villages and reproduce the same in religious congregations. The most disturbing part of their education is that they are not exposed to social studies, science and mathematics. The argument is that these subjects would pollute the young mind and turn them into atheists and munafiqs (deviators). These private madrassas do not subscribe newspapers and magazines. The boarders in the hostels are not allowed to listen to radio news and other programmes. There is no question of getting access to television programmes. They are told that the televisions are nothing but "Satanic Boxes". In other words the students are virtually kept totally insulated from the rest of the world. It is horrific to find boys of very tender age kept within regimented and sordid conditions. Equally disturbing and horrifying is the scurrilous hate campaign indulged in by the Muftis and teachers. To quote one such sermon in a congregation:

> God has made Islam the best religion in the world. Only the believers have the entitlement to be in the Heaven. All others will perish in the hell. Non-believers are to be despised and looked down upon.

Such provocative and rabid communal utterances motivate and prepare the fanatic elements to carry on subversive activities. This is the common language used by the fundamentalists all over the world. This is the language of the jihadi preachers in Bangladesh that gets echoed in India. As already stated there had been a series of attacks on minorities in Bangladesh soon after the 2001 elections. The attackers were reportedly Islamic zealots, mostly ill-educated madrassa products, who were inspired by such communal campaigns. The new recruits are told that they are in the path of Allah and that if killed they will find a place in

Heaven and that their families will be looked after by the ummah. Although there is no trace of any arms training in madrassas in Assam, it is alleged that some of the products of the madrassas are picked up for militancy. As already stated most of the leaders of the Muslim militant groups are products of madrassas; but it could not be ascertained whether the private madrassas provide their infrastructure to the militants.

It is difficult to assess objectively the magnitude of the socio-political problem posed by the private madrassas in Assam due to lack of information. They are not registered. Secondly, it is not known what the students in these seminaries are taught owing to the lack of proper and regulated curriculum. It is indicative of the gravity of the problem. What social service or community service will such products of these private madrassas render after the completion of their courses? Will they not be a huge liability on the society and the country? These and other relevant issues demand a thorough study on the private madrassas in Assam.

The situation in the private madrassas including the Hafizia madrassas is a reflection of the situation now obtaining in Bangladesh, where these institutions have been the breeding grounds and recruitment centres of jihadi forces. In Assam, it could not be ascertained, due to the lack of empirical data, whether private madrassas have become recruitment centres of jihadi elements. Except for newspaper reports and revelation of some of the surrendered militants there is no reliable data on the exact state of affairs in the private madrassas in Assam and their extreneious agenda, if any.

It is relevant to mention that the economically weakest section of the Muslims send their children to the private madrassas knowing fully well that their children have an extremely limited scope for livelihood after passing out of such schools. They know that their children will be employable only in mosques and maktabs and a few madrassas. Yet they send their children to these madrassas because of the fact that there they get two square of meals and shelter for free. They need not spend anything for their education. Since they cannot afford to send their children to any regular school, because of poverty, they find private madrassas the best option.[52]

India's policy

The rise of Islamists in Bangladesh has been felt in India. In all post-Mujib elections in which the Jamaat had been participating, India baiting has been its pronounced plank. The BNP is another party which has been mobilizing public support by using anti-India sentiment to its advantage. Anti-India tirade has become a major political stance in all but the 2001 elections in Bangladesh in the post-Mujib era. To quote Syed Anwar Husain:

> Except India with no other country Bangladesh has issues that divide the nation politically. This is because of the fact that India is a factor in domestic politics. At least in rhetorics (sic), there appears to be a political division among the 'pro' and/or 'anti'-India lines. But, in reality, any party in power irrespective of its ideological mooring and orientation has to adjust itself to the overarching India factor during its tenure.[53]

The Awami League finds it difficult to counter it in a forceful manner despite the fact of its steadfast foreign policy to cultivate friendly relations with India and its expressed gratitude to the Government of India for liberating the country from Pakistani occupation. It is argued that the defeat of the Awami League in the 2001 is to be attributed to the conclusion of Ganga Water Treaty on December 12, 1996 which goes, in BNP's perspective, against the interests of Bangladesh and to the decision of Bangladesh government to facilitate the return and rehabilitation of the displaced Chakmas. Whatever steps the government of Bangladesh took during the time of Sheikh Hasina Wajed to improve India-Bangladesh relations, were severely criticized by both the BNP and the Islamists, as a surrender of Bangladesh's sovereignty. Such rhetoric which is not backed by hard facts, was used as a vote catching strategy.

With the change of Government in Bangladesh in 1996, when the Awami League formed the government and an atmosphere of mutual trust was cultivated, India began to pursue a policy of further expanding its relations with Dhaka. The inauguration of the bus services between Dhaka and Kolkata in June 1999, which was a part of Tract II diplomacy, was the starting point in the pursuit of a meaningful and mutually beneficial relationship between the two countries. Prime Minister Atal Bihari Vajpayee accompanied by a delegation which included the Minister of External Affairs visited Dhaka on June 19 and 20, 1999 on the occasion of inauguration of the bus service between Kolkata and Dhaka in order to underscore the importance of smooth surface connectivity between the two neighbours.[54] During the visit of the Prime Minister, an agreement to extend a credit line of Rs.200 crore to Bangladesh spread over three years, was signed. There were regular high level meetings of the ministers, bureaucrats and defence officers. The most notable was a joint naval exercise in the Bay of Bengal on November 1-4, 1999, the very first since Bangladesh became an independent country.[55] There were setbacks. A border skirmish took place between India's BSF and Bangladesh Rifles in April 2001 following the killing of 16 BSF men.[56] Since then, firing takes place intermittent way by the two forces, making the border tense. Despite the heat generated by the occasional exchange of fire, the Awami League period of 1996-2001 showed symptoms of adjustment and reconciliation in the relations between the two countries which had passed through a strenuous journey since the assassination of Sheikh Mujib. Before the relationship could be strengthened further the 2001 elections brought Begum Khaleda Zia once again and for the second time to power. With Jamaat as a partner of her coalition government, Begum Zia had limited option to initiate any further step to improve relations with India.

Considering the developments leading to the change of government in Bangladesh as a purely domestic matter, Government of India continued to a policy of promoting bilateral relationship with Bangladesh, through greater economic and cultural engagements. The efforts in this direction started with the export of locomotives under credit line in April and extension of ICCR scholarships to students from Bangladesh[57] and sponsoring 250 Bangladeshi teachers in computer application courses in New Delhi in July 2003, under the "Aid to Bangladesh Programme".[58]

The Government of India has a firm policy of non-intervention in the internal affairs of any country in the world in general and its neighbours in particular. It has a broad framework "to strengthen peace and stability in our region" and to enhance cooperation and friendship with the countries in the neighbourhood.[59] Within the broad framework of India's foreign policy, the approach to positive engagement has been pursued, keeping aside the issue of the rise of Islamists in Bangladesh which is a domestic matter of that country. At the same time India raised a voice of serious concern on the issue of violence on the minorities during and after the 2001 elections.[60]

The Islamic fundamentalism, if confined to the boundaries of Bangladesh, could be regarded a matter of domestic concern so long as it does not spread its wing to overreach the soil of its neighbours. The jihadi related activities in Bangladesh, combined with the pronounced and profound hostilities threatening the territorial integrity of its neighbour, have become a borderless problem. The Government of India has the right to express concern and take measures to deal with it. The impact of rise of Islamists is felt in activities of the jihadis, border skirmishes started by the Bangladesh Rifles, growth of madrassas in Assam and West Bengal, which are well-focused in the print and electronic media.[61] This issue, along with the porous nature of the border has been on the top agenda of the student organizations of the region. The All Assam Students' Union, which spearheaded a six-year movement against the foreigners, has been demanding that the Indo-Bangladesh border should be sealed within a limited time frame.[62] There has been growing concern at the ISI's activities in the region through its agents. On rare occasions the issue receives attention of the national forums like the Parliament of India.[63] The Defence Minister strengthened the contention with "human evidence" of ISI's anti-Indian activities from Bangladesh.[64] All this indicate the gravity of the security scenario in the region.

The Government of India has taken up the issue of Bangladesh-based Islamic militancy and its activities in India with its Bangladeshi counterpart in the 7th round of Home Secretary level talks held in Dhaka on August 24-27, 2006 and expressed deep concern on the activities of Indian Insurgent Groups (IIGs) operating from Bangladesh territory and on their links with HuJI[65]. The Bangladesh government dismisses India's concern and allegations saying that no such activities are allowed there. But Dhaka's assertion is patently hollow in view of the fact that the all the top guns of the ULFA are in Dhaka, maintaining links with the ISI for training their cadres,[66] and they plan their terror attacks there. Similarly, all the Muslim militants belonging to North East find Bangladesh as the safe and secure destination for shelter, arms and training. Being strengthened by the logistics extended to them during their training period in that country, they return home to mastermind killings and sabotage in the region. Therefore, the involvement of Bangladesh and its dubious role in aiding and abetting the North East militants is clear.

The two-day conference of the Directors General of Police of North East India held at Guwahati on November 1 and 2, 2006 expressed grave concern at the rise in the activities of jihadi groups in the region who had links with their counterpart in Bangladesh.[67] Their concern was also echoed in the speech of the Governor of Assam, Ajai Singh, who said: "Our intelligence network is not mature enough to tactfully foil the intensified jihadi activities in the North-East."[68] The concern expressed in the conference and the top police officers' addresses thereafter to the press testify to the gravity of the situation which no government would like to ignore.

None can deny the fact that there are contentious issues, as already spelt out in this Chapter, which has continued to plague India-Bangladesh relations for more than three decades. Such issues cannot be resolved all of a sudden; it needs a patient, protracted and positive approach to find a lasting solution. At the same time, leaving aside the contentious issues, the Government of India has conceived of a broad framework to improve India's relations with Bangladesh. One can consider Manmohan Singh's commitment to improve the relationship as reflected in unmistakable terms in his letter to Begum Khaleda Zia, soon after he became the Prime Minister. He wrote that the importance of India-Bangladesh partnership remains a cornerstone of India's foreign policy, which is broadly framed within the commitment to building mutually beneficial relationship with all our neighbours on sensitivity to each other's core concerns" [69] In his letter as also in his interview with *Daily Star* and *Prothom Alo* in November 2005, the

Prime Minister dealt with the bilateral issues concerning Indo-Bangladesh partnership at length. A few of his expressions deserve attention to understand in broader perspective the entire gamut of the partnership. Referring to the strained relationship between the two countries over the years, Manmohan Singh said: "I told her [Khaleda Zia] that as Prime Minister it is my ambition to give the highest priority to relations with neighbours. India-Bangladesh relations are not what they should be, and it should be our combined efforts to find practical, pragmatic pathways to reverse the situation".[70]

The issue of the rise of Islamic fundamentalism is too sensitive to be discussed and debated in and outside the South Block. It is understood that the Government of India wants to play safe on the issue, being apprehensive of hurting the sentiments of the Islamic world. At the same time, it could not ignore the nexus between the Islamists and the North-East rebels operating from Bangladesh with connivance of the Government of that country. The issue is considerably serious in view of the reports that the Taliban fighters and al-Qaeda operators frequent Bangladesh. India has been watching the situation from a close range.[71] The reports of ISI activities in Bangladesh are more disturbing. It is a known fact that Pakistan has not reconciled to its dismemberment and has harbouring designs to foment trouble in India.[72]

Close on the heels of these developments, the Government of India is worried about the close relations that the Government of Bangladesh has been cultivating with China. One report suggests:

> China's role as a defense education provider has also been on the rise in South Asia, a region traditionally dominated by India. The rise of anti-Indian sentiment in Bangladesh, coupled with the rise of Islamic fundamentalism, has led the Bangladeshi government

> to seek closer ties with China. In the past few years, literally hundreds of Bangladeshi officers graduated from PLA educational institutions. China is currently the main supplier of weapons to its armed forces, supplying it with frigates, fighter jets, tanks, armored personnel carriers and other equipment sold at "friendly prices."[73]

In each and every high level meetings between the two countries, the issue is raised by the Indian official functionaries. In the latest move made in March 2007, the Government of India raised the issue, which was responded to by the Bangladeshi counterpart by a mere patent assurance that such activities would not be allowed from that country; the issue of Islamic fundamentalism hardly figures in the bilateral talks.

Such an inclination to keep the issue away from discussion is reflected in the debates and discussions in the parliament. Over a decade or so the sessions of the Indian Parliament had been preoccupied are kept absorbed with party-based self-regarding politics with issues ranging from scams, corruptions, law and order situation, etc. The issues of foreign policy hardly figure.[74] A survey of the debates in the parliament would reveal that there was not a single discussion on Bangladesh since 2001 and on the rise of Islamic fundamentalism in that country. Even the plight of minorities in Bangladesh is not discussed, despite the fact that the Hindus have been leaving the country since 2001, taking shelter mostly in West Bengal.

The impact of ascendancy of the political and militant Islam is felt as flashed in the media from time to time, has been felt in the country in various ways. The incidence of Bangladesh-based terrorist attack on the American Center at Kolkata in January 2002, and bombing in different parts of India including places of worship and passenger trains killing scores of innocent persons, the nexus between the fundamentalists forces and the North East insurgents and Muslim militants, the attack on Hindus in Bangladesh, forcing thousand to flee from the country and take shelter in India, the rise of private madrassas which potentially could be the centres for hate campaign against other communities and recruitment centres for militants are the most disturbing manifestations of the rise of Islamists in Bangladesh. Islamic fundamentalism and militancy is obviously a borderless problem. For its strategic location and geopolitical juxtaposition to Bangladesh, India is undoubtedly vulnerable to all sorts of problems, from militancy to fundamentalism as also exodus of migrants.

REFERENCES

1. Partha S. Ghosh and I traveled from Hatsingimari in Dhubri district of Assam along with the Bangladesh border and covered a distance of about 120 km in April 2006. We were shocked to see how porous our international border with Bangladesh is. See the photographs attached to this Chapter. There are a number of holes on the barbed fence making it easy for anyone including jihadis to cross the border. About 40 km stretch of the border is well protected. We talked to the BSF personnel including an officer who revealed that there has not been any infiltration on this side of the border as the vigil had been strong. But, he said, the cow thief (goru chor) from Bangladesh side used to cross the border and steal cows very often. We were told by the local people that Bangladeshi nationals come for shopping at Hatsingimari Sunday market. One gentleman shared information with us that once Bangla Bhai too came and stayed a couple of days in Mankachar.
2. For a detailed report see "Porous Dhubri Border Aiding Jihadis, *Assam Tribune*, December 19, 2006.
3. There are countless newspaper reports on this issue. The top guns of the ULFA are taking shelter in Dhaka. The cadres of most of the North East insurgent groups are receiving all the needed infrastructure facilities and training in Bangladesh.

4. There are more than 30 jihadi outfits in Pakistan. Most prominent among them are Harkat-ul-Mujahidin, Laskar-e-Tayyeba and Jaish-e-Muhammad. For an in-depth analysis see Stephen P. Cohen, "The Jihadi Threat to Pakistan", *The Washington Quarterly*, Vol. 26, No. 26, Summer 2003, pp. 7-25.

5. Speeches of Khaleda Zia often contain anti-India sentiments. Her favourite issues are Ganges water sharing, transit and corridor pact with India, and the Chakma return and rehabilitation. For a collection of her speeches delivered in Bengali language see Emajuddin Ahamed and Musfiqur Rahman (eds), *Khaleda Zia: Rajnaitik Adarsa and Karmasuchi* (Khaleda Zia: Political Ideology and Agenda) (Dhaka: Asia Publications, 2001).

6. For details see *Times of India* (Sunday Times) report entitled "HuJI's India chief nabbed", June 24, 2007. For the latest twin blasts in Hyderabad on August , 2007 see *Hindu* August 25, 26 and September 4, 2007.

7. It may be mentioned that the audio tapes containing the speeches of the jihadi leaders and Jamaat are easily available not only in big and small cities and towns but also in rural areas.

8. A former diplomat of Bangladesh revealed to me over dinner at his residence on November 28, 2006 that Bangladesh has a fear, however unfounded it might be, that India might any time strike militarily. The fear draws Bangladesh to the diplomatic proximity to Pakistan and China. The fear also provides a rationale for allowing Bangladesh to be a safe haven for the North East militants.

9. Not many works by Bangladeshi scholars and journalists could be found entirely devoted to a narrative analysis on India's role in the liberation of Bangladesh. The recent work of Salam Azad is one such which deserves attention. See his *Contribution of India in the War of Liberation of Bangladesh* (New Delhi: Bookwell, 2006).

10. Iftekharuzzaman, "The India Doctrine: The Relevance for Bangladesh" in M.G. Kabir and Shaukat Hassan (eds), *Issues*

and Challenges Facing Bangladesh Foreign Policy (Dhaka: Bangladesh Society of International Studies, 1989), pp. 18-43.

11. A.K.M. Abdus Sabur, "Some Reflections on the Dynamics of Bangladesh India Relations" in Iftekharuzzaman and Imtiaz Ahmed (eds), *Bangladesh and SAARC: Issues, Perspectives and Outlook* (Dhaka: Academic Publishers, 1992), pp. 130-154.

12. Avtar Singh Bhasin, *India-Bangladesh Relations: Documents – 1972-2002*, Vol. I (New Delhi: Geetika Publishers, 2003), p. xix, for the text of the Treaty, pp.29-32.

13. It is argued that the treaty caused much displeasure among the Bangladeshis. Article 8,9 and 11 delimited the sovereign right of Bangladesh in international affairs. See Amena Mohsin, "Bangladesh-India Relations: Limitations and Options in an Evolving Relationship" in Emajuddin Ahamed and Abul Kalam (eds), *Bangladesh, South Asia and the World* (Dhaka: Academic Publishers, 1992) pp 59-73 and Abul Kalam, "Foreign Policy of Bangladesh: A Reconsideration", *Journal of Asiatic Society of Bangladesh,* Vol. 47, No. 1, June 2002, pp.205-220.

    Partha S. Ghosh writes that it "was heavily weighted in favour of India." See his *Cooperation and Conflict in South Asia* (New Delhi: Manohar, 1995), p. 65.

14. Harun ur Rashid, *Indo-Bangladesh Relations: An Insider's View* (New Delhi: Har-Anand Publications, 2002), p. 18.

15. For details see Lawrence Lifschultz, *Bangladesh: The Unfinisted Revolution* (London: Zed Press, 1989), pp. 36-37.

16. Amena Mohsin however mentions about the court martial of Indian military personnel, see her "Bangladesh-India Relations: Limitations and Options in an Evolving Relationship" in Emajuddin Ahamed and Abul Kalam (eds), *Bangladesh, South Asia and the World* (Dhaka: Academic Publishers, 1992), pp 59-73.

17. Iftekharuzzaman. "The India Doctrine: The Relevance for Bangladesh" in M.G. Kabir and Shaukat Hassan (eds), *Issues*

and Challenges Facing Bangladesh Foreign Policy n. 9, pp 32-33.

18. For the text of the treaty see Avtar Singh Bhasin, *India-Bangladesh Relations: Documents – 1972-2002*, n. 12, Vol. II, pp. 1099-1101.

19. Rehman Sobhan, *Bangladesh-India Relations: Perspectives from Civil Society Dialogues* (Dhaka: Centre for Policy Dialogue and University Press Limited, 2002), pp.54-56.

20. Government of India did not hand over Tin Bigha Corridor to Bangladesh, as the 1974 agreement is for perpetual lease and not transfer. Further, there was widespread protest against the agreement on the Indian side on security related grounds. There has been easy movement of people between the two enclaves in Bangladesh since 1982. For details see Avtar Singh Bhasin, *India-Bangladesh Relations: Documents – 1972-2002*, Vol. IV, n. 12. pp. 1920, 1936, 1946 and 2055-59.

21. About 2.5 lakh Bangladeshi citizens live in 51 Bangladesh enclaves in an area of 7,110 acres under the jurisdiction of Kurigram and Lalmonirhat districts inside Cochbihar District of West Bengal and a similar number of Indian citizens are living in an area of 17,158 acres inside Kurigram, Lalmorihat, Nilphamari and Panchagarh districts of Bangladesh. The mobility of these people are severely restricted. They have no access to education, health care, sanitation, safety, security, family planning, vaccination, voting rights.

22. Iftekharuzzaman and Imtiaz Ahmed (eds), *Bangladesh and SAARC: Issues, Perspectives and Outlook*, n. 10, pp 147-48.

23. Amena Mohsin, "Bangladesh-India Relations: Limitations and Options in an Evolving Relationship" n. 16. quotation, p.64.

24. Akmal Hussain, "The Bangladesh-India Relations, 1972: Seeds of Future Discord" in Muzaffer Ahmad and Abul Kalam (eds), *Bangladesh Foreign Relations: Changes and Directions* (Dhaka: University Press Limited, 1989).

25. Md. Abdul Halim, "Foreign Policy Review" in A.M. Chowdhury and Fakrul Islam, *Bangladesh: On the Threshold of the*

Twenty-first Century (Dhaka: Asiatic Society of Bangladesh, 2002) pp 575-598, especially p. 579.

26. Almost all the writings of Bangladeshi intellectuals with the exception of Shahriar Kabir and Salam Azad demonstrate the anti-Indian feeling taking the issues one after another. In my interactive sessions with Bangladeshi scholars during my visit to Dhaka in November-December, I felt the intensity of their critical, if not totally hostile, views on India's "bullying" tactics on Bangladesh.

27. Harun ur Rashid, *Indo-Bangladesh Relations: An Insider's View,* n. 14, p. 19.

28. It is important to mention here that Bangladesh itself failed to put Ghulam Azam on trial despite his known involvement in the genocide committed by the Pakistani army, al-Badar and Razakars. More importantly, in response to an appeal from the Pakistani Prime Minister to the people of Bangladesh to forget and forgive the mistakes of the past, the Government of Bangladesh decided not to proceed ahead with the trial announced on April 17, 1973 as an act of clemency. For a detailed narration see Harun ur Rashid, *Indo-Bangladesh Relations: An Insider's View, ibid,* pp. 26-27.

29. Rehman Sobhan, *Bangladesh-India Relations: Perspectives from Civil Society Dialogue* (Dhaka: Centre for Policy Dialogue and University Press Limited, 2002), p. 31.

30. *Daily Star*, November 15, 2005.

31. Quoted in *Quarterly Bangladesh Foreign Policy Survey* (Dhaka: Bangladesh Institute of International and Strategic Studies) Vol. 5, No. 3, July/September 1999, p. 9.

32. Swapan K. Bhattacharya, "Does Bangladesh Benefit from Preferential Trade with India?: A Gravity Analysis", *Economic and Political Weekly,* November 27, 2004, pp. 5152-5162, quotation, p. 5161.

33. Mohammad Mafizur Rahman, "Trade and Regional Integration: Bangladesh and SAARC Perspective", *Asia Profile,* Vol. 1, February 2006, pp. 79-93.

34. Anasua Basu Ray Choudhury, "Gas Export from Bangladesh: A Dream Pipe" in Jaideep Saikia (ed), *Bangladesh: Treading the Taliban Trail* (New Delhi: Vision Books, 2006) pp. 150-172.

35. Partha S. Ghosh, *Cooperation and Conflict in South Asia*, n. 13, p.68.

36. Quoting *Hindu* dated February 27, 1979, Partha S. Ghosh writes that the assistance fell from $111 in 1972-73 to $ 7 million in 1975-76, *ibid*, p.88. Siddharth Varadarajan writes that the non-tariff barriers imposed on Indian exports put by Bangladesh government had restricted the trade relations to a considerable extent. See his article "An Overview of Indo-Bangladesh Relations: Perception of Each Other's Foreign Policies" in Farooq Sobhan (ed), *Dynamics of Bangladesh-India Relations: Dialogue of Young Journalists across the Borders* (Dhaka: Bangladesh Enterprise Institute and University Press Limited, 2005), pp. 49-54.

37. Farooq Sobhan (ed), *Dynamics of Bangladesh-India Relations: Dialogue of Young Journalists across the Borders, ibid,* p. 7.

38. Rehman Sobhan, "Political Economy of Bangladesh's External Relations", *Daily Star*, November 4, 2003.

39. For some details see Jaideep Saikia, *Terror Sans Frontier: Islamic Militancy in North East India* (New Delhi: Vision Books, 2004), Appendix I.

40. For details of the Barpeta massacre see Monirul Hussain, "Understanding Barpeta massacre 1994: ethnicity, communalism and state", *Economic and Political Weekly*, May 20, 1995, pp. 1154-1155.

41. The data on the jihadi groups operating in North East are collected from reliable sources, close to the police and other government establishments. A few of the surrendered militants had been interviewed to cross check informal sources of information and to understand the dynamics of motivation, training, fund, areas of operation, links with other militants groups in the region.

42. As reported by one of the surrendered MULTA functionaries when interviewed on October 23, 2006.

43. Jaideep Saikia has presented a detailed list of Islamic militants' camps in Bangladesh in his book *Terror Sans Frontiers*, n. 39, Appendix XII.

44. It is difficult to assess to what extent the MULTA has links with the ISI. In my separate interactions with two of the surrendered leaders of the MULTA I was given the impression that while there had been political discussions between them and the militant groups in Bangladesh, the arms training had been imparted by the Urdu speaking plain clothed 'tough' persons, who did not reveal their identities. They are not sure whether the trainers were ISI agents or functionaries.

45. Intelligence sources reveal that most of surrendered militants including the Surrendered ULFA (SULFA) found Bangladesh to be the best place for 'good preparation' towards realization of their militant objectives. My interactions with both surrendered jihadi and SULFA leaders corroborate the intelligence sources. A sense of security is evident in them, as they feel that the Government of Bangladesh, for its own domestic and international considerations, would not take any measure to drive them out or to restrain their operational activities. However, the Bangladesh government time and again refutes the allegation of hourbouring North East militants on its soil. For a representative comment made by Bangladesh's Foreign Minister M. Morshed Khan see *Daily Star*, September 8, 2004.

46. The huge cache included 1.8 million rounds of ammunition, 1,790 types of arms, 27,020 grenades, 150 rocket launchers, 840 rockets, hundreds of spot rifles, 100 various types of guns. For details see *Daily Star*, April 3 and 4, 2004. Indian newspapers too gave coverage of the seizure of arms and ammunitions. This was the largest single illegal arms consignment to have been intercepted in Bangladesh.

47. On an earlier occasion on June 27, 2003 a huge cache of arms and ammunition had been seized in Bogra. Despite the intermittent raids and seizure of arm by the security personnel,

the arms trafficking has been going in Bangladesh for quite sometime. It is argued that illegal arms go to either Muslim militants or to the North East insurgents.

48. Time and resources did not permit to examine the state of affairs of madrassa education in West Bengal, which shares a long border with Bangladesh and reportedly has a large number of private madrassas. The state of madrassa education in Assam could be treated as a case study.

49. There are about 2,251 Char villages which are inhabited by Muslims, who are known to be immigrants from the then East Bengal and present Bangladesh. It is alleged that the Bangladeshis cross the border and come to Assam and live in these Char areas. There was a huge movement in Assam against the Bangladeshi foreign nationals during 1979-1985. For details of the movement see Monirul Hussain, *Assam Movement: Class, Ideology and Identity* (New Delhi: Manak Publications, 1993).

    For detailed statistical data on the Chars see Government of Assam, *Socio-Economic Survey Report 2002-2003 of Char Areas of Assam* (Guwahati: Directorate of Char Areas Development Assam, n.d). I had visited a few Char areas in Barpeta and Dhubri districts in 2006. Some of these are settled such as Alopatty Major Char which has settlement records since 1885. It is a considerably big Char with a total population around 3700. It has two high schools, one madrassa and one college, one health centre and other government infrastructure. There are small and shifting chars like Khargrachar in Dhubri district, inhabited by around 200 families. There is only one primary school with no other government infrastructure. Most of the Chars look alike.

50. For some details on madrassas in Assam see Jaideep Saikia, *Terror Sans Frontiers*, n.39, pp.147-151.9.

51. I was present in such a congregation. I could gather from my interaction with him that the Mufti, who reportedly studied in Baskandi Madrassa and also did some courses in Deoband, had no basic ideas of mathematics and science. He has not studied any history book, nor is he aware of the Constitutional

provisions. He is not aware of what is happening in other parts of Islamic world. His words reflect the content and tone of retroactive Muftis in Bangladesh. When confronted with hard facts, the Muftis dismiss them as 'propaganda materials' circulated by the West.

52. I interacted with some of the parents/guardians of children studying in Madrassas in different parts of Assam. They live in abject poverty and cannot afford to send their children/ wards to any other school. They reveal given some resources at their disposal, they would have put the young and innocent kids in general schools, where they would have availed of better education.

53. Syed Anwar Husain, *Bangladesh: National Scenario Foreign Policy and SAARC* (Dhaka: Agamee Prakashini, 2003) p.103.

54. Ministry of External Affairs, *Annual Report, 1999-2000*, pp 5-6.

55. *ibid*, p. 5.

56. It was on April 15, 2001 there was an intrusion of Bangladesh Rifles (BDR) in Pyrdiwah in Meghalaya which followed a heavy exchange of fire on April 17 and 18. 16 BSF personnel were killed and their bodies were returned with horrific marks of torture and mutilation. For details of the incidents since April 15 see *Assam Tribune* 16-19, 1999 and also for the concern expressed by the Government of India see Ministry of External Affairs, *Annual Report,2001-2002,* p. 2.

57. *ibid*, pp. 3-4.

58. *ibid, 2003-2004*, p. 3.

59. *ibid*, 2001-2002, p. ii.

60. *ibid*, p. 4.

61. For example *Assam Tribune*, July 19, 2006 carried a detailed narration presented by the Directors General of Police, Assam and Tripura before a press conference on the fundamentalists activities in the region. Also see a news entitled "Bangla-based ultra posing threat to NE" in *Assam Tribune*, July 18, 2006. Most of the Assamese dailies have been publishing news items

to make the public and the government aware of the porous border, influx of Bangladeshi nationals and militancy operating from Bangladesh. In another report published in the said daily entitled " Bangla's DGFI fomenting trouble in NE" dated February 3, 2007 the role of the ISI and DGFI has been flashed in clear terms.

62. *Assam Tribune*, June 30 and July 31, 2006. Home Ministry functionaries made a visit to the border areas to have a survey on the border and assess the situation. For details see *Assam Tribune*, July 29, 2006.

63. The Government of India has found that the "Pakistan Embassy in Dhaka has become a nerve-centre of ISI activity in Bangladesh". *ibid*, 2002-2003, p. 4.

64. For an in-depth analysis on ISI activities see Major General Ashok Krishna, "The Inter-Service Intelligence (ISI) of Pakistan", Institute for Peace and Conflict Studies, Article No. 191, May 25, 1999, http:/www.ipcs.org.in/

65. *ibid*, 2006-2007, p. 4.

66. Vinay Kumar, "ISI Trained ULFA in use of Explosives?", *The Hindu*, December 25, 2003.

67. For details of the conference see *Assam Tribune* and *Sentinel*, November 2 and 3, 2006.

68. *Sentinel*, November 3, 2006.

69. *ibid*, June 1, 2004.

70. *Daily Star*, November 15, 2005.

71. Seema Guha, "India is watching with growing concern" DNA World, http:/www.dnaindia.com/report.asp?newsID=106049 dated 10/31/2006.

72. Besides intelligence and media reports that talk on the design of Pakistan to create problems in India, as a measure of revenge, some of the surrendered militants reported that the "Urdu speaking military trainers' used to say very often that they want see 'thousand cuts on the body polity of India and see it bleeding profusely'".

73. http:/www.pinr.com report.php?ac=view_report& report_id= 562 & languagee_*id*=1 10/5/2006.

74. I had long discussions with P.A. Sangma, former Speaker of Lok Sabha, on a number of occasions during the year 2006 at his Guwahati and New Delhi residences on issues relating to the role of Parliament in shaping India's foreign policy, secularism, migration and political Islam in Bangladesh. He agrees that matters relating to external affairs do not bother the members of Parliament. My own study entitled "Role of Parliament in Shaping India's Foreign Policy" presented in a seminar on "Fifty Years of Indian Parliament" held in April 2002 at India International Centre, confirms the common impression that the Parliament has no time and interest in the foreign affairs of our country. Consequently, issues such as fundamentalism in Bangladesh are not discussed at all. The issue which figured prominently was 9/11 and its possible global consequences.

Weak and mutilated border fence; other side is a Bangladesh village

Entry and exit point: a leveler used to cross the fence

Impenetrable 40 km border fence from Hatsingimari

India-Bangladesh border point, Hatsingimari, Assam

The mighty ocean-like Brahmaputra cutting across the international border

A view of a char on the Brahmaputra within Bangladesh

Khagrar Char: one of the hundreds of shifting river islands (chars)

Temporary settlements in Khagrar Char

A Primary School in a char area

6

FUTURE ENVISIONED

Nothing is static in politics, whether domestic or international. Changes take place with the change of power structure and equation depending on how fast things move. The last century is replete with countless testimonies to such gradual or revolutionary and even violent changes. The Indian subcontinent too experienced heart-throbbing developments, proving, thereby, the universally accepted theory that dynamism prevails over stagnation and the static; it is a matter of time only. It took barely a quarter of a century to see how the 'two-nation theory' collapsed and how a new nation-state emerged out of the eastern wing of Pakistan. The political landscape of Bangladesh too witnessed within a span of again quarter of a century a series of changes, some of which were shocking and violent. Two army Generals ruled the country for a considerable length of time. The recent developments in Bangladesh foretell, probably and unfortunately, another spell of military dictatorship behind the curtain. There had been shift from the basic premises of its secular credentials to Islamization. The Bangladeshi nationalism faced serious challenges from the Islamists, who tried to put the once discarded religious affiliation at the top of the national agenda. The slogan "Muslims first" reverberated in the socio-political environment of Bangladesh so much so that the international community was staring at this scenario with a disturbing question – "Is Bangladesh going to be Talibanized?"

Bangladesh is a Muslim majority country, economically and educationally backward, and therefore, susceptible to pre-modern and retrogressive ideas of religious fundamentalism. The process of converting a traditional Hindu society into an Islamic one in this part of the world took a mere 300 years only, when the Sufis, and not the rulers, accomplished a social engineering of conversion on a massive scale. The transformation had been phenomenal due to several factors, including the prevalence of *Pir-Murid* relationship, as spelt out in Chapter III. The partition of Bengal on religious lines created a flash point of political dispensation that was instrumental in leading to the emergence of East Pakistan – the eastern wing of a newly established state of Pakistan. Islam could not hold together the state, and East Pakistan became the People's Republic of Bangladesh in 1971. It demonstrated the relevance of the ethnic dimension of Bengali Muslims which was shaped by a long tradition of admixture of religion and socio-cultural tradition that gave a distinct personality to the Muslims of Bengal as Bengali Muslims. It also suggests that well-articulated ideas based on reason or chimerical panacea for prosperity could sweep the masses to a great extent.

The influence of religion has remained intact, even after the emergence of a Bengali nation-state. The fact that Bangladesh is a hugely Muslim populated country in absolute terms has been a significant matter in its social and political life. The political environment continues to be charged by this realization. Despite his deep commitment to secularism, the founder of the nation, Sheikh Mujib, had to use the religious sentiment and slogans to mobilize public support. He, however, consciously refrained from communalizing the political life of Bangladesh. But the introduction of Islamic symbols by the Bangabandhu himself made it easy for the then dormant Islamists to pave the way for their reemergence in the post-Mujib politics of Bangladesh. The military rulers used religion and communal forces to legitimize their rule and to cultivate friendly relations with the Islamic countries, particularly the oil-rich Arab ones. Once given a political space, the communal forces and militant groups started showing their teeth. They could be contained and marginalized but not altogether be eliminated.

It is easy to arouse passion in the name of religion in an economically and educationally backward country like Bangladesh, where misinformation tends to encrust facts and truth. As an LDC, Bangladesh is yet to show the symptoms of steady economic growth. The political uncertainties compound the endemic economic situation. Its foreign aid dependence makes it vulnerable to external pressure, which incapacitates the government in checking foreign funds flowing to the aid of the fundamentalists forces. All these tend to play a role in the rise of religious fundamentalism in Bangladesh. The fundamentalists find it easy to mobilize people in the name of religion. It is not unusual, taking Bangladesh as a case, to find a growing feeling among a considerable section of the Muslims that their primary identity stems out of their loyalty to the religion rather than race, identity and nationality.[1]

At the same time, it is difficult to say that religious identity is the overriding factor in all social and cultural domains of the Muslims.[2]

Although the mobilization is not too spectacular in terms of percentage, it is worrisome in absolute terms, in a highly populous country with a small geographical space. Islam is undoubtedly a major factor in Bangladesh. The religious slogans and symbols could be used by political leaders, religious preachers like the Sufis, and also by both political and militant Islamists. How to and to what extent these are used is determined by the political culture of Bangladesh.

The manifestation of the ascendancy of the Islamists in Bangladesh has been pronounced and profound. The arrival of the once hated Ghulam Azam in Dhaka soon after the assassination of Sheikh Mujib and then his rehabilitation, sounded the revival of the Jamaat and along with it, the appearance of militant Islamic organizations in the political process in Bangladesh. The year 2001 is a watershed in the history of Bangladesh when the Jamaat scored a political mileage, leading to sharing power with the BNP. The planned, widespread and serial attack on the minorities including the Ahmediyas, before and after the elections, is a clear indication of the direction in which the country was moving. Those who sympathized with the minorities and talked to the displaced persons taking shelter in India, were also attacked, jailed and harassed; some of them were even killed. The liberal and democratic media, too, faced the onslaught of intolerant Islamists at the instigation of the Jamaat and the Chatra Parishad.

Bangladesh experienced the deadly emergence of the jihadis on August 17, 2004 when a well-planned attack on an Awami League gathering was executed with precision leaving scores of people dead and wounded. It demolished the government's tall claim that the jihadis were not a force to be worried about and that they posed no threat to democracy and social structure. It allowed the monster of fanaticism, in the name of Islam, to grow apace till it acquired the capacity of devastating impact.

The social base of the jihadis suggests that they belong to the poor peasantry, who could not afford modern education for their children; in stead they decide to send their kids to the madrassas, where their education and boarding needs are looked after. All the jihadi organizations depend on the madrassas, spread over all the districts of Bangladesh, for recruitment. Most prominent amongst these are in Dinajpur,

Rangpur, Kurigram, Jamalpur, Sherpur and Chittagong. The children of poor and distressed people, including the displaced Rohingya community of Myanmar, are the most vulnerable to such recruitment. There has been easy flow of funds from the oil-rich Arab countries with which the jihadis expand and promote their activities including procurement of arms and ammunitions. The government of Bangladesh during the period 2001-2006 indirectly supported them by adopting a policy of connivance and appeasement. To state succinctly, the jihadis have a position of advantage; they have dependable recruitment centres, which offer young boys ready to fight and die 'for the cause of God', easy money from foreign sources and the indirect support from the government to pursue their activities. Under the circumstances, the rise of both political and militant Islam in a speedy manner is not unnatural.

The international community, more particularly the West, takes an ambivalent position. They know that as an LDC Bangladesh needs funds for its economic and human development. They used the weapon to pin down the government at times of crisis. The United States forced the Mujib Government to stop importing sugar from Cuba and exporting jute to that country in 1974, when the country was facing famine. The promised and much needed food at the time of famine was not shipped till the government of Bangladesh yielded to the pressure. In 2001 the BNP-led government was pressurized to take away the agriculture portfolio from the Jamaat member, in apprehension that this important ministry would be used to expand Islamist activities in rural areas. In recent times, Western pressure compelled the Caretaker Government to postpone the general elections and to initiate steps to revise the electoral rolls. The US Ambassador to Bangladesh Howard Schaffer reportedly expressed his concern in April 2007 at the terrorist activities in Bangladesh and said that there was a relationship between lack of governance and rise of extremism. He said: "Bangladesh is badly governed. And under those circumstances, there is a tendency to turn moderate Islamic countries, moderate Islamic parties, to more radical groups".[3] The British Government expressed desire to help Dhaka to fight terrorism.[4] The Western countries are aware of the fact that external dependency determines Bangladeshi domestic politics and international relations. At the same time, the West, knowing fully well that its allies in the Middle East are the most dependable and benevolent sources of funds for the jihadis with money flowing in ostensibly in the name of promoting Islam, hardly exerts any pressure on these governments to rein them in.

For India, to officially raise alarm on the rise of fundamentalism in Bangladesh is too sensitive an issue to be pursued with vigour because of the involvement of the religious question. It takes up the issues of intermittent border skirmishes, cross border terrorism and North East militants operating from Bangladesh together with influx of Bangladeshi nationals into the states of the region, in official bilateral forums and meetings. All these are critical issues and solutions to them have become illusory, in view of the not-too-happy relations between the two countries. The Indo-Bangladesh border is porous. In many places there is virtually no border fence because of the mighty river Brahmaputra cutting across the international border. In certain portions of the border on the Meghalaya side, the existence of a lengthy stretch of disputed border incapacitates the Government of India in erecting a fence. A perpetually porous border facilitates not only migration of the Bangladeshi nationals but also cross-border crimes, export of terrorism and easy passage for the militants. Unless a more congenial and cooperative partnership is developed, mere raising the issues, including the question of fundamentalism in Bangladesh, will not produce any concrete results. So long as Bangladesh does not realize the magnitude of the problems posed by the rise of militant Islam seriously and does not feel the need to have bilateral cooperation in handling it, it would remain a vexed and tangled issue, too difficult to pursue unilaterally by the Government of India.

The impact of the conservative ascendancy is felt in India, more particularly in the North East and in West Bengal, for the obvious the reason of proximity. The growth of Islamic militant organizations in the region, such as MULTA in some of the Muslim dominated areas and the mushroom growth of private madrassas in Assam and West Bengal is an indication of the impact. Sustained interrogation of captured militants reveals to the extensive impact of the rise of fundamentalism in Bangladesh.

A 'fragile' state, located in a geopolitically sensitive region, sharing its eastern, northern and western border with India, could be a source of unmitigated troubles. Religious fanaticism has become a global problem and its deadly manifestation is well-understood. As already stated, there has been a steady increase of Islamic fundamentalism in Bangladesh. Judged from the percentage of votes polled, the Jamaat may not be able to muster a support base capable of electorally returning it to form a government on its own strength in the near future. Nonetheless, the ascendancy of the political and militant Islam, in less than a decade, demonstrating its support base in absolute terms is undoubtedly a matter of grave concern, not only for the country but also for India.

The steady rise of the Islamists in Bangladesh is bound to have repercussions in the North East owing to the geopolitical proximity. The recent demand made by a Member of Assam Legislative Assembly, belonging to the immigrant Muslim community, for an autonomous council in some of the Muslim dominated areas of Assam, is a manifestation of a dangerous political ambition capable of destabilizing the state.

Therefore, what is to be done?

As stated in the preceding Chapter, it is a clear policy of the Government of India to promote mutually beneficial partnership, (a better expression than relationship), with all its neighbours. India's Bangladesh policy has been formulated on that broad line. Therefore, despite the existence of rancorous irritants, India's positive approach to Bangladesh has been reflected in its position on various issues such as water sharing, transfer of enclaves, efforts to reduce trade deficit and encouraging DFI to boost latter's economy, judicious release of the Ganges water to meet Bangladesh's requirements and adherence to a policy of non-interference in the internal affairs of Bangladesh. The diplomatic terminologies to define its relations with Bangladesh, as reflected in official statements and reports clarifying that India is committed to promote friendly relations with its neighbour may not alone serve the purpose of handling the problematic relations with Dhaka. A definite long term and short term policy intervention is the need of the critical hour to deal with each and every sensitive issue that dominate the brittle relationship between the two countries.

A few spear points might crystallize India's foreign policy option to handle endemic problems in forging a more meaningful, durable and mutually beneficial partnership between India and Bangladesh.

(i) The Government of India could to take steps to address all the accusations made by the Government of Bangladesh and the people starting from the day one of its independence, December 16, 1971, such as, that the surrender ceremony of the Pakistani army was an all-India affair, sharing of Ganges water is discriminatory etc, so that misconstruction and misinterpretation of information and events, if any, could be obliterated once for all.

(ii) Since it is not possible to take interest in the internal affairs of Bangladesh beyond a permissible point, the Tract II diplomacy could be activated to clear unfounded apprehension about India's role in the region; it is desirable to have more informal and private communication channels and civil society engagements that include exchange visits of students, scholars, artists, sports personalities, literary and Sufi religious figures, and businessmen. Islamic fundamentalism has to be fought from within in close cooperation with the democratic and secular minded people of Bangladesh.

(iii) An economically and educationally backward neighbour pestered with recurrent and unresolved problems, is a perennial source of irritation. In order to help strengthening Bangladesh's economic foundation, a policy to accommodate a few of its demands including release of a certain quantum of water during the lean season could be acceded to as an ad-hoc measure to improve the relations between the two countries. In this way Bangladesh could be engaged in the process of combating not only terrorism but also the Bangladeshi influx into North East India. The emphasis on 'partnership' as often done by Prime Minister Manmohan Singh, rather than on the traditional term of 'relationship', would instill a sense of confidence in the mind of the policy makers of Bangladesh.

(iv) To combat religious fundamentalism, India needs to help Bangladesh in the field of education. A steady growth of modern and liberal education would replace the outdated private madrassas which are the breeding grounds of jihadis and fundamentalists.

(v) A strong border police in the mould of coastal guards could be created to protect India's border with Bangladesh. Mere fencing and deploying the BSF are not enough since these measures become ineffective in protecting the border during monsoon when flood waters flows above the fence. Moreover, the huge and mighty Brahmaputra passes through the international border; policing it against infiltration is too difficult a task to be handled in an orthodox manner.

(vi) The Government of India needs to consider seriously the demand from various corners that photo identity cards should be given to the inhabitants of the Char areas, situated close to the international border.

(vii) There should be better coordination between the Ministry of External Affairs and the Ministry of Home Affairs in dealing with the problems of insurgency and Islamic fundamentalism.

(viii) India has to accord importance to its neighbours. The media, the parliament, and the political parties have to come forward to discuss and debate on issues of common interest faced by our neighbours. The opinion makers, more particularly the media personalities, in Bangladesh could be involved in such discourses.

(ix) The imbalance of trade could be looked into to reduce the trade deficit; the quantum of import from Bangladesh could be raised to a certain extent by extending tariff concession on certain selected quality products.

(x) The question of sharing the river water could be reviewed once again to accommodate Bangladesh's interests. Hopefully, goodwill could be cultivated by releasing some more cusecs of water to Bangladesh during the lean season. The public of Bangladesh has to be made aware that water of other rivers including that of the Brahmaputra flow to their country, without any obstruction and hindrance.

(xi) The West has been taking anti-terrorist measures since 9/11. The Government of India needs to coordinate its efforts with the West to curb and crush the spectre of terrorism in the region. Bangladesh is heavily dependent on foreign aid coming from the West. The West could be persuaded to put pressure on the Government of Bangladesh to take action against militant Islam and sideline religion-based political parties. Such foreign pressure works, as testified to by the recent events during the months of November and December 2006 when the caretaker government was compelled to postpone the elections and to take steps to revise the electoral list. If the issue can be viewed from the perspective of combating international terrorism, India can advance a step further to be a partner in the global efforts to deal with terrorism in a formidable manner. International pressure would force Bangladesh to be a partner in combating fundamentalism of all forms.

(xii) International forums, such as the SAARC and the BIMSTEC, could be used more effectively to draw attention to the various dimensions of the pernicious impact that religious fundamentalism would have in both domestic and international politics in the region, so as to facilitate formulation of a common agenda to combat it. Religious fundamentalism cannot be fought in isolation. There is an urgent need to have a holistic approach to deal with it.

Any foreign policy move towards Bangladesh needs to be examined against the backdrop of the following:

- Although religion did not work as a binding force to keep Pakistan united and prevent the emergence of Bangladesh, it has a space in the social and the political life of Bangladesh.
- Sufism has still a role to play in Bangladesh in tempering the religious zealots and in fortifying liberalism, democracy, religious tolerance and secular values.
- Rise of Islamic fundamentalism in Bangladesh is an outgrowth of the global scenario since the fall of Reza Shah Pehlavi of Iran in February 1979. Internal compulsions and issues facilitated its rise in Bangladesh which can be contained only with the support and participation of the common man, who is definitely not communal.
- The impact of the ascendancy of fundamentalism in Bangladesh has to be neutralized by a series of interventions such as conflict management in the country, border vigil and fortification, modernization of madrassas, greater connectivity and trade relations and cultural exchanges, and concrete measures to develop the economy of the region including Bangladesh. Poverty ridden districts of India and Bangladesh are the fertile grounds that breed fundamentalism.
- The secular forces in Bangladesh are strong and deserve external inputs and support.
- The caretaker government will stay for some time as a transitional phase towards restoration of elected and representative government hopefully by December 2008. Even then a diplomatic channel could be

activated to cultivate sustainable relations with Bangladesh, so that when the new democratically elected government takes over, New Delhi would be able to consolidate the gains of the interim period. The role of the top brass of defence and high level bureaucracy in Bangladesh under the caretaker government, is an indication of perceptive changes towards better future. They will be formidable components in the governance of Bangladesh after the general elections. They will constitute the core of the decision-making structure, which is likely to play the pivotal role in managing internal dynamics and foreign affairs of Bangladesh.

- Bangladesh's susceptibility to external pressure merits consideration.

India, as a regional superpower, has a responsible role to play in ensuring greater stability in the subcontinent. Bangladesh is one the countries in the region which has been facing mounting internal political difficulties, which make it vulnerable to Islamic militancy. It is imperative to seek a wider approach involving other great powers towards preventive measures including development initiatives. What Bangladesh needs is economic performance, better health care and modern education – all of these are inextricably linked with its stability. India has to grab the initiative and play the most critical role as an external facilitator within the broader framework of partnership in the developmental dynamics of Bangladesh.

REFERENCES

1. Zeyno Baran, "Fighting the War of Ideas", *Foreign Affairs*, Vol. 84, No. 6, November/December 2005, pp. 68-78.
2. For an interesting discourse on the issue see Amartya Sen, *Identity and Violence : Illusion of Destiny* (London: Penguin, 2006) Chapter 4.

3. http:/www.countercurrents.org/choudhury250407.htm dated 5/3/2007.

4. In a news conference Charles Style, Deputy Chief Admiral of the United Kingdom revealed this in a news conference during his visit to Dhaka in November, 2006. See *Daily Star*, November 22, 2006.

BIBLIOGRAPHY

Official documents

Amnesty International, *Bangladesh: Attack on Members of the Hindu Community*, (December 2001).

Beverly, Henry, *Reports on the Census of Bengal, 1872* (Calcutta: Secretariat Press, 1872).

Census of India, 1901, Vol. 6, *The Lower Province of Bengal and their Feudatories*, Part I, "Report" (Calcutta: Bengal Secretariat Press, 1902).

Government of People's Republic of Bangladesh, *Speeches of Sheikh Mujib* (Dhaka: External Publicity Division, Ministry of Foreign Affairs, 1972).

Government of Assam, *Socio-Economic Survey Report 2002-2003 of Char Areas of Assam* (Guwahat: Directorate of Char Areas Development Assam, n.d).

Government of India, *Annual Reports* (New Delhi: Ministry of External Affairs, 2000-2007).

Human Development Report, 2005 and 2006.

Quaid-I-Azam Mohamed Ali Jinnah's Speeches as Governor General 1947-48 (Karachi: Pakistan Publication, n.d).

2004 Statistical Yearbook of Bangladesh (Dhaka: Bangladesh Bureau of Statistics, 2005).

Statistical Yearbook of Bangladesh, 2004

US Department of State, *Bangladesh: International Religious Freedom Report 2005*, http;//www.state.gov/g/drl/irf/2005.

The World Bank, *Pursuing Common Goals: Strengthening Relations between Government and Development NGOs* (Dhaka: University Press Limited, 1996)

Books

Abecassis, David, *Identity, Islam and Human Development in Rural Bangladesh* (Dhaka: University Press Limited, 1990).

Ahamed Emajuddin, *Foreign Policy of Bangladesh: A Small State's Imperatives* (Dhaka: University Press Limited, 1984).

Ahamed, Emajuddin, *Military Rule and the Myth of Democracy* (Dhaka: University Press Limited, 1988).

Ahamed, Emajuddin and Mushfiqur Rahman (eds), *Khaleda Zia: Rajnaitik Adarsha O Karmashusi* (Khaleda Zia: Political Ideology and Agenda) (Dhaka: Asia Publications, 2001).

Ahmad, Aziz, *Studies in Islamic Culture in the Indian Environment* (London: Oxford University Press, 1964).

Ahmed, Imtiaz (ed), *Women, Bangladesh and International Security: Methods, Discourses and Policies* ((Dhaka: University Press Limited, 2004).

Ahmed, Kamaruddin, *Social History of East Pakistan* (Dacca: Orient Longman, 1969).

Ahmed, Moudud, *Era of Sheikh Mujbur Rahman* (Dhaka: University Press Limited, 1983).

Ahmed, Moudud, *Democracy and Challenge of Development: A Study of Political and Military Interventions in Bangladesh* (Dhaka: University Press Limited, 1995).

Ahmed, Rafiuddin, *The Muslims of Bengal 1871-1907: A Quest for Identity* (New Delhi: Oxford University Press, 1981).

Ahmed, Rafiuddin (ed), *Islam in Bangladesh: Society, Culture and Politics* (Dhaka: Bangladesh Itihas Samiti, 1983). See Introduction part and Sheikh Mujib's secularism, MN Roy quotation pp. 190-191.

Ahmed, Rafiuddin (ed), *Religion, Nationalism and Politics in Bangladesh* (New Delhi: South Asia Publication, 1990).

Ahmed, Rafiuddin (ed), *Understanding Bengal Muslims: Interpretative Essays* (New Delhi: Oxford University Press, 2001).

Ahmed, Siraj-udddin, *Bangabandhu Sheikh Mujibur Rahman* (Dhaka: Bhaskar Prakashini, 2001).

Ahmed, Sufia, *Muslim Community in Bengal: 1884-1912* (Dacca: Oxford University Press, 1974).

Akhtar Banu, UAB Razia, *Islam in Bangladesh* (Leiden: E.J. Brill, 1992).

Alamgir, Muhiuddin Khan (ed), *Land Reform in Bangladesh* (Dhaka: Centre for Social Studies, 1981).

Alamgir, Muhiuddin Khan, *Development Strategy for Bangladesh*, 2nd Edition (Dhaka: National Institute for Local Government, 1986).

Ali, A.N.M.M. Shaukat, *Politics and Land System in Bangladesh* (Dhaka: National Institute of Local Government, 1986).

Ali, A.M.M. Shawkat, *Faces of Terrorism in Bangladesh* (Dhaka: University Press Limited, 2006).

Anderson, Benedict, *Imagined Communities: Reflections on the Origin and Spread of Nationalism* (Lodnon: Verso, 1994).

Appleby, R. Scott, Samuel C. Heilman, James Piscatory *et. al.*, *Accounting for Fundamentalism: Dynamic Character of Movements* (Chicago: University of Chicago Press, 1994).

Archer, Blood, *The Cruel Birth of Bangladesh: Memoirs of an American Diplomat* (Dhaka: University Press Limited, 2002).

Ayoob, Mohammad, *et al.*, *Bangladesh: A Struggle for Nationhood* (Delhi: Vikas Publications, 1971).

Awwal, Maulana Abdul, *Jamaater Asal Chehara* (The True Portrait of the Jamaat) (Dhaka: Agami Prakashini, 1993).

Azad, *Hindu Somprodai Keno Bangladesh Tyag Koreshe* (Why are Hindu Community Leaving Bangladesh) (Kolkata: Punosho, 2001).

Azad, Salam, *Contribution of India in the War of Liberation of Bangladesh* (New Delhi: Bookwell, 2006).

Azam, Ghulam, *A Guide to Islamic Movement* (Dhaka: Orient Press, 1968).

Azam, Ghulam, *Jamaate Islamir Karmaniti* (Policies of the Jamaat-i-Islami) (Dhaka: Publication Division of Jamaat-i-Islami, 1990).

Aziz, K.M. Ashraful and Clarence Maloney, *Life State, Gender and Fertility in Bangladesh* (Dhaka: International Centre for Diarrheal Disease Research, 1985).

Barakat, Abul, *Bangladeshe Maulobader Orthaniti* (Fundamentalist Economy in Bangladesh) (Dhaka: Mukti Bhawan, 2005).

Baxter, Craig, *Bangladesh: A New Nation in an Old Setting* (Boulder, Colorado: Westview Press, 1984).

Baxter, Craig, *Bangladesh: From a Nation to a State* (Boulder: Westview, 1997).

Begum, Khurshida, *Tension Over the Farakka Barrage: A Techno-Political Tangle in South Asia* (Dhaka: University Press Limited, 1987).

Bhasin, Avtar Singh, *India-Bangladesh Relations: Documents – 1972-2002*, Vol. I-V (New Delhi: Geetika Publishers, 2003).

Bhutto, Zullfikar Ali, *The Great Tragedy* (Karachi: Vision Publications, 1971).

Biswas, Sukumar and Hiroshi Sato, *Religion and Politics in Bangladesh and West Bengal: A Study of Communal Relations* (Tokyo: Institute of Development Economics, 1993).

Bradley-Birt, F.B., *Dacca: The Romance of an Eastern Capital*, First Published in 1914 (Guwahati: Spectrum Publication, 1992).

Brass, Paul R. and Marcus F. Franda (eds), *Radical Politics in South Asia* (Cambridge: MIT Press, 1973).

Centre for Policy Dialogue, *Crisis of Governance: A Review of Bangladesh's Development 1997* (Dhaka: University Press Limited, 1998).

Centre for Policy Dialogue, *Demographic Dynamics in Bangladesh: Looking at the Larger Picture* (Dhaka: Pathak Shamabesh, 2003).

Chakrabarti, Ratan Lal, *Bhasha Andolaner Dalilpatra* (Documents of Language Movement (Dhaka: Bangla Academy, 2000).

Chaudhury, Rafiqul Huda and Nilofar Raihan Ahmed, *Female Status in Bangladesh* (Dhaka: BIDS, 1987).

Chakravarty, S.R. (ed) *Society, Polity and Economy of Bangladesh* (New Delhi: Har-Anand Publications, 1994).

Chatterjee, Basant, *Inside Bangladesh Today: An Eye-witness Account* (New Delhi: S. Chand & Co., 1979).

Chatterji, Suniti.Kumar, *Origin and Development of Bengali Language*, Vol. 1, (Calcutta: University of Calcutta Press, 1926).

Chatterji, Suniti Kumar, *Languages and Literatures of Modern Bengal* (Calcutta: Bengal Publishers, 1963).

Chowdhury, Abdul Momin, *Dynastic History of Bengal, 750-1200* (Dacca: Asiatic Society of Pakistan, 1976).

Chowdhury, A.M. and Fakrul Alam, *Bangladesh: On the Threshold of the Twenty-first Century* (Dhaka: Asiatic Society of Bangaldesh,2002).

Das, Suranjan, *Communal Riots in Bengal 1905-1947* (Delhi: Oxford, 1991).

Daula, Aman-ud, , *Ghulam Azamer Nagarikatta Mamla* (About Ghulam Azam's Citizenship) (Dhaka: Dibya Prakash, 1993).

Deutsch, Karl W., *Nationalism and Social Communication: An Inquiry into the Foundations of Nationality* (Cambridge, Mass: MIT Press, and New York: John Wiley and Sons, 1953).

Eaton, Richard Maxwell, *The Rise of Islam and the Bengal Frontier, 1204-1760* (Berkeley: University of California Press, 1993).

Eickelman, Jon W. Anderson, Mark Tessler, *New Media in the Muslim World: The Emerging Public Sphere* (Bloomington: Indian University Press, 2003).

Emerson, Rupert, *From Empire to Nation* (Cambridge, Mass: Harvard University Press, 1960).

Esposito, John L., *Iranian Revolution: Its Global Impact* (Miami: Florida International University Press, 1990).

Esposito, John L., *The Islamic Threat: Myth or Reality* (New York: Oxford University Press, 1999).

Franda, Marcus, *Bangladesh: The First Decade* (New Delhi: South Asia Publishers, 1982).

Geertz, Clifford, *Islam Observed: Religious Development in Morocco and Indonesia* (Chicago: University of Chicago Press, 1971).

Ghosh, Partha S., *Cooperation and Conflict in South Asia* (New Delhi: Manohar, 1995).

Guhathakurta, Basanti, *Ekattaorer Smriti* (Memories of Seventy One) (Dhaka: University Press Limited, 2000).

Hafiz, M. Abdul and Rob Khan (eds), *Nation Building in Bangladesh: Retrospect and Prospect* (Dhaka: BISS, 1982).

Haq, Maulana Mansurul (ed), *Mr. Mawdudir New Islam* (Mr. Mawdudi's New Islam) (Dhaka: Lalbag, Jamia Quraniya Arabia, 1985).

Haq, Mohammad Enamul, *A History of Sufism in Bengal* (Dhaka: Asiatic Society of Bangladesh, 1975).

Haque, Ahmed Safiqul, *Politics and Administration in Bangladesh: Problems of Participation* (Dhaka: University Press Limited, 1988).

Hardy, Peter, *The Muslims of British India* (Cambridge: Cambridge University Press, 1972).

Hasanuzzaman, Al Masud, *Role of Opposition in Bangladesh Politics* (Dhaka: University Press Limited, 1998).

Hossain, Golam, *General Ziaur Rahman and the BNP: Political Transformation of a Military Regime* (Dhaka: University Press Limited, 1988).

Hulme, David, *Finance against Poverty* (London: Routledge, 1996).

Hunter, W.W., *The Indian Musalmans: Are They Bound in Conscience to Rebel Against the Queen?* Second Edition (London: Trubner, 1972) esp. chapter 1 and 2.

Huntington, Samuel P., *The Clash of Civilization and the Remaking of the World Order* (New York: Simon & Schuster, 1996).

Husain, Syed Anwar, *Bangladesh: National Scenario Foreign Policy and SAARC* (Dhaka: Agamee Prakashini, 2003).

Hussin, Mutalib, and Taj ul-Islam Hashmi, *Islam, Muslims and the Modern State: Case-Studies in Thirteen Countries* (London: Macmillan, 1996).

Hussain, Muhammad Delwar (ed), *Bangladesher Rajnitite Dharma O Dharma Niropekdhata* (Religion and Secularism in the Politics of Bangladesh (Dhaka: Prerona Prokashan, 1993).

Hussain, Monirul, *The Assam Movement: Class, Ideology and Identity* (New Delhi: Manak Publications, 1993.

Ilias, Khandakar Mohammad (ed), *Bangladesher Samaj Biplobe Bangabandhur Darshan* (Bangabandhu's Philosophy for Social Revolution) (Dhaka: Bangladesh Parishad, 1979).

Iqbal, Mohammad Jafar (ed), *Bish Bachar Pore* (Twenty Years After) (Dhaka: Mohana Pradasani, 1993).

Islam, A.K.M. Azharul and Shah Muhammad Habibur Rahman, *Bangladesh School O Madrassa Sikshaniti O Pathyakram* (School and Madrassa Education and Curriculum in Bangladesh (Dhaka: Islamic Academy, 2003).

Islam, Nurul, *Development Planning in Bangladesh: A Study in Political Economy* (Dhaka: University Press Limited, 1979).

Islam, Sahidul, *Jongider Nepothey 'RAW'-Mossad* (In the Background of the Militants 'RAW'-Mossad) (Dhaka: Professor's Publications, 2006).

Islam, Sirajul, (ed), *History of Bengal 1704-1971* (Dhaka: Asiatic Society of Bangladesh, 1998).

Jahan, Rounaq, *Pakistan: Failure in National Integration* (New York: Colombia University Press, 1972).

Jahangir, Borhanuddin Khan, *Bangladeshe Jatiyotabad Ebong Moulabad* (Nationalism and Fundamentalism in Bangladesh) (Dhaka: Agami Prakashini, 1993).

Jansen, Erik G., *Rural Bangladesh: Competition for Scarce Resources* (Dhaka: University Press Limited, 1986).

Jatiyo Ulema Parishad, *Jamaat Unmasked: The True Colour of a Fundamentalist Party* (Dhaka: Council for National Religious Scholars, 2001).

Johns, Anthony and Nally Lahoud (eds), *Islam in World Politics* (New York: Routledge, 2005).

Kabir, Muhammad Ghulam, *Minority Politics in Bangladesh* (Dhaka: New Delhi: Vikas, 1980).

Kabir, Muhammad Ghulam, *Changing Face of Nationalism: The Case of Bangladesh* (New Yoirk: South Asia Publishers, 1994).

Kabir, Shahriar (ed), *Ekattarer Ghatok Jamaat-i-Islami: Atit O Bartaman* (The Killers of 71 Jamaat-i-Islami: Past and Present (Muktijuddha Chetona Bikas Kendra, 1989).

Kabir, Shahriar, *Resist Fundamentalism: Focus on Bangladesh* (Dhaka: Central Committee for Resisting Killers and Collaborators of Bangladesh Liberation War of 1971, 1999).

Karim, Muhammad Abdul, *Social History of the Muslims of Bengal* (Dacca: Asiatic Society of Pakistan, 1959).

Kaishar, Ashraf, *Bangladese Rajnaitik Hatyakanda*, (Political Assassinations in Bangladesh) (Dhaka: Maula Brothers, 1998).

Karlekar, Hirenmay, *Bangladesh: Next Afghanistan* (New Delhi: Sage, 2005).

Khan, Mohammad Ayub, *Friends, Not Masters: A Political Autobiography* (Karachi: Oxford University, Press, 1969).

Khan, Muin-ud-din Ahmad (ed), *Selection from Bengal Government Records on Wahhabi Trials, 1863-1870* (Dacca: Asiatic Society of Pakistan, 1961).

Khan, Zillur R., *Martial Law to Martial Law: Leadership Crises in Bangladesh* (Dhaka: University Press Limited, 1984).

Kissinger, Henry A., *The White House Years* (Boston: Little Brown, 1979) pp. 842-919 Devotes 76 pages to defend US position on Bangladesh.

Kochanek, Stanley, *Patron-Client Politics: Patron and Business in Bangladesh* (Delhi: Sage, 1993).

Lawrence, Bruce, *Shattering the Myth: Islam Beyond Violence* (Princeton: Princeton University Press, 1998).

Lifschultz, Lawrence, *Bangladesh: The Unfinished Revolution* (London: Zed Press, 1989).

Limaye, Satu P. *et. al.*, (eds), *Religious Radicalism and Security in South Asia* (Honolulu, Hawaii: Asia Pacific Centre for Security Studies, 2004)

Lumbard, Joseph E.B., *Islam, Fundamentalism and Betrayed Tradition: Essays by Western Muslim Scholars* (Bloomington: World Wisdom, 2004).

Majumdar, Gayatri Sen, *Buddhism in Ancient Bengal* (Calcutta: Navana, 1983).

Majumdar, R.C., *History of Bengal* (Dacca: University of Dacca, 1943).

Majumdar, R.C., *History of Ancient Bengal* (Calcutta: G. Bharadwaj & Co., 1971).

Maloney, Clarence, *Behavior and Poverty in Bangladesh* (Dhaka: University Press Limited, 1986).

Maniruzzaman, Talukdar, *The Bangladesh Revolution and Its Aftermath* (Dhaka: university Press Limited, 1988)

Marty, Martin E. and R. Scott Appleby, *Fundamentalism Observed* (Chicago: Chicago University Press, 1994).

Mehdi, Al, *Dharmaniropekshotar Fanchi Sai* (Hang Secularism) (Dhaka: Al Amin Prakashan, 2006).

Miller, Carol and Jessica Vinion (eds), *Women's Employment in the Textile Manufacturing Sectors of Bangladesh and Morocco* (Geneva: UNDP, 2002)

Mitchison, Rosalind J. and G. Ter Haar, *The Freedom To Do Gods Will: Religious Fundamentalism and Social Change* (London: Routlege, 2003)

Mohammad, Hasan, *Jamat-e Islami Bangladesh: Netritto Sangathan, Adarsha* (Jamat-I- Islami of Bangladesh: Leadership, Organization and Ideology) (Dhaka: Academic Publishers, 1993).

Morrison, Barrie, *Political and Cultural Regions of Early Bengal* (Tucson: University of Arizona Press, 1974).

Maniruzzaman, Talukdar, *The Bangladesh Revolution and Its Aftermath* (Dacca: Bangladesh Books International, 1980).

Maniruzzaman, Talukdar, *Group Interests and Political Changes: Studies of Pakistan and Bangladesh* (New Delhi: South Asian Publishers, 1982).

Mullick, A.R., *British Policy and the Muslims of Bengal, 1757-1856*, 2nd Edition (Dhaka: Bangla Academy, 1977).

Murshid, Tazeen M., *The Sacred and the Secular: Bengal Muslim Discourses, 1871-1977* (Calcutta: Oxford University Press, 1995).

Mutalib, Hussin and Taj ul-Islam Hashmi, *Islam, Muslims and the Modern State: Case-Studies in Thirteen Countries* (London: Macmillan, 1996).

Nahar, Sultana, *A Comparative Study of Communalism in Bangladesh and India* (Dhaka: Dhaka Prokashon, 1994).

Nair, M.B., *Politics in Bangladesh: A Study of Awami League 1949-58* (New Delhi: Northern Book Centre, 1990).

Nehemia, Levtzion (ed), *Conversion to Islam* (New York: Holmes and Meier, 1979).

Nirjatoner Dalil – 2001 (Document on Atrocities) (Dhaka: Sanmilita Samajik Andololon, 2002).

Niyogi, Puspa, *Brahmanic Settlements in Different Subdivisions of Ancient Bengal* (Calcutta: R.K. Mitra, 1967).

Novak, James J., *Bangladesh: Reflections on the Water* (Bloomington: Indiana University Press, 1993).

Phadnis, Urmila, *Ethnicity and Nation-building in South Asia* (New Delhi: Sage, 1989).

Qamruzzaman, Muhammad, *Adhyapak Ghulam Azamer Sangrami Jibon* (The Struggled Life of Professor Ghulam Azam) (Dhaka: Al Falah Printer, 1989).

Quddus, Muhammad A., *Pakistan: A Case Study of a Plural Society* (Calcutta: Minarva Associates, 1981).

Rabassa, Angel M. *et.al.*, *The Muslim World after 9/11* (Santa Monica: RAND Corporation, 2004).

Rashid, Aminur and Mostafa Firoz, *Pramany Sangsad* (Authentical Parliament) (Dhaka: Tathya Seva, 2002).

Rashid, Harun-or-, *The Foreshadowing of Bangladesh: Bengal Muslim League and Muslim Politics, 1936-1947* (Dhaka: Asiatic Society of Bangladesh, 1987)

Rehman, Sobhan, *Bangladesh: Problems of Governance* (Dhaka: University Press Limited, 1993)

Riaz, Ali, God Willing: *The Politics of Islamism in Bangladesh* (New York: Rowman and Littlefield, 2004).

Rizvi, S.A.A., *A History of Sufism in India* (Delhi: Munshiram Manoharilal, 1978).

Robinson, Francis, *Atlas of the Islamic World since 1500* (Oxford: Phaidon Press, 1982).

Roy, Asim, *The Islamic Syncretistic Tradition in Bengal* (Princeton: Princeton University Press, 1983).

Rubbee, Khondaker Fuzli, *The Origins of the Musalmans of Bengal* (Calcutta: Thacker, Spink and Co. 1895).

Ruthven, Malise, *Fundamentalism: The Search for Meaning* (New York: Oxford University Press, 2004).

Saikia, Jaideep, *Terror Sans Frontier: Islamic Militancy in North East India* (New Delhi: Vision Books, 2004).

Saikia, Jaideep (ed), *Bangladesh: Treading the Taliban Trail* (New Delhi: Vision Books, 2006).

Saklayen, G., *Bangladeser Sufi Sadhak* (The Sufi Austere of Bangladesh) (Dhaka: Islamic Foundation, 1982).

Sarkar, Bibhuranjan, *Cleansing of Religious Minorities in Bangladesh* (Dhaka: Citizens' Voice, 2002).

Sarkar, Jagadish Narayan, Hindu-Muslim Relations in Bengal: Medieval Period (Delhi: Idarah-i-Adabiyat-i- Delli, 1986).

Schwartzberg, Joseph E. (ed), *A Historical Alas of South Asia* (Chicago: University of Chicago Press, 1978).

Sen, Amartya, *Argumentative Indian* (London: Penguin, 2005)

Sen, Amartya, *Identity and Violence: The Illusion of Destiny* (London: Penguin, 2006)

Sen, Dinesh Chandra, *The Folk Literature of Bengal* (Calcutta: University of Calcutta, 1920).

Sen, Dinesh Chandra, *History of Bengali Language and Literature* (Calcutta: University of Calcutta, 1954).

Sharif, Ahmed *et.al.* (eds), *Ekattarer Ghatok O Dalalra Ke Kothay* (Where are the Killers of 71 and Collaborators) (Dhaka: Mukti Juddho Chetona Bikash Kendra, 1987)

Siddiquee, Noore Alam, *Islam in Bangladesh Politics: The Role of Ghulam Azam* (London: Routledge, 2004).

Sisson, Richard and Leo E. Rose, *War and Succession: Pakistan, India and the Creation of Bangladesh (Berkeley: University of California Press, 1990).*

Sivan, Emmanuel, *Radical Islam: Medieval Theology and Modern Politics* (New York: Yale University Press, 1988).

Sobhan, Farooq (ed), *Dynamics of Bangladesh-India Relations:*

Dialogue of Young Journalists across the Borders (Dhaka: Bangladesh Enterprise Institute and University Press Limited, 2005)

Sobhan, Rehman, *Bangladesh: Problems of Governance* (Dhaka: University Press Limited, 1993)

Sobhan, Rehman (ed), *Bangladesh-India Relations: Perspective from Civil Society Dialogues* (Dhaka: Centre for Policy Dialogue and University Press Limited, 2002)

Spate, O.H.K. and A.T.A. Learmonth, *India and Pakistan: A General and Regional Geography* (London: Methuen, 1967).

Subrahmanyam, K., *Bangladesh and India's Security* (Dehra Dun: Palit and Dutt, 1972).

Thapar, Romila, *From Lineage to State: Social Formations in the Mid-First Millennium BC in the Ganga Valley* (New Delhi: Oxford University Press, 1984).

Tibi, Bassam, *The Challenge of Fundamentalism: Political Islam and the New World Disorder* (Berkeley: University of California Press, 1998).

Trimingham, J. Spencer, *The Sufi Orders in Islam* (London: Oxford University Press, 1971).

Umar, Badaruddin, *Juddhotoro Bangladesh* (Post-War Bangladesh (Dhaka: Mukhadhara, 1975).

Umar, Badaruddin, *The Emergence of Bangladesh: Class Struggle in Eat Pakistan (1947-1958)* (New York: Oxford University Press, 2004)

Umar, Badaruddin, *The Emergence of Bangladesh*, Volume 2, *The Rise of Bengali Nationalism, 1958-1971* (New York: Oxford University Press, 2006).

Weekes, Richard, *Pakistan: Birth and Growth of a Muslim Nation* (Princeton: Von Nostr and Company, 1964).

Wink, Andre, *Al-Hind: The Making of the Indo-Islamic World*, Vol. I, *Early Medieval India and Expansion of Islam, 7th-11th Centuries* (Leiden: E.J. Brill, 1990).

World Bank, *Bangladesh: Government that Works: Reforming the Public Sector* (Dhaka: University Press Limited, 1996) p. 101.

Zafarullah, Habib (ed), *The Zia Episode in Bangladesh Politics* (New Delhi: South Asia Publishers, 1996)

Zaheer, Hasan, *The Separation of East Pakistan: The Rise and Realization of Bengali Muslim Nationalism* (New York: Oxford University Press, 1994).

Ziring, Lawrence, *Bangladesh: From Mujib to Ershad: An Interpretative Study* (Dhaka: University Press Limited, 1984).

Articles

Absar, Syeda Sharmin, "Women Garment Workers in Bangladesh", *Economic and Political Weekly*, July 20, 2002, pp. 3012-3016.

Ahamed, Emajuddin, "Current Trends of Islam in Bangladesh", *Economic and Political Weekly*, June 18, 1983, pp. 1114-1119.

Ahamed, Emajuddin and DRJA Nazeen, "Islam in Bangladesh: Revivalist or Power Politics?", *Asian Survey*, August 1990, pp. 395-408.

Ahmad, Mumtaz, "Madrassa Education in Pakistan and Bangladesh" in Satu P. Limaye *et.al.*, *Religious Radicalism and Security in South Asia* (Honolulu, Hawaii: Asia Pacific Center for Security Studies, 2004) pp. 101-107

Ahmed, Abu Nasar Saied, "Indo-Bangladesh Relation and its Implications for Northeast India" in C.Joshua Thomas (ed), *Engagement and Development: India's Northeast Neighbouring Countries* (New Delhi: Akansha, 2006)

Ahmed, Rafiuddin, "Redefining Muslim Identity in South Asia" in Martin E. Marty and R. Scott Appleby (eds), *Accounting for Fundamentalisms* (Chicago: University of Chicago Press, 1944) pp. 669-705.

Ahmed, Samina, "Politics of Bangladesh: The Paradox of Military Intervention in Virender Grover (ed), *Bangladesh: Government and Politics* (New Delhi: Deep and Deep Publications, 2000) pp.97-129.

Ahsan, Rana Razzaque, " An Introduction to the Trends of Bengali Muslim Thought, 1905-1947, *Journal of Asiatic Society of Bangladesh,* Vol. 43, No. 1, 1998, pp. 37-62

Akhtar Banu, Razia UAB, "The Fall of Sheikh Mujib Regime: An Analysis", *Indian Political Science Review,* Vol. X, No. 1, January 1981, pp 1-19.

Akhtar Banu, Razia UAB, "Jamaat-i-Islami in Bangladesh: Challenges and Prospects" in Mutalib, Hussin and Taj ul-Islam Hashmi, *Islam, Muslims and the Modern State: Case-Studies in Thirteen Countries* (London: Macmillan, 1996) pp. 80-99.

Amin, Sajida *et al.*, "Contraception and Religiosity in Bangladesh" in Ronald McDonald Gavin Jones at al., *The Continuing Demographic Transition* (London: Oxford University Press, 2004) pp. 268-289.

Anisuzzaman, "Religion and Politics in Bangladesh" in S.R. Chakravarty (ed) *Society, Polity and Economy of Bangladesh* (New Delhi: Har-Anand Publications, 1994) pp. 40-51.

Ansari, M.H., "Militant Islam", *Radical Humanist,* May 2002 pp7-11 and June 2002, pp 30-34

Baran, Zeyno, "Fighting the War of Ideas", *Foreign Affairs,* Vol. 84, No. 6, November/ December 2005, pp. 68-78.

Begum, Hasna, "Rights of Women in Bangladesh", *Journal of Asiatic Society of Bangladesh,* Vol. 35, No. 1, June 1990, pp. 21-36.

Bhattacharya, Swapan K., "Does Bangladesh Benefit from Preferential Trades with India: A Gravity Analysis", *Economic and Political Weekly,* November 27, 2004, pp. 5152-5162.

Bose, Sarmila, "Anatomy of Violence: Analysis of Civil War in East Pakistan in 1971", *Economic and Political Weekly,* October 8, 2005, pp. 4463-4471.

Brass, Paul R., "Elite Groups, Symbol Manipulation and Ethnic Identity among the Muslims of South Asia" in David Taylor and Malcolm Yapp (eds), *Political Identity in South Asia* (London: Curzon Press, 1979).

Brasted, Howard V., "Islam and Identity in South Asia: At the Crossroads of Confusion and Confrontation" in Anthony H. Johns and Nally Lahoud (eds), *Islam in World Politics* (New York: Routledge, 2005) pp.105-126.

Cohen, Stephen P., "The Jihadi Threat to Pakistan", *The Washington Quarterly*, Vol. 26, No. 26, Summer 2003, pp. 7-25.

Custers, Peter, "Islamisation and More Aid for the Generals", *Economic and Political Weekly*, June 25, 1988, pp. 1317-1318.

Dasgupta, Rajarshi, "Representations of Communalism: A Study of Recent Print Media Reports in Bangladesh", *Asian Studies*, Vo. XXII, January-December 2004, pp. 39-70.

Eaton, Richard M., "Islamization in Bengal: Some Aspects of Socio-religious Background" *Dhaka University Studies*, Vol. 47, No. 1, June 1990, pp. 71-79.

Eaton, Richard M., "Who are the Bengal Muslims? Conversion and Islamization in Bengal" in Rafiuddin Ahmed (ed), *Understanding the Bengal Muslims: Interpretative Essays* (New Delhi: Oxford University Press, 2001) pp. 26-51.

Ehteshami, Anoushiravan, "Islam as a Political Force in International Politics" in Anthony H. Johns and Nally Lahoud (eds), *Islam in World Politics* (New York: Routledge, 2005) pp. 29-53.

Fealy, Greg, "Islamization and Politics in Southeast Asia: The Contrasting Case of Malaysia and Indonesia in Anthony H. Johns and Nally Lahoud (eds), *Islam in World Politics* (New York: Routledge, 2005) pp. 152-169.

Franda, Marcus, "Ziaur Rahman and Bangladesh Nationalism", *Economic and Political Weekly*, Annual Number, March 1981, pp. 357-380.

Gait, Edward A., "The Muhammadans of Bengal" in *Census of India, 1901*, Vol. 6, *The Lower Province of Bengal and their Feudatories*, Part I, "Report" (Calcutta: Bengal Secretariat Press, 1902).

Geertz, Clifford, "Religion as a Cultural System" in *Anthropological Approaches to the Study of Religion*, Association of Social Anthropologists, Monograph No. 3 (New York: Praeger, 1965) p. 4

Ghosh, Bipattam, "Bangladesh: Factors Contributing to its Emergence" in Verinder Grover (ed), *Bangladesh: Government and Politics* (New Delhi: Deep Deep, 2000) pp. 11-29.

Ghosh, Partha S., "Bangladesh at the Crossroads: Religion and Politics", *Asian Survey*, August 1990 pp. 795-808.

Ghosh, Partha S., "Conservative Ascendancy in Bangladesh", *South Asian Survey*, Vol. 12, No. 2, 2005, pp. 247-265

Grain, Philip, "General Elections in Bangladesh", *Handbook of Election Reporting* (Dhaka: Society for Environment and Human Development, 1995) p. 113.

Halim, Mohammad Abdul and Kamal Uddin Ahmed, "Foreign Affairs: Safeguarding National Interest" in Habib Zafarullah (ed), *The Zia Episode in Bangladesh Politics* (New Delhi: South Asia Publishers, 1996) pp. 125-139.

Hardy, P., "Modern European and Muslim Explanation of Conversion to Islam in South Asia: A Preliminary Survey of Literature" in Nehemia Levtzion (ed), *Conversion to Islam* (New York: Oxford, 1979) pp. 68-99.

Hashmi, Taj ul-Islam, "Islam in Bangladesh Politics" in Mutalib, Hussin and Taj ul-Islam Hashmi, *Islam, Muslims and the Modern State: Case-Studies in Thirteen Countries* (London: Macmillan, 1996) pp. 100-138.

Hashmi, Taj ul-Islam, "Islamic Resurgence in Bengal: Genesis, Dynamics and Implications" in Satu P. Limaye *et.al.*, *Religious Radicalism and Security in South Asia* (Honolulu, Hawaii: Asia-Pacific Centre for Security Studies, 2004) pp. 35-72.

Hollen, Christopher Von, "The Tilt Policy Revisited: Nixon-Kissinger Geopolitics and South Asia", *Asian Survey*, Vol. XX, No. 4, April 1990, pp. 339-361.

Hossain, Akhtar, "Anatomy of *Hartal* Politics in Bangladesh", *Asian Survey*, Vol. XL, No. 3, May/June 2000, pp. 508-529.

Hossain, Kazi Tobarak, "The Santals of Bangladesh: An Ethnic Minority in Transition", *Journal of Asiatic Society of Bangladesh*, Vol. 49, No. 2, December 2004, pp. 389-396.

Hussain, Monirul, "Understanding Barpeta massacre 1994: ethnicity, communalism and state", *Economic and Political Weekly*, May 20, 1995, pp. 1154-1155.

Hussain, Syed Anwar, "Islamic Fundamentalism in Bangladesh: Internal Variables and External Inputs" in Rafiuddin Ahmed, *Religion, Nationalism and Politics in Bangladesh* (New Delhi: South Asian Publsihers, 1990).

Iftekharuzzaman and Mahbubur Rahman, "Nation Building in Bangladesh: Perceptions, Problems and Approach" in M. Abdul Hafiz and Rob Khan (eds), *Nation Building in Bangladesh: Retrospect and Prospect* (Dhaka: BISS, 1982).

Iftekharuzzaman. "The India Doctrine: The Relevance for Bangladesh" in M.G. Kabir and Shaukat Hassan (eds), *Issues and Challenges Facing Bangladesh Foreign Policy* (Dhaka: Bangladesh Society of International Studies, 1989) pp. 18-43.

Islam, Syed Serajul, "The State of Bangladesh under Zia", *Asian Survey*, Vol. 24. No. 5, May 1984.

Jahan, Rounaq, "Bangladesh in 2002: Imperiled Democracy, *Asian Survey*, XLIII, No. 1 January/February, 2003, pp. 222-229.

Kalam, Abul, "Foreign Policy of Bangladesh: A Reconsideration", *Journal of Asiatic Society of Bangladesh,* Vol. 47, No. 1, June 2002, pp.205-220.

Klaiman, M.H., "Bengali" in Bernard Comrie (ed), *The World Major Languages* (New York: Oxford University Press, 1990).

Kochanek, Stanley A., "The Rise of Interest Politics in Bangladesh", *Asian Survey*, Vol. XXXVI, No. 7, July 1996, pp. 706-718

Kochanek, Stanley A., "Bangladesh in 1996: The 25th Year of Independence", *Asian Survey*, Vol. XXXVII, No. 2, February 1997) pp. 136-38.

Kochanek, Stanley A., "Bangladesh in 1997: The Honeymoon Is Over", *Asian Survey*, XXXVIII, No. 2, February 1998, pp. 149-141.

Kochanek, Stanley A., "Governance, Patronage Politics and Democratic Tradition in Bangladesh", *Asian Survey*, Vol.XL, No. 3, May/June 2000, pp 530-550.

Lintner, Bertil, "Bangladesh: A Cocoon of Terror", *Far Eastern Economic Review*, April 4, 2002.

Lintner, Bertil, "Religious Extremism and nationalism in Bangladesh" in Satu P. Limaye *et. al.*, (eds), *Religious Radicalism and Security in South Asia* (Honolulu, Hawaii: Asia Pacific Centre for Security Studies, 2004) pp. 413-436.

Maloney, Clearance, "Bangladesh and its People in Prehistory", *Journal of the Institute of Bangladesh Studies*, Vol. 2, (1977) pp. 17-22.

Maniruzzaman, Talukdar, "Bangladesh Politics: Secular and Islamic Trends" in Rafiuddin Ahmed (ed), *Islam in Bangladesh: Society, Culture and Politics* (Dhaka: Bangladesh Itihas Samiti, 1983) pp. 185-219.

Maniruzzaman, Talukdar, "The Fall of the Military Dictator, 1991 Election and the Prospect of Civilian Rule in Bangladesh", *Pacific Affairs*, Summer,1992.

Mohsin, Amena, "Bangladesh-India Relations: Limitations and Options in an Evolving Relationship" in Emajuddin Ahamed and Abul Kalam (eds), *Bangladesh, South Asia and the World* (Dhaka: Academic Publishers, 1992) pp 59-73

Nasr, Seyyed Vali Reza, "Mawdudi and the Jama'at-i-Islami; The Origins, Theory and Practice of Islamic Revivalism" in Ali Rehana (ed), *Pioneers of Islamic Revival* (New York: Zed Publication, 1994) pp. 98-124.

Obeidullah, ATM, "Local Government of Bangladesh: An Introduction or an Institution?" *Journal of Asiatic Society of Bangladesh,* Vol. 43, No. 2, December 1998, 38-67.

Perry, Alex, "Deadly Cargo", *Time*, October 21, 2002, pp. 22-25.

Rahman, Khan Md. Lutfor, "Minorities in Bangladesh and their Alienation: Causes and Implication", *Journal of Asiatic Society of Bangladesh*, Vol. 41. No. 2, December 1996, pp. 299-314.

Rahman, Mohammad Mafizur, "Trade and Regional Integration: Banglaesh and SAARC Perspective", *Asia Profile*, Vol. 1, February 2006, pp 79-93.

Rahim, Enayeur, "Bangladeshe Jamate Islamir Uttaran" (Rise of Jamat-i-Islami of Bangladesh) in Muhammad Jafar Iqbal (ed), *Bish Bachar Pare* (Twenty Years After) (Dhaka: Mohana Pradasani, 1993).

Rashid, H., "Some Notes on the Chittagong Hill-Tracts and its Tribes", *Journal of Asiatic Society of Pakistan*, Vol. XII No. 1, 1967) pp. 171-173.

Rashid, Sadek, "Mayoral Elections in Bangladesh: Consolidation of the Ruling Classes, *Economic and Political Weekly*, February 26, 1994, p. 482.

Rashiduzzaman, M., "The Awami League in the Political Development of Pakistan", *Asian Survey*, Vol. X, No. 7, July 1970, pp. 574-587.

Rashiduzzaman, M. "The Liberals and Religious Rights in Bangladesh", *Asian Survey*, 34 (1994) pp. 974-90.

Rashidduzzaman, "Bangladesh in 2000: Searching for Better Governance?" *Asian Survey*, Vol. VLI, No. 1, January/ February 2001, pp. 122-130

Rashiduzzaman, M., "Bangladesh in 2001", *Asian Survey*, Vol. XLII, No. January/February, 2002, pp 183-191.

Riaz, Ali, "Bangladesh in 2004: The Politics of Vengeance and Erosion of Democracy, *Asian Survey*, Vol. XLV, No. 1, January/February, 2005, pp. 112-118.

Riaz, Ali, "Bangladesh in 2005: Standing at a Crossroads", *Asian Survey*, Vol. XLVI, No. 1, January/February 2006, pp. 107-113

Rizvi, Gawher, "Democracy, Governance and Civil Society in South Asia", *Pakistan Development Review*, Vol. 33, No. 4 1994, pp. 593-624.

Roy, Asim, " Bengali Muslim and the Problem of Identity", *Journal of Asiatic Society of Bangladesh*, Vol. XXII, No. 3, 19, December 1977, pp. 192-199.

Sabur, A.K.M. Abdus Sabur, "Some Reflections on the Dynamics of Bangladesh India Relations" in Iftekharuzzaman and Imtiaz Ahmed (eds), *Bangladesh and SAARC: Issues, Perspectives and Outlook* (Dhaka: Academic Publishers, 1992) pp. 130-154.

Sengupta, Dipankar and Sudhir Kumar Singh (eds), *Minorities and Human Rights in Bangladesh* (New Delhi: Spandan, 2003) pp. 89-114.

Shehabuddin, Elora, "Bangladesh in 1998", *Asian Survey*, XXXIX, No. 1, January/ February 1999, pp. 148-154.

Shehabuddin, Elora, "Bangladesh in 1999: Desperately Seeking a Responsible Opposition", *Asian Survey*, Vol. XVL., No. 1, January/February, 2000, pp. 181-188.

Sobhan, Rehman, "External Dependence and the Governance of Bangladesh", *Journal of Asiatic Society of Bangladesh*, Vol. 37, No. 1, June 1992, pp. 1-32.

Ullah, Mohammad Sahid, "Election Coverage and the Neutrality of State-run Broadcast Media: The Experience of Two Parliamentary Elections in Bangladesh", *Journal of Asiatic Society of Bangladesh*, Vol.45, No. 2, 2000, pp. 121-136.

Umar, Badaruddin, "Problems of Left Unity in Bangladesh", *Economic and Political Weekly*, July 21, 1990, pp. 1576-1577.

Wise, James, "The Muhammadans of Eastern Bengal", *Journal of Asiatic Society of Bengal*, Vol. 63, 1894).

Zakaria, Farid, "The Rise of Illiberal Democracy", *Foreign Affairs*, November-December 1997, pp. 22-42

Newspapers:

The Assam Tribune (Guwahati)
The Sentinel (Guwahati)
Daily Star (Dhaka)
Ittefaq (Dhaka)
Protom Alo (Dhaka)
Telegraph (Guwahati edition)

INDEX